UN FIN ISHED

UNFINISHED: Ideas, Images, and Projects
from the Spanish Pavilion at the 2016 Venice Architecture Biennale

Published by Actar Publishers and the Ministry of Development
Editors: Iñaqui Carnicero, Carlos Quintáns Eiras
Managing editor: Ángel Martínez García-Posada
Graphic design: Mikhail Grinwald
Cover: Ramon Prat Homs
English translation: Vincent Morales, Kathy Lindstrom
Copyediting: Mikhail Grinwald, Helen Elizabeth Gyger

Distributed by Actar D
New York:
440 Park Avenue South, 17th Floor
New York, NY 10016
T +1 212 966 2207
salesnewyork@actar-d.com

Barcelona:
Roca i Batlle 2
08023 Barcelona
Spain
T +34 933 282 183
eurosales@actar-d.com
info@actar.com
actar.com

ISBN: 978-1-945150-68-5
Library of Congress Control Number: 2017953121
A CIP catalogue record for this book is available from the Library of Congress, Washington D.C., USA.

This book is set in Roboto and Neuton.

IDEAS, IMAGES, AND PROJECTS

UN FIN ISHED

FROM THE SPANISH PAVILION

AT THE 15TH VENICE ARCHITECTURE BIENNALE

EDITED BY
IÑAQUI CARNICERO, CARLOS QUINTÁNS
WITH ÁNGEL MARTÍNEZ

UNFINISHED

CURATORS
Iñaqui Carnicero, Carlos Quintáns Eiras

SCIENTIFIC COMMITEE
Santiago de Molina
Jacobo García-Germán
Ángel Martínez García-Posada

DOCUMENTATION AND EDITING
Nuria Prieto González
Beatríz Vilahoz Herrero
Óscar Fuertes Dopico
Ángel Montero Pérez
Hugo Malvar Álvarez

EXHIBITION DESIGN
Iñaqui Carnicero
Carlos Quintáns Eiras
Lorena del Río
Marcos Cortes Lerín, collaborator

STRUCTURE
Song Ren
Echeocai

PRINTING AND FRAMING
Museoteca

PRODUCTION AND INSTALLATION
Luigi D'Oro & ARGUZIA S.R.L. with
Flaminio Bovino
Giovanni Spagnoletti
Chiara Mazzarella
Micol Riva

WEB
Estudio Caravana

TRANSLATION
Kathy Lindstrom

TECHNICAL SUPPORT FOR THE INTERVIEWS
Elena Toumayan
Johanna Grazel

GENERAL COORDINATOR
Francisco Mangado, Spanish Government
General Coordinator of Architectural Biennales

COORDINATION
Eduardo Aragoneses, Sara León (Fomento)
Monique Lambie (AC/E)
Alejandro Romero (AECID)

Spanish Pavilion, La Biennale di Venezia 2016
15th International Architecture Exhibition
REPORTING FROM THE FRONT
May 28–November 27, 2016

The publishing coordination produced for the exhibition Unfinished at the 15th edition of the International Architecture Venice Biennale were supported by the Arquia Foundation

fundación arquia

ACKNOWLEDGEMENTS
Amale Andraos
Barry Bergdoll
Mark Cruvellier
Kenneth Frampton
Eva Frank
Sou Fujimoto
Carlos Mínguez
Terence Riley
Jorge Silvetti
Andrea Simitch
Martino Stierli
Nader Tehrani
Meijeen Yoon
Val Warke
Sarah Whiting

Cornell University, Department of Architecture
Storefront for Art and Architecture

Sutega
Ondarreta

la Biennale di Venezia
15. Mostra Internazionale di Architettura
Partecipazioni Nazionali

GOBIERNO DE ESPAÑA — MINISTERIO DE FOMENTO

GOBIERNO DE ESPAÑA — MINISTERIO DE ASUNTOS EXTERIORES Y DE COOPERACIÓN — cooperación española

AC/E ACCIÓN CULTURAL ESPAÑOLA

CONTENTS

INTRODUCTION: ARCHITECTURE *NON FINITO*

IÑAQUI CARNICERO

The theme proposed by the main curator of the Venice Architecture Biennale often reacts ideologically to that of the previous one. For many years the selected title defined a relatively lax framework that permitted the incorporation of a large number of prestigious architects who, in addition to magnificent architecture, brought glamour to the Giardini during the days of the inauguration. Surprisingly, in the last Biennale, Rem Koolhaas proposed focusing all of the attention of the exhibition on architecture itself. The "Elements of Architecture" exhibition was organized around an investigation analyzing the design of fundamental elements used to construct architecture in different historical periods and contexts. The result was tremendously effective in resolving the contradiction between his position as curator of an exhibition positioned against architecture as spectacle, and his own condition as an architectural celebrity. The exhibition contents were generated through the analysis of building fragments, the majority of them anonymous, which left the so-called "starchitects" out of the conversation.

This year Alejandro Aravena introduced a different perspective with the title "Reporting From the Front," claiming the practice of architecture as an instrument for improving the living conditions of the least privileged members of our society. If in the 2014 exhibition Koolhaas invited all national pavilions to reflect on how each country had absorbed modernism, this year Aravena proposed sharing the main challenges that architecture has had to deal with in recent years. A visit to the Biennale's national pavilions would serve not only to contemplate the latest avant-garde projects, but also to learn about, and perhaps anticipate, possible conflicts in different geographical contexts that the profession may have to face in the near future.

Spain is probably one of the countries where the impact of the economic crisis of 2008 has affected most deeply the practice of architecture. There are not many places on the planet where such an incredible amount of structures were built in a short period of time, in many cases with no other intention than feeding the voracious appetite of the motor that was driving the economy. The lack of reflection with respect to the necessity of these projects resulted in many cases in abandonment due to the economic unviability of their completion or maintenance. Their appearance in the Spanish landscape has generated a collection of unfinished buildings, which exemplify the madness of recent years, when the consideration of change, adaptability and evolution over time was removed from the formula for making architecture. Nobody knows how long these structures will remain in this unfinished state. Some of these contemporary ruins will be adapted to new uses, yet others will remain for many years frozen as useless objects in the landscape.

The hope that if we could report and share this sad situation so other emerging economies wouldn't fall into the same mistakes, was the starting point of the exhibition. "Unfinished" was materialized in the central space of the Spanish Pavilion with a hanging movable structure where the work of seven photographers was condensed in fifty-five images with a critical vision of the disasters of the real estate bubble.

Some of the most critical narratives were articulated by the photographs by the collective Cadelasverdes, whose series "Spanish Dream" included everyday domestic scenes in surprisingly unfinished architectural backdrops. These snapshots were taken in half-finished structures with raw interior spaces, where the quotidian nature of the scenes strike us as the inhabitants behave obliviously to the fact that they are living in a ruin. Not much economic effort would be needed to make these ruins inhabitable again.

Photographer Adrià Goula in his work "Re-edificatoria" documents half-built, half-demolished structures in a stage when it is still possible to read the traces that reveal the construction process. The spaces lack any type of refinement or embellishment and are dominated by the raw materials that were never hidden by finishes.

Central space of the Spanish Pavilion at the Venice Biennale. Photographs by Luis Diaz and Juan Rodríguez.

The collective "Roundabout Nation," with a series of aerial pictures, documented infrastructures executed in virgin landscapes where the architecture that was meant to complete the urban operation never arrived and the roads and roundabouts remained as isolated geometries scattered throughout the territory.

The power of these photographs is intrinsically linked with a strong element of criticism, but besides their political position toward the system, these snapshots, captured in different moments of the construction process, have the astonishingly evocative capacity of freezing an early stage of architecture, when the work is not yet finished. Only the evolution over time will reveal the success or failure of the operation. The contemplation of these ruins not only reveals the minimum actions necessary to complete the construction process, but also suggests a reflection on their behavior over time. Ultimately these images attempt to elaborate on the idea of unfinished architecture.

The dictionary indicates the following synonyms of "unfinished": unadorned, crude, formless, imperfect, raw, rough, under construction, unfashioned, unperfected, unpolished, unrefined. All of these adjectives conjure in the imagination of designers a type of architectural intervention that perceives the existing built environment as a constraint upon which we can leave an important but impermanent mark. In this way, architects become a link in the chain of a structure's life. Through the concept of the "unfinished" we may understand the desirability of a perpetual state of evolution of the constructions that define our societies. The architecture of the unfinished leaves a door open to the unexpected, and to ideas and interventions of the future, many of which we may not yet be aware of. Unfinished architecture blurs the signature of the architect as an author and transforms the piece into a collaborative work that involves actions over years of use.

The original trace of Diocletian's Palace in Split could be considered as a project that ended in the fifth century with the construction of the residence for the Roman emperor. However, it is more interesting to understand it as an unfinished project that began with the definition of the floor plan of the palace and still today continues serving as a master plan for the city. An aerial view reveals the rectangular perimeter of the palace as well as its ancient main halls which are today transformed into piazzas, public buildings and other urban spaces. The houses that have been built over the years since the fall of the Roman Empire, instead of starting from scratch, assumed the remains of the palace as found objects available for reuse. The layout of the palace originally responded to the functional individual needs of the emperor, but also was sufficiently generic to allow its transformation throughout the following centuries into a construction that today belongs to the public realm.

When we examine the notion of "Unfinished" throughout history we discover examples that demonstrate the role of the architect in society not as a designer that starts from scratch but as an analytical mind that examines the existing environment in order to discover constraints upon which to build a new mark. This is especially obvious during the Baroque period in Rome.

The Baroque architects' reaction toward the ruin was that of true artists who recognize and respect the ruins not as untouchable monuments, but as elements that are still active in the present. The layout of Piazza Navona is based on the plan of the Roman Circus that previously occupied the same space. Instead of adopting a protectionist attitude by filling the piazza with ancient columns and excavated stones, the Baroque architects granted the Romans the supreme honor of inspiring their designs through the incorporation of the imprint of their buildings.

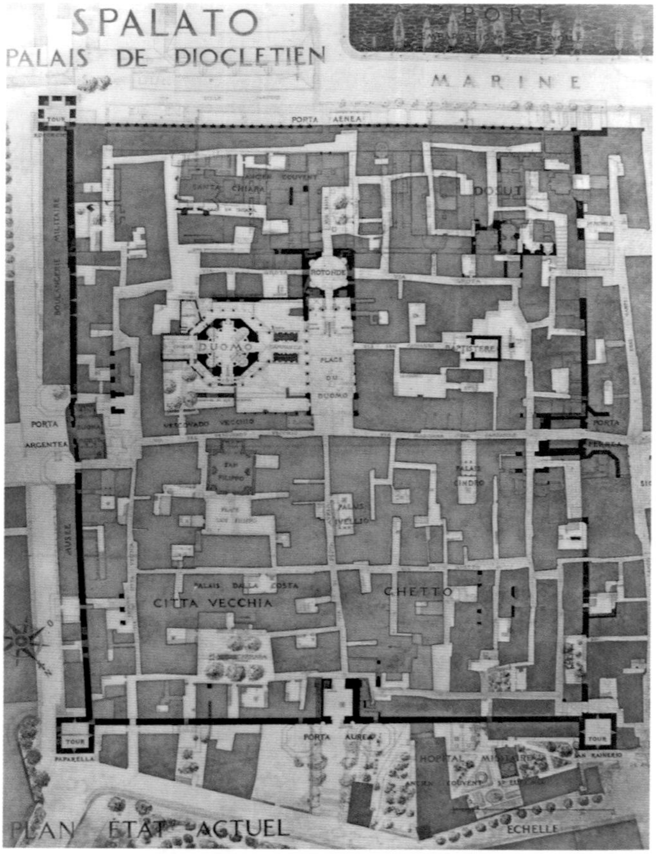

Overall plan of the city of Split with the remains of Diocletian's Palace.

The Imperial Forum in Rome before and after the excavations ordered by Mussolini.

The fact that the plan only served as the constraining geometry for the new design does not represent any lack of respect for the Roman ruin, but rather a creative attitude that understands the ancient city as a living context susceptible to being used and reinterpreted from an artistic point of view instead of as a museum of dead monuments from the past. A similar understanding of an architecture that arises from the consideration of constructed yet unfinished elements can be noted in other urban spaces, such as Piazza di San Ignazio, Piazza di Spagna or the Quai di Ripetta in Rome.

We can also recognize reactions toward periods of scarcity in the reuse of pieces from previous constructions. Especially interesting is the period in history when the concept of style was not important and architectural elements, designed originally according to one particular stylistic direction, were reused to complete another building. The beauty of Santa María in Trastevere is linked to this juxtaposition of fragments from previous constructions.

Inhabitation becomes a critical question to evaluate the success of certain urban operations, originally designed with one purpose, but modified over the years to respond different needs of society. Henry Hope quotes the writer Auguste Hare, who claims that between 1870 and 1903 archaeologists destroyed more of the artistic beauty of Rome than the Goths or the Vandals in any of their invasions. Hope renders this reality by comparing two engravings: one of the Roman Forums in the seventeenth century, and another after the archaeological excavations of 1935 ordered by Mussolini in the Via di Fori Imperiali, which unearthed columns and remains of ancient temples that had been buried repeatedly by the constant overflows of the Tiber River. The rows of houses, the tree-lined avenues and the quaint adaptations of the Roman monuments occupied by humble programs shown in the first engraving had all disappeared in the second. The magical space represented in the scene, where passersby could walk in close proximity to the capitals of the buried temples, was lost. In the second perspective, the fragments of the Roman ruins have been cleaned up to remove any trace of occupation. The ruins have been converted into mere objects of contemplation, generating the desolate landscape of a bombed-out city inhabited only by tourists.

The Italian expression *non finito* is used to define artistic expressions whose value resides in their unfinished condition. In some cases the incompleteness of the work is produced voluntarily by the author, while in others technical difficulties impede completion, or even the unexpected death of the artist. At some moment the author's intent meets with an unexpected event that humanizes and contextualizes the artwork. We can find examples in painting and sculpture by important artists such as Leonardo or Michelangelo. Architecture is not too far removed, if we observe the variables that can occur during the design and construction process that modify the author's initial intentions. These interferences are opportunities to understand up to what point, far above the specific needs of the client, architecture belongs to society and therefore should evolve along with the culture willing to respond to future needs.

Cave di Cusa is located three kilometers south of Campobello di Mazara in the Italian province of Trapani. This quarry was first used in the sixth century BC to extract the stone for the temples of Selinunte. With the arrival of the Carthaginians led by Hannibal the quarry was abandoned abruptly in the year 409 BC. It is still possible today to observe the original rock sculptured into cylindrical forms, in an early stage before becoming a column in a temple that was never built.

The unfinished obelisk of the city of Aswan (Assuan) would have been the largest element of cut stone in the world, if it had not been fractured during the quarrying process and therefore abandoned. The work could never be completed, but like the stones at the Cave di Cusa, a perpetually unfinished object was produced as the result of an unexpected event.

Fragments of columns carved out of stone in the quarries of Cave di Cusa for Temple G in Selinunte.

Unfinished Obelisk in Asuan.

These stones never left their place of origin and were never used for their intended purpose, however their unfinished condition reveals a phase in the quarrying process that we would otherwise never have known.

But besides reporting this situation in response to the main call, it was important to illustrate how architects have been dealing with this period of economic scarcity.

"Unfinished" proposes to draw attention to the process and not only the result and to view architecture as unfinished, in constant evolution and as something that serves humankind, in a moment of uncertainty with respect to the profession which makes this an especially relevant consideration for our time.

The ultimate goal of the "Unfinished" exhibition is to present a selection of built works developed during these years of scarcity where the economy of means has triggered unexpected and ingenious solutions. Some of these offices have demonstrated how creativity can be used as a powerful tool against economic constraints and can subvert the negative aspect of the crisis to develop an architecture that is no longer linked with the concept of spectacle.

The fifty-five architectural interventions exhibited in the perimeter spaces of the Spanish Pavilion were selected in an open call where more than 500 works were presented. They epitomize a way of understanding the constructed environment as unfinished and in constant evolution. The economy of means compels us to modify design strategies, sometimes through simplification and at other times by incorporating previous structures or anticipating future adaptations. Architecture without place (because there is no more real estate), without its own facade (because one already exists), without its own structure (because it consolidates and uses the existing one), without new spaces (because it reuses the old ones), without a single author (because it is the result of the work of many people), or whose beauty arises as a result of yielding to difficult initial constraints that limit possible actions.

The selection of these built works responded to the open call that was framed under the *Unfinished Manifesto:*

-Unfinished Architecture blurs the signature of the architect as an author and transforms the piece into a collaborative work that involves actions over years of use.

-Unfinished Architecture defends strategies of adaptation, transformation and occupation of abandoned or incomplete structures that are taken as a given constraint, allowing unexpected solutions.

-Unfinished Architecture examines typologies that became obsolete after the difficulty of adaptation to fulfill new demands.

-Unfinished Architecture defends demolition as a powerful tool to architecturally intervene in our cities.

-Unfinished Architecture defends the consideration of the future ruin of the building.

-Unfinished Architecture examines how certain architectures are more likely to be considered as part of a chain that could be continued by others.

-Unfinished Architecture analyzes how the cost of a building should be considered in relation to its life span.

-Unfinished Architecture promotes dialogue between the old and the new.

It is the intention of this book to expand the content of the "Unfinished" exhibition, recognized with the Golden Lion as the best national pavilion at the 2016 Venice Architecture Biennale. Fifty-five photographs from seven different artists, fifty-five built works addressing nine categories of Unfinished, eleven interviews with relevant voices in the academic context and five critical articles are contained in this book.

It is not the goal of this compilation of ideas to conclude with certainties, but rather to keep the conversation open.

CONSTRUCTING THE UNFINISHED

SANTIAGO DE MOLINA

When he was twenty years old, he looked up, saw the sky, once again, saw the earth, with great attention. It was true, then! God had done nothing but sketch the word. He left nothing but ruins. Ruins this oak, albeit its beauty. Ruins the water that breaks softly against the shore. Ruins the sun itself. Ruins all of these signs of beauty, as the clouds prove well, more beautiful still.
Only the sun has had a full life, perhaps, he told himself. Hence its simple and uncreated semblance. Since then, he likes nothing but the sketches in the work of painters. The line that closes on itself seems to betray the cause of this god who has preferred the anguish of search over the joy of the work that is finished.

—Yves Bonnefoy, "L'inachevable"[1]

At the beginning of the novel *The End of the Affair*, Graham Greene wrote: "A story has no beginning or end: arbitrarily one chooses that moment of experience from which to look back or from which to look ahead. I say 'one chooses' with the inaccurate pride of a professional writer . . . "[2] Maybe people of letters can choose the narrative moment when to begin their story, they may even be able to choose the instant when to end it. But it is different to truly finish writing a piece, which is subject to an endless polishing process, where there is no room for inaccuracy from the point of view of the author's pride and where the dissatisfaction that every writer experiences perpetuates itself.

In the realm of the arts, the unfinished managed to have significant character on its own merits, and even its own masters centuries ago. Ascanio Condivi, Michelangelo's disciple and biographer, awarded him with the title of master of the *non finito*.[3] All he needed to do was to let the inner characters emerge from the stone to consider that the most important part of the piece was done. That which was not finished in Michelangelo's work became significant as an act in itself. Vasari, in his *Lives* stated: "All things which are far removed, be they paintings, sculpture or whatever, have more beauty and greater force when they are a beautiful sketch [*una bella bozza*] than they are finished."[4] Nonetheless, Vasari himself suggested that the unfinished, in Michelangelo's case, was also the product of a permanent feeling of dissatisfaction with his work.

1 BONNEFOY, Yves, "L'inachevable,", from *Les raisins de Zeuxis et d'autres fables*. Montauk: Monument Press, 1987. Translated for this text by Vincent Morales Garoffolo.

2 GREENE, Graham, *The End of the Affair*. New York: Viking Press, 1951.

3 SCHULZ, Juergen, "Michelangelo's Unfinished Works," *The Art Bulletin*, Vol. 57, No. 3 (Sep., 1975), pp. 366-373. Likewise, a reference to other reasons for the *non-finito* in Michelangelo's work can be found, given by T. Brunius, who speculates that the unfinished offered the possibility that in the future the work could be seen with a charm similar to that conveyed by the ruin. (T. Brunius, "Michelangelo's non finito," *Contributions to the History and Theory of Art*, 1967)

4 VASARI, Giorgio, *Lives of the Most Eminent Painters, Sculptors, and Architects*. New York: Abrams, 1979 (first edition 1550), p. 45.

Michelangelo's unfinished statue of the apostle Saint Matthew, 1503.

The incomplete became so popular over the centuries that it even generated an aesthetic of the unfinished, and with it, its own debates. The idea of the *non inito* first triumphed during the Renaissance, and it gave artists the power to declare that a piece was finished on their own free terms, regardless of what the rest of society had to say. Pietro da Cortona, in his *Treatise on Painting and Sculpture* from 1652, justified the abandonment of uncompleted works by the Florentine master by saying the great artists need not feel guilty for not finishing a piece, because the idea behind it was more important than actually carrying it out. In art history, the unfinished has long been the source of debate: from the rise in artists' prestige that allowed them to declare that a piece was finished—that it was art—to the preeminence of the idea itself as the main pillar of artistic expression.

However, in the field of architecture, the simple line that defines the meaning of a project, or its mere habitability, marks a limit that has always prevented any sort of possible romantic dalliance in that direction.

Apparently, architecture never felt it was part of the realm of the unfinished, perhaps because architecture itself never thought it was finished in the same sense that the term had in the world of art, even once a project was inaugurated and inhabited. The historical processes in which architecture was produced were always so prolonged that they outlasted entire generations and even their original authors. The shared authorship of built works, which also occurred during the Renaissance, and the need to use materials that just could not be wasted, made this discipline safeguard itself against the menacing monster of the unfinished.

On the other hand, architecture, at a certain moment, simply submerges itself into time before it considers itself finished. No matter how much a building is occupied, inhabited and used as expected, architecture has always worked with parameters that were different from those applied to the notion of ending in the sense of finishing.

Nowadays, however, we can see how the unfinished constitutes a wide range of unrealized or partially realized works. The category "unbuilt" encompasses a broad spectrum of what are apparently ill-fated projects, arrested before they were completed and, therefore lacking, it seems, a future (and even any spurpose). In our time, the architecture of the unfinished adds another meaning to the term, one that is generated by what was once an unimaginable growth of construction which has produced works that have been left half-finished, all over the place. These remains, this "unfinished" architecture, makes up a territory that must be examined because it offers a clarifying insight into the profound changes that contemporary architecture is experiencing. Just like the stars that have died in the firmament whose light still reaches us, the notion of the unfinished sheds light on a wide field full of paths that lead to the same vessel: time.

To think about an architecture of the unfinished means to think, therefore, about the way time meddles with architecture, and this enables us to ask ourselves if it does so in any specific way.

In this text, the unfinished-time dialectic will be illustrated by two images. In the first, we will observe what it means to build an incomplete project undertaking an unfinished work does not guarantee its anticipated finishing in the future. In the second, undertaking an unfinished work does not guarantee its anticipated finishing in the future.

Oventon Down. 1960.

Oventon Down, excavation, 1992.

In Overton Down, Wiltshire, a county in southwest England, a tumulus and a ditch were formed in 1960. The structure was twenty-seven meters long and seven meters wide, and the idea was to find out how, with the passing of time, the geometry of the terrain and the materials buried inside it would degrade. The experiment is supposed to last 128 years. It is monitored from time to time and different samples are taken with the aim of seeing how it evolves as a whole. The last tests will be run in 2088.

In 1964, the first results were obtained: the shape of the entire structure had changed and discoloring was observed in the material that was buried. After fifty-six years, the entire site, both the tumulus and the ditch have been seeded with dozens of plant species, which have been carefully studied and documented to record the process by which nature is invading the ruins. For the untrained eye, it all looks like a carefully planted meadow. The strange ditch has given shelter to a solitary pair of trees, serving as a huge, mysterious planter for them. This experiment has now been declared a World Heritage Ste. The future will tell whether this work, closely related to the "earthworks" and field sculptures of the 1960s and 1970s, is capable of revealing anything that is not already known to architecture itself by means of studying its many ruins.

From this experiment, some aspects need to be highlighted regarding the unfinished. The first is that this work never reached a finished state of construction. Not even when it was inaugurated in the 1960s could it have been considered finished, because the goal of this experiment was none other than to see how time would leave its imprint on the site.

On the other hand, it cannot be concluded that, in a literal sense, this is a ruin. The only thing that can be stated is that an open time cycle exists that is responsible for softening edges, opening cracks and dissolving the entire structure. Here, a real continuity between the disciplines of archaeology and architecture can be discerned. In this case, the unfinished does not entail of frustration, since the goal of this project is not inhabitation. The unfinished is an inherent part of the experiment. There is no chance of failure, unless there is nothing left to learn from the samples extracted, unless the experiment is abandoned and forgotten. (However, it is important to keep the words failure and frustration in mind, for later).

Since it is a time vessel, this experience at Overton Down shows the spirit of all "open works" and it allows us to imagine how, at each stage, the architectural form turns into a valuable transmitter of messages. Or, at least, into a magnificent supplier of information.

The second case worth looking at is located in Rome. At the beginning of the first century AD and during the following three hundred years, twenty-six million broken amphorae were deposited near the site of an ancient port. Those amphorae contained the oil that was used in the city on a daily basis. The oil traveled across the Mediterranean Sea inside these ceramic vessels, which were later abandoned, since it was costlier to reuse them than to throw them away and make new ones in their places of origin. Nowadays, this pile of broken pieces of pottery is one more mound in the city, in addition to the seven natural and original hills that made up ancient Rome's topography. This mound is called the Monte Testaccio, and it was located within the Aurelian walls. Today, we can hardly tell it is there, camouflaged as it is, barely thirty-five meters high, looking like a simple, grass-covered hillock.

This heap of broken pots was laid out following a precise structural pattern: they were covered in layers of lime to prevent bad smells, retaining walls were built and an inner structure was implemented to maintain its stability as time went by. At present this mound constitutes a fascinating ruin that is capable of giving us information about Roman uses and customs, even more so than the writings of the city's historians. There lies the history of an unfinished garbage dump which has turned into a vessel of Rome's own eternity.

By looking at the Monte Testaccio we can see how its finalization, as a project, was never planned. Its ending simply happened. In its time, this ending might have come about because of a change in customs or for commercial or historical reasons. The thing is that the construction of the Monte Testaccio was simply left unfinished, whether due to its abandonment or to its inability to hold any more residue.

The Testaccio district In Rome in 1625, showing Monte Testaccio surrounded by wasteland.

This pile of broken amphorae places us before a quandary regarding antiquity: Should ancient piles of refuse receive the same careful treatment as the ruins of temples? Or, more importantly regarding the intentions of the unfinished: Can something that was never intended to become a construction in the sense we understand architecture, something that in principle did not have a purpose and therefore we cannot consider finished, be declared a ruin and remain as untouchable as a museum object?

At the Monte Testaccio the coalescence of construction and time makes most of those questions hard to answer, but they might be sufficient to clarify the real issue behind the unfinished.

The questions regarding the experiment at Overton Down and the Testaccio mound are difficult to answer for various reasons. One of them, and not the least important, is that in fact, neither has a specific author. This makes it impossible to ask what their true intention was.

However, in modern architecture, the role of the author, the architect, in carrying out a project is crucial for various reasons. In architecture, authorship makes architects responsible for their work. And not only that. When faced with a project, its author not only becomes responsible for it, but also, as Georg Lukács said, for everything that is done with it, including its interpretations and derivatives. All architects, from the perspective of the unfinished, are considered responsible for the ruins that their work will produce.

From this perspective, let's say that Anthemius of Tralles, besides being the deviser of the Hagia Sophia established his influence, is the subsidiary creator of hundreds of mosques that felt its weight and magnetism as their source of inspiration. From a Lukácsian standpoint, every architect bears the weight of their work's power of persuasion through time, regardless of whether they managed to finish the work or not, since they are responsible for what is done with it and for the meanings they are able to convey. In the same way, artists such as Rembrandt or Homer have extended the influence of their unfinished works to this day. Moreover, aren't Mozart's *Requiem*, Walter Benjamin's *Arcades Project*, Schubert's *Unfinished Symphony* or Robert Musil's *The Man without Qualities* unfinished works that are valuable in their own right, despite the minor detail of their incompletion diminishing their promise, without their lack of a resolution subtracting an iota of value from what they have achieved?

Perhaps, given this relationship between author and work, but also due to a series of means that have been wasted, there exists in unfinished architecture an unconcealed anxiety regarding frustrated endeavors. Or at least a conscious but unattainable struggle for the survival of the project through time and for its good use to redeem it. If authors are unable to take charge of the unfinished aspects of their work, then who would become responsible for doing so?

The Neue Nationalgalerie in Berlin is an unfinished project by Mies van der Rohe, who died before its completion. However, as a project, it is not incomplete, we cannot say that it was left to its own devices. The work was finished without Mies. Just like ancient cathedrals, where large endeavors were unfinished because of the sudden disappearance of their authors or their successors. This work was, by Mies's death, sufficiently developed, detailed and advanced so that its authorship was not questioned. The truth is that even poems, as Valéry said, are never finished, they are simply abandoned. The history of the great projects of the past shows us that the spirit of the unfinished does not need an author, but it does require the will to persevere and overcome the fatigue that every project entails, and it does require a sufficiently resonant meaning.

Monte Testaccio, Rome.

Monte Testaccio, archaeological excavation. Rome.

From the moment in which the work is considered done, from the moment in which the work is left to its own devices, not only does the architect cease to have power over it, but the inhabitants become both responsible for it and responsive to it—responding to it, giving it a response. Perhaps they will also become its keepers and guardians to pass it on to future generations. That is when they become its interpreters and critics, establishing the same bonds that a parent has with a newborn baby. It is precisely tthen that, in the field of architecture, one of the dramatic aspects of the unfinished resides. If those inhabitants are nonexistent, if the work remains uninhabitable, then the ruins of the work remain orphaned in such a way that they stand out like a generalized failure that implicates society as a whole.

Therefore, in the unfinished we can discern the failure of wasted, dispersed and soulless means. This might be the reason why the spirit of the unfinished is perhaps the main material with which the "junkspace" that Rem Koolhaas describes is built, that is, the main ingredient of the global city in which we live. The image of the unfinished belongs to the realm of the unborn, a field that is hungry for meaning, eager to give meaning to something and always expecting the future to make sense of the work and make it legible. This is why all unfinished things refer to the precedent of a Tower of Babel that aspired to a dream that mankind, with all its hubris, was unable to attain. Everything that is unfinished has something of the fall of Icarus to it. It is the indelible trace of a disaster. The unfinished is always ghostlike. It bears, after all, one of the most persuasive symbols of human failure.

In that sense, the unfinished is a ruin whose future has been amputated. It is a ruin whose design was not completely prefigured and therefore its development is not subject to a clear intention. The unfinished is a disordered state of possibility mixed in with an array of improbability. This is why within the unfinished lies an indefinable but real collective frustration, a fatigue that is hard to cure: "fatigue is way of being that is poorly known; little is said about it; it is a color of life that does not even have the prestige of the heinous or the damned, what words can we use to talk about fatigue? However it is the dimension of time: infinite, it is infinity itself... fatigue but not weariness."[5]

Even so, the unfinished must be differentiated from that which is merely abandoned. The unfinished is that which cannot be completed, that which turns interminable. The abandoned, to the contrary, entails surrendering without a fight, the personification of fatigue. People who abandon themselves are those who do not take care of their appearance—be it their hygiene or their manners, who are not in shape. That is, abandonment has a clear chronology. Abandonment is gradual but dateable. However, this does not occur with the unfinished, since setting a date would be a way of certifying its conclusion.

Therefore, how can the chronology of the unfinished be pieced together? How does the gradual *unfinishing* of a work take place?

We know that in the construction of architecture everything has its own pace and time goes by in unique ways. In architectural design, slow, regular steps coexist with a final rapid succession of events that pile up and trample over each other when the last actions are taken. The inner workings of a project include periods of impasse and delay, overlapping and waiting. During this process, the unfinished is an incident, a moment in which things just happen, without a bang, in a clear and finite movement that is, nevertheless, open. Because there is a time during the process when not everybody is aware that the architecture will be unfinished. There will be those who will continue visiting the site, working on the project, and even making an effort to start everything up again and continue the endeavor . . . Hence, unfinished architecture is a special malformation of the time in which architecture is developed.

5 BARTHES, Roland, *El Susurro del lenguaje: más allá de la palabra y la escritura*. Barcelona: Paidós, 1994, p. 229. Translated for this text by Vincent Morales Garoffolo.

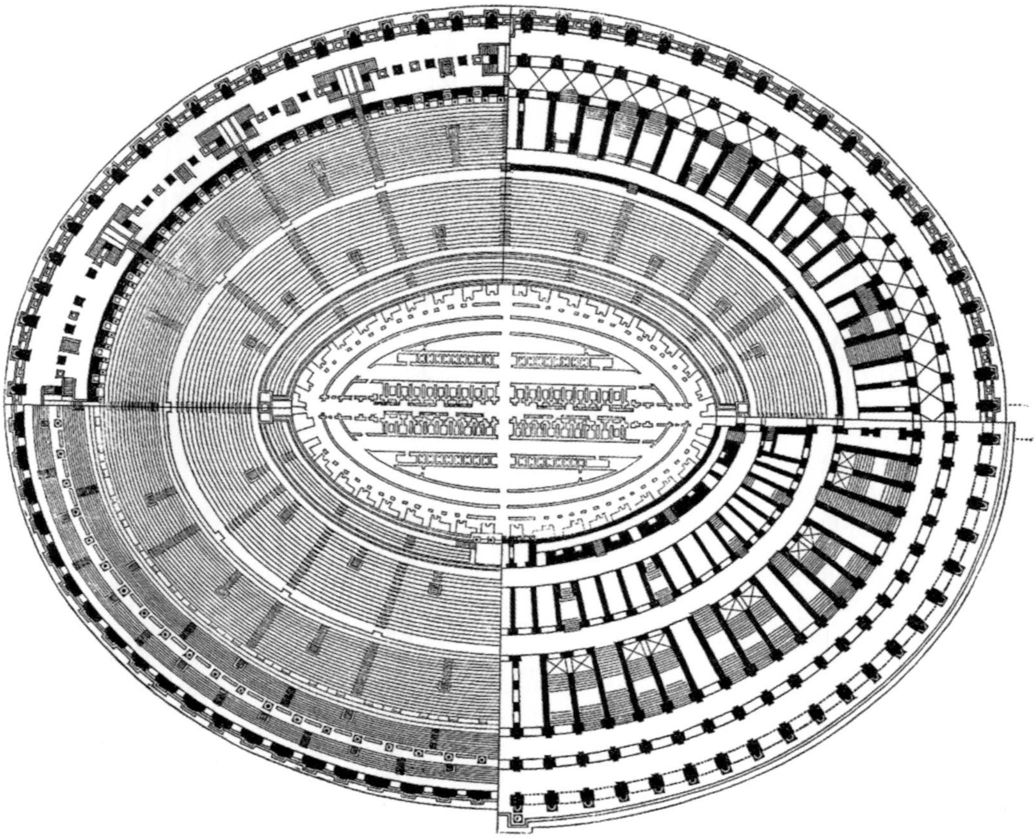

The Coliseum, Rome. Plan.

A project can be declared finished because its inhabitants occupy and use it, but when something ends up unfinished it is because there is a period in which the work enters a process of absences, it begins to lack visitors, until the ruinous emerges. Then, some inconsequential valuable parts are removed, rust appears and weeds begin to grow. Since its surroundings have not been developed, the project becomes inaccessible. Until its fences collapse and it becomes part of nature... That is, the moment in which a work is declared unfinished is not clear, it cannot be pinpointed, things just happen, things gradually become unfinished. They are not intentionally unfinished. They are not un-ended. Ruin simply takes place.

Some time ago Robert Smithson said that architecture does not fall into ruin but that ruin becomes part of architecture from the moment its construction begins. We know that time, like an insatiable woodworm, incessantly undermines every building. Nothing can guarantee the survival of architecture, neither its form, nor its symbology, nor its material, nor the institution that sustains it, nor the place where it is located. The woodworm of time does its job, it bores holes, demolishes, tears down and reconfigures shape until it is exterminated or transformed into something very different. Therefore, who cares whether a project is finished or not?... Only those who expect the work to be used and to serve as shelter, only those who expect to inhabit it according to its function. Hence, what corresponds to the unfinished, just like the ruinous, is the impossibility of a conventional use.

After its employment as an arena for almost five centuries, the Roman Coliseum was used as a church and a place to worship the martyrs who had been sacrificed there; after that, for hundreds of years it became a quarry (fig.9). It survived as a ruin thanks to the cannibalistic use of its materials for other buildings, not because of its monumentality or its historical value. Then, a more dignified use was given to it in order to ensure its survival, once the extraction of materials endangered its existence. When Sixtus V became Pope, he tried to turn it into a spinning mill. The plan was to place the workshops on the ground floor and dwellings for the workers on the upper levels. "He had already begun to excavate the earth and to level the street working with seventy wagons and a hundred laborers, so that if the Pope had lived only one year more the Coliseum would have become the first workers' settlement and large-scale unit of manufacture."[6]

By now we know that the unfinished, as a ruin, is a part of time, but, of what specific time? Doesn't the unfinished configure or contain its own time system, one that is different from that of the ruin?

Conceptually, the unfinished confronts us with two options: either to declare all architectural work as something immersed in the river of time, and therefore to understand it as something that is unfinishable (from the construction to the ruin); or to insist that architecture has a moment of optimal use, of sampling (and that we are faced with a truly classic work when that time is extended), even though we assume that the work will inevitably be devoured by time. In between these two states, the unfinished would be a mere link, hence worth nothing. If nothing can be finished, then the unfinished would cease to produce even the least bit of frustration. Its dramatic aspect would not exist. However, we have seen that the drama exists when energies are wasted and neither a significant, nor even a useful, result is reached.

That is, the unfinished means a situation that is doubly transitive regarding time, since it refers on the one hand to an ideal, unattained object and on the other it manifests itself as a difference, as something that contrasts with that ideal state in which the object becomes part of its contemporaneity and is surrounded by a context of other works. In short, it only exists when it appears as a differentiated state capable of underlining it and making it present with respect to itself and to the time in which the work would have reached its maturity. Consequently, the unfinished is a portrait of time from a specific double perspective.

6 FONTANA, Doménico, *Libro secondo in cui si ragiona di alcune fabriche fatte in Roma et in Napoli*. Naples, 1603, p. 18 (quoted in GIEDION, Sigfried, *Space, Time and Architecture*. Cambridge, MA: Harvard University Press, 1941, p. 106).

The Winged Victory of Samothrace. Louvre Museum, Paris.

Paul Klee, *Angelus Novus*, 1920. Museum of Israel, Jerusalem.

This represents theoccupation of an intermediate time between the past and the future that does not fit in with either one. Neither does it fit within the instant of the pure present that takes place between two well-known winged images: the Victory of Samothrace and Walter Benjamin's Angel of History.

Margarite Yourcenar says that the Victory of Samothrace becomes more of a wind from the sky and the sea than the woman that she once was.[7] The sculpture, eaten away and eroded, is a prow that points to the future, consumed by the wind of the new that beats against it and that encourages us to fight against the fatigue of what is to come. The figure, with its folds lashed by the invisible wear of what is yet to come and that drives life itself, encourages propelling forward with hope. To be the spearhead toward the future is exhausting but memorable. The Victory of Samothrace shows how future eras need heroes that decisively lead the way, regardless of the fatigue this entails. This image stands in sharp contrast with that of the "Angelus Novus" that Walter Benjamin invoked, which is an angel that raises its silent wings toward the past.

"A Klee painting named 'Angelus Novus' shows an angel looking as though he is about to move away from something he is fixed contemplating. His eyes are staring, his mouth is open, his wings are spread. This is how one pictures the angel of history. His face is turned toward the past. Where we perceive a chain of events, he sees one single catastrophe which keeps piling wreckage upon wreckage and hurls it in front of his feet. The angel would like to stay, awaken the dead, and make whole what has been smashed. But a storm is blowing from Paradise; it has got caught in his wings with such violence that the angel can no longer close them. This storm irresistibly propels him into the future to which his back is turned, while the pile of debris before him grows skyward. This storm is what we call progress."[8]

The architecture of the unfinished stands on the thin red line between these two images. It gives shape to a fault. It is an object with a certain depth in the present, a present dislocated from the fleeting, because the meaning its past conveys is persistent and has already been lived (it is the sign of failure) and the possibilities its future has to offer are so scant that its latency can barely be perceived. The unfinished inhabits a mobile present, slightly dislodged from the now. It is an instant that stands slightly in the past, or a now that is slightly anticipated. As if the present of the unfinished occupied a thick space, not a point, between those two images, that of the future or that of the angel of history.

If architecture is the only efficient place to keep time, to store it and to enhance it, then for this same reason the incomplete does not have this containing capacity. It is a broken vessel.

At this point we can say that the time of the unfinished which we experience nowadays is equivalent to a time of ruins. And it does not matter if the way we arrive at the ruin now occurs in a totally different way: when the work is concluded it seems to acquire new meanings and tones; sometimes, beautifully, these tones are settled and soft. This slow, rotting process begins with what the Japanese, who are experts in nuances, call "saba," which literally means "rust" rather than patina. "Saba" is the inimitable rust, the charm of the old, the mark of time on things that Benjamin called "aura." A coat that ends up being more meaningful than the special encrusting that mankind calls history.

7 YOURCENAR, Marguerite, *That Mighty Sculptor, Time*. New York: Noonday Press, 1993 (first edition *Le temps, ce grand sculpteur*, Paris: Éditions Gallimard, 1983).

8 BENJAMIN, Walter, "Theses on the Philosophy of History," in *Illuminations*. New York: Schocken Books, 1969, p. 257.

Greek temple of Segesta, Sicily. Italy.

Thomas Cole, Greek temple of Segesta, 1843.

Afterwards, time will open up lines up in places that at first were unseen; and later on, fissures. It will open skylights. Only a few remains will continue upright. These ruins will be capable of evoking past times, will preserve their meaning, in part, and will acquire the breath of the old. They will hide mysteries regarding their inhabitants and they will allow us to dream about a distant, perhaps even a savage, past. All said, even from the stance of the romantic meaning that ruins have.

However, only a few unfinished projects reach the status of ruin. And when they do, they continue to be signifiers of that double trait. We know that the Greek temple of Segesta, in Sicily, belongs to the category of an unfinished ruin. We know this because the fluting on its columns was never carved. This is the most visible sign of incompleteness. Apart from that, the ruin has neither has a cella nor anything other than a perimeter of marble columns on a stylobate. There is no trace of them ever having been covered by a tympanum. But, to us, these remains are enough. The temple at Segesta is an unfinished building, however, it is a story the ending of which matters little. Not even its evocative nature as a ruin matters much. What does, is its power as stones laid out in a certain order, its setting, its ability to be a wall and a colonnade that can be traced and walked around. It matters, probably, for different reasons than it mattered to the ancient Greeks, however these remains have become transcendent for the generations that have followed.

The temple at Segesta shows us that the future is capable of recovering the unfinished thanks to the small glimmer of hope that the ruin has to offer. Even though, most of the time, this added transcendent is reached thanks to the incorporation of new materials. Procedures that are similar to those that a surgeon, dentist or prosthetist carry out. Thanks to the growths on a work that is supposedly finished, we have seen the emergence of changes in its meaning and tone, to the point of changing its meaning and establishing a conversation, and even changing it completely. The latter becomes part of the history of architecture that has been built over what was already built, ranging from the successive extensions of the Mosque in Cordoba until its conversion into a cathedral, to the materialization of the palace of Charles V in its relationship to the Alhambra, to mention should be:

two canonical cases... That is, the extensions that some projects have undergone have turned them into unfinished projects even though they were complete works to begin with.

We have seen how the unfinished has turned into a sign of our times, however, the debate around the concept is fully connected with some of perennial architectural issues because in the unfinished lies the issue of time, lies the yearning to find a usefulness and a meaning for architecture. In it lies, in short, the same set of problems that are part of all contemporary architecture. In this way, unfinished architecture constitutes an emblem, practically a heraldry in itself that does not cease to hide its feelings, a mix of frustration and quiet hope regarding what we expect of the architecture of the future.

It is hard to find a happier ending for the story of the unfinished. It would not only be a paradox, but an impossibility. The unfinished deserves an advantage over the in-definition of what is to come: the possibility of becoming something else, later on. This is a solace, like leaving it all pending on an expectant ellipsis...

UNFINISHED: COMMON MISREADINGS, MODELS, AND TYPES

JACOBO GARCÍA-GERMÁN

COMMON MISREADINGS

There are three simplistic ways in which the point of the theme proposed by the curators of this year's Spanish Pavilion at the 2016 Venice Biennale can be missed. Three ways that can lead to easily trivializing its proposal and transforming the issue into a fashionable subject.

The first would be to consider this "call for the unfinished" a search for low-cost and modest architecture, or even for "architecture without architects," carried out by agents who question architecture, who, by nature, consider it a suspicious act and therefore search for bottom-up, instant actions. Actions-turned-architecture that can tolerate a ruthless scrutiny on their immediate functional appropriateness, and that can be presented as naively as many of the hands that, literally, give them shape. The simpler, cheaper and more unassuming, the better: self-made and low-cost.

The second obvious line would be the celebration of a novel achievement, of a certain "new beauty" in the raw-by-necessity finishing of an architecture which, due to budget constraints and an urge to return to the basics, rediscovers the seduction of the untreated, unrefined, unpolished and imperfect. All while recovering, along the way, several modernist or avant-garde paradigms (process, collage, Cubism, Arte Povera...) the result of which is, in appearance, a statement of authenticity that pairs material expression with "real" experience: raw and unpolished beauty.

The third misunderstanding would have to do with a generational and cultural shift, one in which a generally younger and disenchanted breed of architects rises to criticize the establishment and strives to shift the rules of the game away from capitalism and power. A new generation that uses the word "starchitect" with disdain, and that regards collective effort and teamwork as ideological values in themselves, regardless of the factual (architectural or not) result: anti-system and collectiveness.

Each one of these three simplifications could instantly lead to a certain confrontation between poles within the profession. Each one would try to moralize its virtues as positions, based upon what apparently are "positive" and "universal" values: sincerity, solidarity, social consciousness, economy of means, participation, etc. And each one of these three lines of thought could recover, voluntary or involuntarily, certain affiliations and doctrines that have appeared in art and architecture throughout the twentieth and twenty-first centuries, certain modernist and contemporary paradigms that re-emerge, this time, perhaps, defused from their original experimental capacities, to merge and turn unfinished into *the ultimate paradigm to end all paradigms.* After the pipe-dream of parametricism and the scepticism it has raised, minimalism's final decline into irrelevance, ecology's incapacity to produce form and character, the misgivings toward deterministic architecture's approach to program and market demands in a post-economic-crisis context, and the saturation that neo-pop, neo-kitsch and other baroque revivals have brought about, the "unfinished" might appear to be the final answer, the final theory, one that is sufficiently open in order to incorporate difference and time as factors, sufficiently tuned toward the collective effort, sufficiently political to be driven by conversation and negotiation and sufficiently formal and visual to be instantly recognized and marketable.

But of course, we all know these are misunderstandings... Why? Because in these three attitudes, (self-made and low-cost, raw and unpolished beauty, and anti-system and collectiveness), a degree of fundamentalism can begin to be discerned, a degree of limiting ideology and a sense of discrimination toward all other value systems and working protocols. A degree of exclusiveness that could lead the practitioner of any of these three lines to dismiss other procedures, to consider them aligned with the status quo, or lacking some sort of moral contemporary commitment. Or even worse, nowadays "unfinished" has become a trend, and as such, a formula. Particularly in reference to material expression, leaving elements and surfaces crudely exposed. Something we can now find all over the Western world, from private homes to the interior design of shops and restaurants, in what could be even understood as a purge of the bad conscience produced by the omnipresence of images from "other" latitudes reminding us about real rawness and necessity.

In this sense, the selection of the concept, even of the word "unfinished," by the curators of this year's Spanish Pavilion couldn't have been more critical, even perversely critical, as it sheds light on what is now an accepted paradigm in contemporary architecture, while at the same time it aims to open the field to new interpretations of the term, giving greater sophistication to its first and more direct connotations.

And, of course, the theme acts as a thermometer that, somehow, measures the state of things not only in Spanish architecture but in Spain in general, even though at the same time it risks flattening differences under an umbrella of sameness. It is almost as if the curators had thrown this—"unfinished"—net and then sat back, wondering and amused at the extent of their trap, seeing up to what point architects are willing to relate their work to this do-goodism, and are able to rewrite their buildings and designs to align them with the nine categories cleverly placed throughout the net.

Given the heterogeneity of the selection and the plurality of the works shown in the Spanish Pavilion, and once the predictable the notion of unfinished have been revealed, how can we transform what is already a cliché into any reflection that tries to steer away from political correctness and aesthetic intensity? In a provisional (unfinished) way, I would like to launch some complementary hypotheses regarding what could be considered an open understanding of the term, to try to avoid the immediacy of the three automatic reactions mentioned above and perhaps to outline another Unfinished Manifesto.

CALLE
DE
HILARIÓN ESLAVA
TELEBANCO
Dona sangre!

UNFINISHED MANIFESTO

Unfinished is not a material but a cultural condition. Unfinished measures the success of architecture inasmuch as architecture is unfinished because it becomes a collective concern, it turns collective.

In architecture, this process of collectivization is facilitated by certain devices and obstructed by others. It is enhanced when architecture steps back and reveals its virtues gradually, and it is blocked when architecture overacts. Unfinished architecture prevails over time when it is sufficiently decoded as to permit its rewriting.

The value of the unfinished travels in time and can only be traced along lines that move away from the immediate present toward the future and toward the past.

Unfinished, as a line toward the future, has to do with the openness that a work of architecture possesses in cultural terms once it is completed and left to the free interpretations of the onlooker. This openness equates to the work's capability for inquiry and activation.

Unfinished, as a line toward the past, is measured through the layers of conscious or unconscious meaning radiating from the work of architecture. These layers also equate to the work's capability for inquiry and activation.

If an unfinished architecture is that which has a degree of ambiguity in its intentions, so that it can be spontaneously apprehended by the audience, then over-determination, functional specificity and formal and material intensity are at odds with this necessary in-definition.

If an unfinished architecture is that which has a certain density in its character, from where to trace threads of invisible connections across time, then invention and singularity should give way to other, more subtle devices.

In other words, the idea of considering our relation to architecture as "unfinished business" happens when architecture produces the necessary frame for a certain reaction to occur, be it singular or collective. This reaction is both performative and cultural and it is exerted by the user, the viewer and the observer: the audience of architecture.

All architecture that closes this required openness will therefore become isolated from any unfinished reaction. Usually, the more architecture is based upon any sort of paradigm or established discourse (parametricism, minimalism, ecology, participation...), the less it will be left to its own devices, left merely as isolated fromsufficiently unjustified by external explanations to permit new readings and interpretations: to become unfinished.

UNFINISHED TIMELINE

So, to put it bluntly, paradigmatic architecture means closed, not unfinished architecture.

Recent architectural thinking seems to have treated this dilemma in complementary ways. Going back to the timeline idea expressed above, if the only way to legitimize a work of architecture as unfinished is to critically observe its relation to time, and if, as stated, this relation goes back and forth, let's consider two possible contemporary architectural procedures which are sceptical of established paradigms and commonplaces and, at the same time, could lead toward the unfinishedness of architecture: Real Models and Typological Commitment.

The first of these techniques questions the finalist tendency toward single objectives in working processes, that is, the prepoderance of cause-and-effect as a residue of modernist reasoning. It underlines the need to introduce a certain playfulness into creative processes, enabling the result to appear as a possibility among many others, thus embracing the uncertainties behind the real intentions and goals of a work of architecture. Even if these uncertainties are minute and short-lived, they narrow the gap between the work and the observer.

The second focuses upon the current re-emergence of a certain "typological revival" in contemporary architecture (a revival which has made history and memory fashionable once again), although this time it is observed through the filter of imitation, serialization, repetition or reproduction in a sort of cold, un-nostalgic and operational way. Types and prototypes are reconsidered not only regarding their morphological and symbolic condition but also in a performative way, through their capacity to produce effects in real use. This commitment could open up the field of interpretation once again, and thus facilitate singular appropiations of generic and atavic architectures. By working with certain neutrality in character and expression, these mechanisms bring the viewers into the game by means of apparent naturality, familiarity and convention, only to make them realize, soon after, that things were not as straightforward as they thought.

REAL MODELS

According to Danish artist Olafur Eliasson, the experimental nature of art has shifted. It has gone from being something that occurred during production processes in studios or laboratories, to becoming a condition that reaches the user or spectator of a work. Experimental and unpredictable components, which depend on aspects that have yet to be defined or controlled and that were distilled traditionally during working processes, nowadays are extended to the moment the work is received by the public. This does not affect the degree of material perfection or completeness of the work of art, or its elaboration. It does not mean the work is semi-finished or in any need of being completed physically, by third parties. It means that only through the user's reception and reaction does the work achieve a cultural meaning, by means of an appropriation process that necessarily incorporates a social and interactional dimension into the piece. In Eliasson's view, this implies a certain presence and physicality. In this way, what was experimental in the laboratory now becomes part of the public arena. The idea of democracy that is implicit in a work of art or architecture today would then depend on its generating and gathering capacity, on how it produces certain effects and unexpected reactions. Metaphor, simplicity, formal clarity, geometry and material seduction play an important part in this legibility.

Atendo
Atendo

If, in the typically modernist process, as described in Bruno Latour's *Laboratory Life* and other parallel studies, the uncertainties of an experimental path, its questions and incoherencies, are progressively omitted for the sake of the readability of the final product, for Eliasson the negotiable condition of his works make these just an option in which "experience is not based on an essence found in the work itself but on an option activated by the users."[1] When the piece stops being a physical representation of some abstract reality and begins equating reality and model, (a model is understood, in this case, as the step traditionally taken before the physical formalization of ideas), at that precise moment, models become real. If "before models were conceived as rational stations on the way for a perfected object,"[2] now the final work *is* a model. It is no longer the final step in an optimized production process that leads in a convergent path to a result that has been stripped of all superfluous aspects, and thus becoming inevitable, rather, it is a reality made up of models that coexist and offer alternative versions.

A model is not a previous, experimental example, a schematic design that only afterward will acquire the qualities that synchronize it with reality (scale, tectonics, etc.).[3] The model is reality itself, and in this apparent maladjustment, in this apparent accident, a gap appears for the spectator's or user's subjective interpretation and their own appropriation of the work.

What is achieved here is an inversion of the procedure of time and creation: the model is no longer the last layer in a process that has taken place outside of itself, in the world of abstract ideas; this process must take place upon the model itself. The experimental nature is displaced to how the work is used and understood, because this work, as a model, is not presented as an end product and it lacks inherent values. It does not show off its causes proudly but it professes, instead, an inquisitive function; it demands an answer.

What consequences does this have for architecture? Working with models suggests leaving behind some of the traditional tools used for codifying architecture, such as scale, tectonic narratives, or the legibility of compositional elements. Instead, certain abstract conditions that enable the process to remain open without "architecturalizing" it until the last moment are valued. This permits tuning into the effects that are associated with the model with the subjective response of the user, instead of the model becoming a mere representation of pre-existing disciplinary codes. It also suggests that repetition, serialization and randomness may result in a certain creative loss of control over the final result. The fact that models simply "appear" in the real world, "are" reality, seems to give a new conceptual lightness to the work of the architect. Somehow, leaving the tracing of those links with reality to the works themselves, thus eliminating complex discourses to justify interventions and the sophisticated explanations and expectations with which architects usually support their production before it enters the world, is a form of professional liberation.

Working with models presupposes repetition and serialization as tools for practice. Repetition is entrusted with the generation of a sufficient number of events for the work to move away from generalities. The creative events that take place along the way breathe life into the work, bringing to light differences to produce "interferences and crosslinks"[4] by insisting on repetition. These make the process become a kind ofautomatic reaction and introduce an element of controlled chance.

1 ELIASSON, Olafur, *Los Modelos son reales*. Barcelona: Gustavo Gili, 2009, p. 8.

2 ELIASSON, Olafur, op. cit, p. 10. IIt seems necessary to clarify that in English, the original language in which Eliasson's text was written, the term "model" refers both to the conceptual sense employed here and to a three-dimensional form, usually a miniature of something else.

3 ELIASSON, Olafur, op. cit., p. 10.

4 For further discussion of the concept of "model" as used by Eliasson, see BALLESTEROS, José Alfonso, "Modelos," *Pasajes de Arquitectura y Crítica* N. 108 (2009).

Brian Eno and Peter Schmidt invented *Oblique Strategies*,[5] a card game that consists of a collection of quick instructions intended to unlock creative blockages during working processes. Throughout the game, there are many references to finding variations within repetition, leaving accumulation and the uncritical extension of sequential steps as the shapers of form, without worrying about narrative coherence: "repetition is a form of change," "once the search is in progress, something will be found," "change nothing and continue with immaculate consistency," "overtly resist change," "just carry on," etc. However, while interest in repetition, serialization and self-referential autonomy have been traditionally considered mechanisms that belong to minimalist 1960s artists such as Donald Judd or Carl Andre, the idea of model inverts this autonomy and turns it into a contingent condition, dispossessed of codifications, and a path toward the engagement between work and audience.

When working with models, typically minimalist ideas such as repetition and serialization that focus on autonomy, become interdependent notions that move between necessity and chance, just as Jacques Monod described in 1970.[6] And it is this introduction of eventuality, as Eliasson explains, that permits the appropriation of a work by third parties, turning it into an unfinished event.

The Eno and Schmidt instructions do not initiate a process from scratch; nor do they introduce accidental or unconscious conditions. On the contrary, they suggest subtle vibrations which are capable of redirecting the path, and of driving processes away from the predictable. The introduction of an element of surprise is also important for the intended openness, for the intended empathy between object and subject. Therefore, working with models is a way of looking for excuses to light a spark upon which, as expected, certain evolutionary actions will take place and will crystallize to shape a possible result.

In architecture, these procedures connect with many mechanisms that belong to the realm of artistic practices, but at the same time they may help to close the gap between architecture and society, and therefore place the work of architecture within the territory of the unfinished, the inquisitive and the unresolved.

5 See http:/www.enoshop.co.uk/: "The Oblique Strategies constitute a set of over 100 cards, each of which is a suggestion of a course of action or thinking to assist in creative situations".

6 MONOD, Jacques, *El Azar y la Necesidad*. Barcelona: Tusquets Editores, 1993, p. 24 (first edition *Le Hasard et la Nécessité*, Paris: Editions du Seuil, 1970).

TYPOLOGICAL COMMITMENT

By applying the label Typological Commitment to the Spanish net, we might find another possible but perhaps unexpected way for approximating architecture to a collective understanding and, in doing so, turning it into a set of—unfinished—problems.

Typology is once again in vogue.[7] It has become the new neo-avant-garde. After two decades of sculptural, foreground over backdrop, formal and objectified architecture, the city has once again become the focus of our attention, and urban fabrics continuities, fringes, limits, densities and backgrounds have turned into architecture's concerns. Architecture suddenly aspires to become blurred with its background, to become invisible, dispassionate. Black and white is the new green. Axonometric projections have displaced glossy, oversaturated renderings. Aldo Rossi has returned to the lecture halls, where he is being discussed, rediscovered, re-assembled... Venturi and Scott-Brown are hailed once again as radical architects. O.M. Ungers complements OMA, and OMA's earlier works have become the object of study of scholars, more so than OMA's "Bigness" and programmatic work, which now, somehow, seems dated.

A whole new breed of talented, mostly European, young practices, related in one way or another to this revival, have taken over the scene.[8] Practices that work on small-scale projects, "normal" commissions, which lack experimental ambition, and who are not afraid to explain their work in terms of cultural continuity with their predecessors. Architectural practices that are aligned with a certain recovery of craftsmanship, formal legibility, straightforwardness and even pragmatism. In any case, their work is a far cry from the material and geometrical complexities of a few years back, as well as from the grand narratives that have to do with novelty and experimentation, on the one hand, or social issues, politics or sustainability, on the other.

The reasons behind this apparent return to architectural modesty, this return to the discipline,[9] are quite obvious in themselves: exhaustion from the formal flamboyancy that the market economy has brought about; the economic crisis, paired with a strong energy crisis and its accompanying political issues; the adoption of star-architecture by Asian and Middle Eastern economies, and the omnipresence on our screens of the same flat-coloted, contoured, "happy-land" renderings that flatten differences and send an increasingly banal message. All of these recurrences and exaggerations have backlashed, sending architecture toward a new direction, toward a certain sobriety. In academic circles, the prowess and arrogance exhibited by the digital world, parametricism, 3D modelling, etc., or, alternatively, the political correctness of sustainability and ecology, have given way to a new realism, one which presents normalness as a possible provocation.

Buy why call this commitment? Why should we consider this new realism as something other than a form of nostalgia, or even a snobbish imposture?

Why should an architecture that appears to revert back to history be understood as something besides a conservative stance? And, to be even more critical, are we talking about a mere revival or about new theoretical positions, design techniques and operational strategies, which heighten those that were once termed postmodernist more than fifty years ago?

7 This can be observed in the concurrent shifts, over the last three years, in the focus of academic programs worldwide, the reemergence of certain graphic devices and the resurgence of forgotten authors from the so-called postmodern period.

8 Several nuclei can be identified in European cities such as London, Brussels, Berlin, Zurich, or Barcelona and Madrid, that share these concerns and who are actively participating in this recuperation of "normalness". For a further insight see GARCÍA-GERMÁN, Jacobo, and GONZÁLEZ DE CANALES, Francisco, *A Minor Architecture* (exhibition and catalogue), Galería Espacio Valverde, Madrid, 2017.

9 Understanding "discipline" as the conscious use of historical reference in the employment of devices such as geometry, form, materiality, program and character.

PABLO

Perhaps, precisely what makes these positions (despite their particular features and differences) forward-looking is the issue at hand: the fact that the low-profile message of normalness is a way of proceeding that is far more effective than other presumably proactive attitudes, in order to turn architecture into a collective concern. That is, to make architecture an issue of proximity, an open door. And it is through this open door that architecture, once again, is left unfinished. If twentieth- and twenty-first-century Pop Art has shown us that one of the best mechanisms to close the gap with the viewer was to make art easy, familiar, in touch with the everyday and related to personal memory, hence producing a bond, or empathy stronger than any other elitist art form (or architecture) could aspire to, then we can suspect that this return to normalness, via history, is an actualization of those attitudes: disciplinary revival as the new pop.

This reaction is not a new thing: one could argue that Neo-Realism in art, architecture, cinematography, etc., emerged in the early 1950s from the keen observation of the crude reality of a postwar economy, and that out of an "aesthetic of necessity" came the most radical of theoretical positions in architectural thinking since.

What makes this revival a new thing are the tools used in working and design processes themselves. After the advent of the digital age, with the enormous amount of historical residue and information available, and given the speed as well as the immediacy of contemporary production, any proposition in terms of historical, disciplinary recovery is bound to lack depth, becoming, instead, an exercise in postproduction, almost a ready-made[10] project. And it is because of this we can speak of "commitment" as an attitude: the disciplinary revival, as some have termed it, is exerted lightly, without a hint of persuasion or the will to proselytize its stance. This lightness sets it apart from any paradigmatic, ideological attitude. If not long ago, in the postmodern era, the best manipulation of historical precedents was carried out from a hyperconscious perspective, with the weight of selections and recombinations charged with some sort of moral stance, today the attitude is closer to that of the disc jockey or recombiner of precedents from the far and the near past. History has been *de-ideologisized.* At the same time, in our post-historical age, the use of past references has flattened them, hierarchies no longer exist. And so this commitment, as that attitude which throws the dice with faith and risk alike, can be seen as a novelty in what was once a cautious and methodical architectural approach to continuity, without revolutions.

If Real Models imply the suspension of any definite meaning assigned to a given object or form, postponing judgment and, in doing so, making way for the collective in the evaluation and contingent understanding of architecture or art, Typological Commitment, a parallel move toward dispossesing architecture from active expression while grounding its geometries, orders, character, etc., in historical precedents, is proposed as a soft, invisible way toward the establishment of empathy between architecture and user, without eliminating its critical capacity. As in some of the best mid-twentieth-century modernist architecture, Typological Commitment puts forward the generic while expecting possibility and the unpredictable. This is attained through strong organizational schemes, using traditional notions such as wall, room, door, partition and other conventional devices, a far cry from contemporary fluid and un-hierarchical options. At the same time, and due to a certain spatial (and also facial) muteness, these apparently rigid dispositions nurture an inbuilt tolerance, the capacity to be reconfigured and reinterpreted over time, which makes them the ultimately successful, unfinished architecture.

10 One line of thought that has recently deployed ready-made procedures deriving from Marcel Duchamp while considering our contemporary digital era, which has great relevance to the architectural world, can be found in BOURRIAUD, Nicolas, Postproduction. Culture as Screenplay: *How Art Reprograms the World*. New York: Lukas & Sternberg, 2002.

MODELS AND TYPES: GENERIC INSTALLATION, SUBJECTIVE INFRASTRUCTURE

Paradoxical provisional ending for *unfinishedness*: an immediacy, urgency and proliferation of architectural production on one side versus the recovery of generic gestures and orders related to memory on the other. Models and types: models that are repeated with such spontaneity that they turn architecture into an installation; types that shift from being pure infrastructure to become critical and subjective once again. However, in both attitudes lies the idea of appropriation via decontextualization. The strategy of subtlety defamiliarizing with the aim of producing an arresting moment, a second glance. Or, in other words, architecture overcoming its role as a mere problem-solver, its cause-and-effect reasoning, the application of paradigmatic thinking and a preestablished set of aesthetic and ideological guidelines.

Only by means of pulling away from these inertias and thus opening the symmetrical process of producing and using architecture to the unexpected, can architecture become, paradoxically, radical again. Radical being the maladjustment between object and subject in the hope of starting a conversation, thus reaching an unfinished nature.

Accompanying this text are photographs corresponding to *Atlas Madrid Entropia*, an ongoing collaboration between architects Jacobo García-Germán and Eduardo Prieto with photographer Juan Rodríguez. This project traces the contingencies of the passing of time and the vicissitudes exerted by use and decay on a set of buildings, some of them well-known constructions, in the city of Madrid. This archive can be seen, in the context of Unfinished, as the mute register of the complex interchanges between user, city and architecture. Inasmuch as these buildings can somehow proudly show their scars and offer them as proof of their survival and adaptation capacities, they legitimize themselves as afflicted actors in the infinite processes of unfinished performances taking place in the city; infinite unfinished dialogues and rewritings. This work was first shown in the exhibition "Atlas Madrid Entropia, CentroCentro Cibeles, Excmo. Ayuntamiento de Madrid," February to May 2016, with the accompanying catalogue.

ABOUT THE NOTION OF PRESENT IN ARCHITECTURE

ÁNGEL MARTÍNEZ GARCÍA-POSADA

1

Time present and time past
Are both perhaps present in time future
And time future contained in time past.
If all time is eternally present
All time is unredeemable.
What might have been is an abstraction
Remaining a perpetual possibility
Only in a world of speculation.
What might have been and what has been
Point to one end, which is always present.

—T. S. Eliot, "Burnt Norton"

The proposal of the Spanish Pavilion for the 2016 Venice Biennale was introduced by a quote from Marc Augé regarding unfinished buildings and the beauty of the uncertainty between past, present and future: "Unfinished buildings have the beauty of that which could have been. Of that is not yet there. Of that which might be one day." In other words, these thoughts were a reminder of the Aristotelian categories of potential and act that are homologous to the practice of art. The understanding of the world itself as form and matter, can be seen as a vision of reality with an artistic affiliation that the philosopher had. Moreover, it seems pertinent to evoke the famous opening of T.S. Eliot's *Four Quartets* in its poetic fusion "What might have been and what has been point to one end, which is always present." This operative interpretation, which is also contemporary, integrates and transcends lament and values paths that have branched off from the main road, and was likewise the proactive formula that the argument of the curators, Iñaqui Carnicero and Carlos Quintáns, hoped to convey and that this text, a propos of an expanded understanding of the notion of idiomatic in architecture, would like to comment on.

A kind of lyrical symmetry exists between that which is unfinished and that which is already on its path to ruin. Around this asymptote, which one can move closer to or move away from, like the peak of Sisyphus's mountain, there exists a shimmering band in which it is hard to see if something is about to be finished or if it was ever considered done and, therefore, lies within the next phase, degradation. In a well-known short essay, by Marguerite Yourcenar, under the apt title *That Mighty Sculptor, Time*, this precise explanation can be found: "On the day when a statue is finished, its life, in a certain sense, begins. The first phase, in which it has been brought, by means of the sculptor's efforts, out of the block of stone into human shape, is over; a second phase, stretching across the course of centuries, through alternations of adoration, admiration, love, hatred, and indifference, and successive degrees of erosion and attrition, will bit by bit return it to the state of unformed mineral mass out of which its sculptor had taken it." We architects may well feel inclined to identify both with Sisyphus and the stone. Albert Camus admitted in the book he dedicated to this myth that: "Each atom of that stone, each mineral flake of that night-filled mountain, in itself forms a world. The struggle itself toward the heights is enough to fill a man's heart. One must imagine Sisyphus happy."

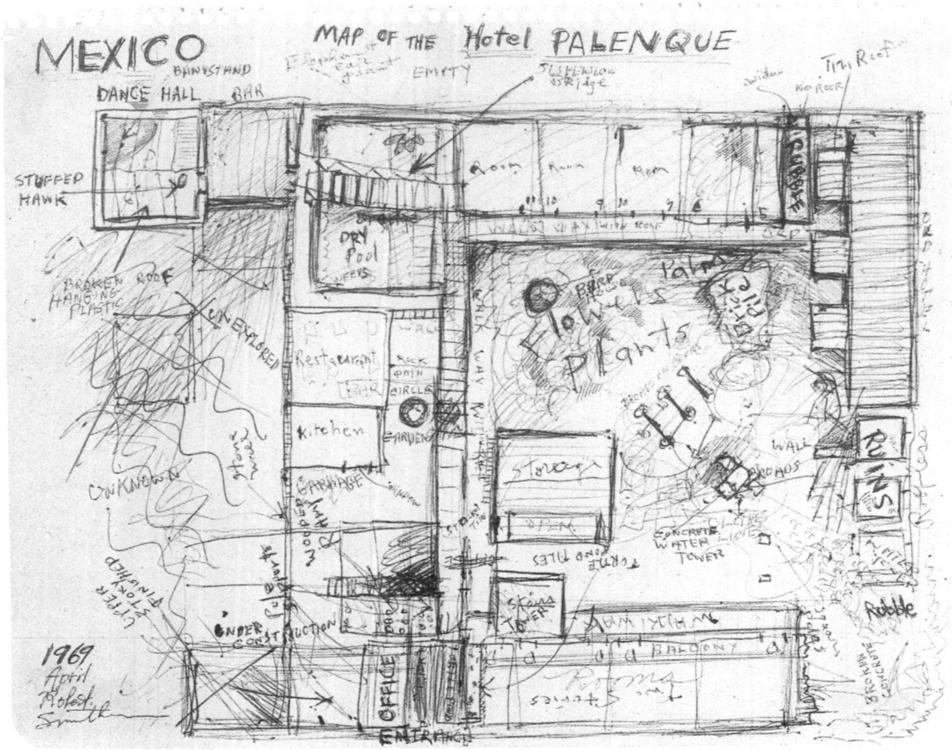

Robert Smithson. Plan drawing of the *Hotel Palenque*, 1969. Estate of Robert Smithson.

Robert Smithson. Photographs of the *Hotel Palenque*, 1969. Estate of Robert Smithson.

ABOUT THE NOTION OF PRESENT IN ARCHITECTURE

During the narration of the film about his work *Spiral Jetty*, Robert Smithson—who carried stones back and forth during his short but intense career—included images of prehistory and dinosaurs taken from the Museum of Natural History in New York, a place he visited often as a child, along with other images that showed the construction process of the spiral. "I needed a map that would show the prehistoric world as coextensive with the world I existed in." As early as 1966, in one of the first texts he ever published, "Entropy and the New Monuments," he delved into this idea of a future that looks toward the past, adding that the feeling of a far past and a distant future had its origin, in part, in his experiences as a young boy at the Museum of Natural History, "there the cave-man and the space-man may be seen under one roof." He often quoted Vladimir Nabokov: "the future is but the obsolete in reverse." Smithson accepted the explanation of the origin of the universe as the evolution of a nebulous spiral of stars. He also accepted the theory that cosmic time was marked by a process of expansion and contraction, hence his identification of the distant future with the most remote past. The ambiguous shape of his spiral could be perceived unfolding and as coiling at the same time. "Following the spiral steps we return to our origins."

In light of how the proposal of the Spanish Pavilion has been articulated, it may seem convenient to find a symbolic connection with the fact that in the critical summer that led to the financial crisis of 2008, with its epicenter in the collapse of Lehman Brothers, at the Museo Nacional Centro de Arte Reina Sofía in Madrid the work *Hotel Palenque* was shown. The piece registered an experience Smithson had in 1969 during a trip to the Yucatan Peninsula. The series of images showed the different stages of the hotel's state: traces of demolitions and new construction, obsolescence and renovation. Smithson was drawn to that overlapping of construction processes and contemporary ruins. He had the feeling that the hotel was built with the same spirit used by the Mayans in the erection of their temples. There was a window from which those precise monuments, the ones Smithson had gone to visit, could be seen. The images on display belonged to a slideshow that was part of a lecture he gave to students at the University of Utah in 1972. These slides did not include a single image of the temples—"you have to go there to see for yourself, and I hope that you go to the Hotel Palenque so that you learn something about how the Mayans are still building"—and they are an intriguing example of an interconnected narrative. On the map he drew of the hotel he indicated the existence of "unexplored areas" behind the restaurant, or "unknown" territories close to the kitchen. The group of photographs and drawings gave shape to the notion of entropy he approached in his works and texts. His work could be considered that of an "entropologist" and his career could be interpreted as a process of "de-sedimentation" of places through revealing their strata.

Just a few months before appearing in the show in Madrid, Nicolas Bourriaud, in an interesting project called *Estratos* curated for PAC Murcia in which he tried to explicitly convey some of the links between recent art and archaeology, used this same piece by Smithson as a metaphor to illustrate the concept of excavating the past, revealing the multiple layers of time that make up our daily life. In a Smithson-like description of that incomplete, almost raw construction, a predominant state did not exist. That amalgam of moments, that stark palimpsest was more attractive given its confusion. Bourriaud's concern at the time, his interest in the way contemporary art turns time into a new spatial dimension, also feels close. *Hotel Palenque* was a building under construction and a contemporary ruin at the same time. Regardless of its modesty, the beautiful drawing of the hotel's plan on a sheet of notebook paper had something Piranesian in the way it searched for preceding, not necessarily finished, times and its attempt to converge other spatial dimensions onto a plan drawing.

Dinosaurs on their way to the New York World's Fair, 1964. Photograph by John Orris, the New York Times Archive.

In my beginning is my end. In succession
Houses rise and fall, crumble, are extended,
Are removed, destroyed, restored, or in their place
Is an open field, or a factory, or a by-pass.
Old stone to new building, old timber to new fires,
Old fires to ashes, and ashes to the earth
Which is already flesh, fur and faces,
Bone of man and beast, cornstalk and leaf.
Houses live and die: there is a time for building
And a time for living and for generation.

—T. S. Eliot, "Burnt Norton"

Campo Marzio, a series of engravings based on a virtual plan of Rome published by Giovanni Battista Piranesi in 1761, besides documenting the remains of Roman glory he had already begun in *Antichitá* in 1756, was a project in which, given the author's knowledge regarding the reproduction of Roman architecture, a new plan of the city was created where the preexisting vestiges grew until they collided with one another. The course of the river Tiber, the Pantheon, the empty space of Piazza Navona, Hadrian's mausoleum or the Theater of Marcellus were barely recognizable. The architect revealed and altered layers of the past, as if it were possible to escape history, creating a new present, perhaps looking ahead toward a new ending, like Eliot recites in his verses. In Smithson's 1977 article "A Tour of the Monuments of Passaic, New Jersey"—nowadays a work of reference—we can find a lucid interpretation of the reality of the periphery built by humankind as a premature ruin. In a unique exercise of comparative monumentality around the limits of eternity, he asked himself: "Has Passaic replaced Rome as The Eternal City? If certain cities of the world were placed end to end in a straight line according to size, starting with Rome, where would Passaic be in that impossible progression? Each city would be a three-dimensional mirror that would reflect the next city into existence. The limits of eternity seem to contain such nefarious ideas."

We can recognize a possible scenario of similarities in Rome's own unfinished nature. Thus, the incomplete gate left by Sangallo when he died, in spite of the hundreds of bastions for the defense of the city that his project foresaw, or thebosses that appear only on a corner of what would have been Bramante's Palace of Justice, are fragments that the city has absorbed to the point of blurring the lines between the pages of its history. Also mentionable is the bulking Monte Testaccio that Santiago de Molina explains herein, made out of the accumulation of ceramic residue from imperial times, as an extreme case of dissolution between artifice and nature, of a mix of times by accumulation, an almost geographical testimony of the condition described by Eliot further along the verses quoted above. In all of those stanzas the poet repeated like a mantra, back and forth, the canto "in my beginning is my end," "in my end is my beginning."

Robert Smithson next to the Colosseum in Rome, 1959. Estate of Robert Smithson.

Robert Smithson as a child at the Museum of Natural History in New York. Estate of Robert Smithson.

If Aristotle's productive interpretation of the world as a dual ensemble of form and matter referred to its artistic interpretation, this archaeological analogy of a time over which we move forward and backward by means of artistic creation gives breath to the architectural and artistic path that resounds in the content shown in the Spanish Pavilion. In "Excavation and Memory," a short text by Walter Benjamin, this real and symbolic link between creation and retrospection was already laid out, a propos of that interpretation of the double path throughout time: "Memory is not an instrument for exploring the past, but rather a medium. It is the medium of that which is experienced, just as the earth is the medium in which ancient cities lie buried. He who seeks to approach his own buried past must conduct himself like a man digging... For the 'matter itself' is no more than the strata which yield their long-sought secrets only to the most meticulous investigation. That is to say, they yield those images that, severed from all earlier associations, reside as treasures in the sober rooms of our later insights—like torsos in a collector's gallery. It is undoubtedly useful to plan excavations methodically. Yet no less indispensable is the cautious probing of the spade in the dark loam. And the man who merely makes an inventory of his findings, while failing to establish the exact location of where in today's ground the ancient treasures have been stored up, cheats himself of his richest prize. In this sense, for authentic memories, it is far less important that the investigator report on them than that he mark, quite precisely, the site where he gained possession of them. Epic and rhapsodic in the strictest sense, genuine memory must therefore yield an image of the person who remembers, in the same way a good archaeological report not only informs us about the strata from which its findings originate, but also gives an account of the strata which first had to be broken through."

In Franz Kafka's narration of the cconstruction of *The Great Wall of China*, he came to realize that its execution was discontinuous and dispersed and he outlined the question of whether it ever reached a finished state.The story fictionalized the following conjecture about how it was built: 500 meters were raised from one side and 500 meters from the other, until they met; then, instead of continuing the completed kilometer, the workers were taken to other regions, where the same steps were repeated, leaving that kilometer of wall standing alone, like a piece of land art *avant la lettre*, awaiting a distant and remotely possible future continuation. This resulted in gaps that took years to close, some after an improbable official conclusion, which made him suspect that there existed many empty stretches that were never erected. For those of us who follow the history of humanity through its projects and buildings—one riddled with branching paths such as those mentioned in Augé's quote or Borges's metaphysics—the process described by Kafka, the homogenous application of this architectural knowledge to all times, is probably the best way to satisfy the unreachable need of perpetuity: a linear production in time, continuous in its circularity, would have privileged the last, solidly erected traces. The improbable state of total construction and perfect closure would have brought about a succession of stretches of wall that belonged to multiple periods, a mix that would have set, in orderly succession, what in so many buildings, or cities, appears superimposed, or like a Hotel Palenque standing in a circle, with each phase following the previous one in line after being randomly shuffled. Like another justification for that Kafkaesque form, one that is more whimsical and mundane. As if it were impossible to retain the workers and make them lay stone upon stone in the middle of nowhere, far from their homes. One could imagine the parties thrown every time a segment of the wall was finished, how good it felt to contemplate the stretches that had been concluded on their return to their places of origin, the longed-for rest at each of their homes a way of placating their impatience and despondency.

Robert Smithson walking on *Spiral Jetty*, Great Salt Lake, Utah, 1973. Photograph by Giancarlo Gorgoni.

Mark Tansey. *Purity Test*, 1982. Curt Marcus Gallery, New York.

ABOUT THE NOTION OF PRESENT IN ARCHITECTURE

The segmented existence of the 117 kilometers of Hadrian's Wall between England and Scotland could illustrate one of those finished and abandoned stretches of wall that await an uncertain, upcoming conclusion in Kafka's story. Guillermo Altares describes a similar building process to that narrated by Kafka in "The First Wall of the West." Every Roman mile a small fort was built, up to a total of seventy-nine. Between each fort there were two guard towers that served as communication points. A moat ran along the front, and a deeper moat defended the back side of the wall. It is approximately four meters high, although in some cases it made use of natural elevations. To the north, the land of barbarians, there were seventy-six access points. To the south there were fifteen gates that allowed crossing the moat.

Under the rules of Trajan and Hadrian, both of whom came from the Spanish city of Italica—a place visited on school fieldtrips, year after year, by this author—the Roman Empire reached its zenith, in terms of prosperity and expansion of its territory. Hadrian wanted to fortify its most unstable boundary, the northern frontier, with a system of fortifications that included a wall between England and Scotland, and on some strategic locations along the Rhine and the Danube. However, his was a time of peace, the provinces were content and, for the most part, the situation was calm. Buildings were being erected throughout the empire, Hadrian himself promoted the construction of hundreds of public facilities during his travels. The wall, which was never finished and that is, in its own right, a kind of mysterious territorial project, was more a symbol than a need. Today, it remains a symbol, this time of the national identity of both the Scots and the English.

It is pleasant to see an incomplete analogy between the Kafkaesque episode and our architectural endeavors. Our works are never concluded, they never close a perfect circle, there are always flanks that remain open. This does not matter, all walls are more metaphysical than structural, none end up enclosing anything, in the same way that their strategically fragmentary construction process fails to guarantee the perfect defense. Instead, they are more of an invitation to carry out a secretive conquest. What's more, none of our structures can contain the life of their inhabitants completely. Nor can the economy of a nation rely completely on the sole activity of construction.

The city is often described as a discontinuous and hazardous amalgam of texts, just like the layout of the stretches of walls in Kafka's story. Architecture is a writing in time, an imperfect remedy against oblivion. Writing and architecture become diluted, like fleeting lines on a current. Territories and cities could be understood as statues that have been given shape throughout the centuries, layer by layer, sediment by sediment. To study architecture over the years is a way of discerning the biographical sketch of humankind, all architecture is an accumulation of intertwined eras. When we are thrown into hostile territory, we need to devise a network of causes and effects in order to prolong our survival, to feel that we will continue to live and, when we look back, to feel like we are a part of a long line of history. In contrast with other organisms, we are capable of fantasizing about what has already happened and about what is to come, we play at peeking into the past and venturing into the future. Art and science are the children of imagination, being able to create alternative worlds makes us special as a species. Artists and scientists are writers that intercede between fiction and reality, yesterday and tomorrow. The convergence of the three times, past, present and future, mentioned by Octavio Paz when he hailed modernism. He sustains the cliché that the past is a country separated from ours by a long interval of time, however, we think that a stroke is a short-circuit capable of bridging times and distances. A solitary time train running in a single direction does not exist; sometimes we come across a coach that comes from the past and, for a moment, we have it right next to us, to our side, in our present.

Alfredo Jaar. *Venezia, Venezia*, 2013. Photographs by Agostino Osio.

2

For man is that creature without any fixed age, who has the faculty of becoming, in a few seconds, many years younger, and who, surrounded by the walls of the time through which he has lived, floats within them but as though a basin the surface-level of which is constantly changing, so as to bring him into the range now of one epoch, now of another.

—Marcel Proust, "In Search of Lost Time"

A few years ago, the use of multiple similes to talk about the collapse of an economy based on housing speculation turned into a trite habit. Among these terms, some of the most used referred to means of travel, by land, air and sea; spoke in the wheel, flat tires, tunnels, bursts, collisions, shipwreck, drifts, run aground, among others. Those simplistic and clumsy euphemisms that referred to a certain collective failure, soon ceased to be novel and became commonplace, which made the situation doubly pathetic. The proactive taxonomy of abstract categories formulated for the Spanish proposal in the Biennale, and its strategy to promote design approaches regarding how to subvert this negative situation and turn it into a positive action, is, however, doubly appropriate.

Even if I run the risk of being redundant, I will try to expand beyond clichés, I hope, one of those journalistic expressions, that of the maritime accident. Diving experts claim that it is difficult to express the feelings one has when submerging into the sea to explore a sunken ship. To the thrill of the historic find, of the encounter with a submerged past, they add the research into the possible causes of the shipwreck and the intense marine life that these artificial reefs create. We also recognize an aura of beauty in the contrast that exists between the modern technology of neoprene suits and assisted breathing mechanisms, and the old swollen timber that, in its rings, still reflects the history of the trees those planks once were. Statistics say that some of the places where it is possible to dive in order to observe these centuries-old, stranded scenarios have turned into the focal points of tourism. The reader might enjoy accompanying me in my navigation through certain analogies with the matter at hand.

Alfredo Jaar. *Venezia*, Venezia 2013. Photographs by Agostino Osio.

During the summer of 2014, an article by Alberto García Palomo for *El País* titled "The mystery of sunken ships," reported on the wish that many diving companies have to be able to offer an ancient treasure within their operating grounds. The journalist had documented the existence, back then, of thirty-odd sunken ships that could be visited, most of which were shipwrecks. He also explained a controversial situation: the wish that diving companies, and even some municipalities, had to sink ships on purpose in order to expand their businesses and their supply. However, red tape and pressures from environmentalists have slowed this lucrative trend. One could say that while the construction industry returns to cruising speed above ground, some investors are considering sinking boats for pleasure. It is paradoxical to design a boat, by definition something that has to float, to later sink it. This is as unnatural, but in the opposite direction from director Werner Herzog's ludicrous image of a huge steamship on top of a mountain, which would become the origin of *Fitzcarraldo* and emerge as the visionary project of the movie's main character, played by Klaus Kinski. In Portugal, in 2012, the company Ocean Revival, with the support of the European Union and other means of patronage, sank four ships that were between 40 and 100 meters long in order to create a man-made reef. Since then, some Spanish initiatives, that have run aground due to bureaucratic and legal obstacles, have tried to emulate the initiative. Regardless of this, the Ministry of Agriculture, Fisheries and the Environment approves of creating these artificial reefs since an abundance of marine life springs up around these sunken ships, something that can result in a means of direct protection of fishing habitats as well as the regeneration of resources. Specialists advise that there are two necessary prerequisites for this: to decontaminate the wrecked ship and to adapt it so that diving can be practiced safely. Environmentalists claim, on the other hand, that the point is not to create new forms of biodiversity, but to protect that which already exist and that the activities proposed can actually become toxic. In any case, more research into the deposits is need, just like, we could say, any architectural research into the waters of the past.

I was reminded of that article when I heard about the argument behind the proposal of the curators Carnicero and Quintáns, in their strategic search for some of the regenerating mechanisms that some recent Spanish architecture has displayed in order to make the most of the large amount of abandoned structures that the past situation has left us. I also recalled that ridiculous joke about the story of the Titanic: if you watch the movie in reverse it is about a bunch of zombies that emerges from the sea, takes over a ship, becomes rich and travels to England to play bridge. Anyway, there are multiple possible shared models between that piece of news and the operative interpretation of the Biennale's theme. Those who are amused by merely contemplating the beauty of some submerged remains or in the comparable presence of halted and abandoned structures that have not reached their final state are not of our interest. However, what will interest us are those who approach their reactivation by diverse means orchestrated by architectural design, just like the paradoxical intensity summoned around a sunken ship, but due to unexpected causes rather than provoked events. I would like all of this to be understood more metaphorically than literally, and I would not like anybody to see in the specific story of a shipwreck, for example, the explicit desire to contextualize. However, I would like the reader to see that, perhaps there are many ways to stay afloat, like the proposal of the Spanish Pavilion has attempted to spread and promote. In a beautiful article in *Culturas,* the supplement of *La Vanguardia,* under the title "The Cycles of Time," Antoni Martí wrote about the cycle of catastrophe and ruin, or the cycle of regeneration and life, using, once again, Eliot's verses. There are times when certain ruins are not a sign of regression but the most pertinent and handy attribute of progress. Benjamin, once again, had already formulated this: sometimes it is necessary to found the concept of progress upon a previous notion of catastrophe.

Alfredo Jaar. *Venezia*, Venezia 2013. Photographs by Agostino Osio.

Likewise, let us recall wat is known as the paradox of Theseus, which has certain similarities if we apply it to architectural heritage. It was formulated by Plutarch as follows: "The ship on which Theseus sailed with the youths and returned in safety, the thirty-oared galley, was preserved by the Athenians down to the time of Demetrius Phalereus. They took away the old timbers from time to time, and put new and sound ones in their places, so that the vessel became a standing illustration for the philosophers in the mooted question of growth, some declaring that it remained the same, others that it was not the same vessel." In different disciplines, ranging from psychology to history, the discussion is still the same: if, on the one hand, each of the parts were replaced one by one or if, on the other, the replaced parts were stored away and were used later on to rebuild another boat, which, if either would be Theseus's original ship. This controversy is similar to the quandary that exists between Western and Eastern cultures regarding heritage preservation: in Western culture, perpetuity has to do with the continuity of matter; in some Eastern cultures, it has to do with the permanence of a certain essence, as the ongoing renovation of Japanese temples shows us.

In 2013, as Chile's representative at the Venice Biennale, the artist Alfredo Jaar presented the work *Venezia, Venezia,* a 1:60 replica of the Giardini, the venue that hosts most of the permanent pavilions of the event. A mechanism allowed the replica to emerge from a five-meter-wide by five-meter-long by one-meter-high metal tank that contained from the city's canals. This emergence occurred 24,860 times during the event, to later be submerged once again. The artist referred to the "24.860 opportunities to imagine a different order, a kind of cultural democracy open to all, a poetic attempt at questioning the obsolete model of national pavilions because, in today's world, cultures flow." Regardless of another possible interpretation that places the piece somewhere between politics and poetics, a view mentioned at the time by the art media, the artist invited the spectators to imagine other possibilities with this site-specific work. The repeated image of submersion and flotation had something about it that spoke of the geography of the city itself, which is in the process of sinking. However, to us it seemed to be, besides this, a strong image that resembled the *Spiral Jetty* that Smithson created, which emerged from and disappeared into the lake depending on the water level, and also reminded us of our metaphorical sunken ships.

In the pictures that show Robert Smithson walking on the spiral and into the water, he seems immersed in his own thoughts, perhaps imagining that by walking on water he was also walking on the universal story of time, in accordance with the formal similitude of his work with that of a universe that expands and contracts. In his articles, Smithson questioned the work of his contemporaries and friends Donald Judd, Carl André, Robert Morris or Dan Flavin, who seemed to be eliminating time from their pieces. The 6.000 tons of basalt and earth that sunk into the Great Salt Lake were placed there when the body of water was practically dry. Two years later, when the piece was *finished*, the water reached its usual level and the spiral was swallowed up. The proliferation of images from the time have prolonged the moment in which the spiral appeared above the surface, although during most of its existence, those stones have been below the waterline. With the advent of the new millennium a drought revealed them once again and the basalt structure remerged for the first time in thirty years. This idea had driven Smithson's work even though he was never able to see his piece *finished* (salt was an essential component of it, since crystallized molecules also grow following a spiral layout, thus reproducing the same structure that was the origin of the universe; "each cubic salt crystal echoes the *Spiral Jetty* in terms of the crystal's molecular lattice"). After decades under water, the salt from the lake, encrusted into the stone, had turned the jetty white. To this day, the spit of earth and stone continues to be exposed to the water cycle, like a sculpture is exposed to time, unfinished and subjected, also, to the entropy created by the many admirers who visit it.

Alfredo Jaar. *Venezia*, Venezia 2013. Photographs by Agostino Osio.

Toward the end of 2009 news emerged that the conservators of the Dia Art Foundation, in charge of safeguarding some the most important land art works and responsible for the preservation of part of the Robert Smithson collection, warned that the *Spiral Jetty* was gradually dissolving. This alarming announcement did not mention the inexorable natural erosion of the piece whatsoever, which was part of the artist's original idea, but the degradation it was suffering due to the many visitors who, on their pilgrimage to the site, took bits of it back to their homes as souvenirs of their emotional experience. This geography of earth and water, which could unfold or curl up forward or backward, just like the angel in Benjamin's story, illustrates a definition of art and architecture as an account of transferences and movement that is permanently open-ended, and paints a portrait of the artist or architect as an amateur who transfers things from one place to another, both real and allegorical, orwho navigates in any direction of time whatsoever and whose works are, inexorably, open. In *The Shape of Time*, George Kubler postulated a study of history in which time was not linear nor chronological, but a way of tracing relationships between ideas that stand alone along the line of evolution, like the Kafkaesque wall that was so influential for American artists in the 1960s and 1970s—among them Smithson—and whose wake is recognizable to our day.

Some of the projects shown in the Spanish Pavilion at the 2016 Venice Biennale are based on this wise, but not melancholic, redemptive choice of an ambiguous time that passes over the present, toward the past and toward the future. As mentioned above, if anything makes humankind unique as a species, it is the urgency with which it needs to establish links that go back and forth. In his essay *The Tightrope Walker*, Andres Neuman writes: "One of the prodigious powers that writing has is how it makes it possible to reconstruct the past, not only to go back and represent it, but also to transform it. To remember while writing is an act of utopian retrospective... To search for lost time does not mean merely to return, but to choose new paths. To conquer another memory... Science fiction has wanted to focus on one of the basic functions of writing: to remind us of the future. To evoke times that who knows will ever come." This same alluded convergence of past, present and future, even of other pasts, presents and futures, takes place through the architectural project.

The different projects on display in the Spanish pavilion, shown under different categories with the well-aimed overall title of *Unfinished*, exemplify architecture's creative capacity to expand the present to the past or to the future. Among these projects I would like to mention one that I saw built—or un-built—in real time, due to my proximity to its authors, to its location and to its program, a venue for the cultural activities of the university where I have been teaching, along with the architects of this work, for a decade: the project for a contemporary art and exhibition center in a former convent in the center of Seville, the work of María González and Juanjo López de la Cruz, built in 2013. The proposal interprets the former, sixteenth-century convent in which it is inserted as a setting that has been altered over and over again over the centuries, showing multiple traces and scars from this process. The series of alterations suggested "a continuous metamorphosis that transcends styles and dilutes the certainties of heritage," in the architect's own words, "an intervention that does not strive to be conclusive and that offers, like a tale that has no end, an intermediate moment that had to take place, from which all options are, once again possible, a space as an ellipsis, waiting for the next exhibition to finish it off." The action of revealing a better version of the space, hidden by the different finishings of previous interventions, activated the project and turned destruction into something as natural as construction itself: recovering the transparent relationship with the patio, tearing through existing finishing materials and discovering, behind them, a hidden and latent building, as if revealing a portrait similar to the drawing of the *Hotel Palenque* over its walls, unmasking floors, walls and ceilings.

Alfredo Jaar. *Venezia*, Venezia 2013. Photographs by Agostino Osio.

Gordon Matta-Clark expressed like no one else the need to counter the act of destroying, as art, or the act of building, as architecture. Matta-Clark stood on his own and face to face with buildings when there was nothing left of them but matter and, like an inverted architect, he paid careful attention to the acts of cutting, sectioning, disassembling, perforating, and tilting, a care that is usually reserved for the acts of building, assembling, connecting, piling and leveling: "Buildings are fixed entities in the minds of most people. The notion of mutable space is taboo, especially in one's own house. People live in their space with a temerity that is frightening. Home owners generally do little more than maintain their property." Once, the artist stated that the best reaction that he had ever received to his work next to the Pompidou in Paris where he drilled a hole into a ruinous block of flats that was set for demolition to make way for the museum, came from an old door lady who said: "Oh, I see the purpose for that hole—it is an experiment in bringing light and air into spaces that never had enough of either." Matta-Clark performed his actions on condemned buildings, which he wounded in order to awaken them during their last hours, to turn them into characters of a drama and show them as pure, raw material. This raised people's curiosity, nostalgic feeling and pity, elevating the act of returning matter to matter to the level of artistic feelings. Matta-Clark made cracks in buildings, he produced entities, architectural objects from other architectural objects. His task was not to give shape, but to metamorphose, a destructive act as well as a constructive one. In our work in the urban context it has become ever more common to approach things that are already there in order to think of another ending for them.

In his *A History of Eternity*, Jorge Luis Borges wrote: "One such obscurity, neither the most challenging nor the least beautiful, keeps us from ascertaining the direction in which time moves. It is commonly held to flow from past to future, but the opposite notion, established in Spanish verse by Miguel de Unamuno, is no less logical: Nocturnal the river of hours flows/from its source, the eternal tomorrow... Both directions are equally probable-and equally unverifiable". Jorge Manrique's verse from *The Coplas on the Death of his Father* is well-known in Spain, "our lives are as fated as the rivers." In *Austerlitz*, W. G. Sebald asked himself: "Every river, as we know, must have banks on both sides, so where, seen in those terms, where are the banks of time?"

When we navigate through history we hear the murmur of centuries, a polyphony of voices with which we spin a net of fictions in order to end up building something that does not slide through our fingers. An ancient phrase says: "sailing is necessary, living is not necessary." Memory, like time, is a fluid state. Perhaps the task of historians, archaeologists, artists or architects consists in giving it shape, in finding a way to narrate time or to understand it, to make it visible. Aristotle also wrote that poetry is a more elevated form than history because it tells what happens as if the facts had been traversed by a chain of reasoning that organizes them toward a certain finality. It is true that we are made out of two substances: one, that is tangible, is subjected to a place and a time; the other, thought, is unfinished as long as we live, can navigate following spatial-temporal ports, return to the past and move to the future, conceive things that are no longer there or that no longer exist, design others that have never been.

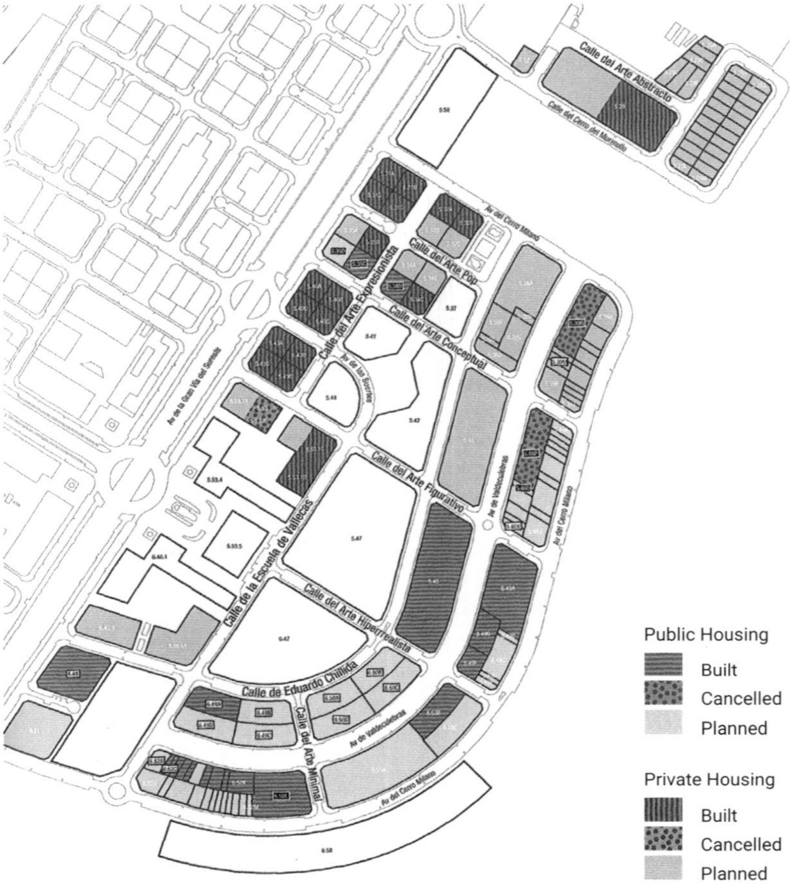

Madrid, Ensanche de Vallecas. Museo Nacional Centro de Arte Reina Sofía, Madrid.

Hans Haacke. *Castillos en el aire*, 2012. Museo Nacional Centro de Arte Reina Sofía, Madrid.

3

A place is condensed time, multiple times. Not only its present but a labyrinth of time and different periods which is interwoven into a landscape and constitutes itself, in the same way that folds and wrinkles and expressions recorded by happiness or sadness do not even mark a face, but are the face of that person, who never has the age or the spirit of that moment alone, but that of all ages and spirits of life. Landscape as face, man in the landscape like a wave in the sea.

—Claudio Magris, "Endless Journey"

In 2012, coinciding with the exhibition *Castillos en el aire (Castles in The Air)* that the Reina Sofia dedicated to him, Hans Haacke conceived a well-aimed site-specific piece that linked the context that housed it with his own career. He also explained why he had chosen that title, which, besides being an image from a tale, was yet another one of those phrases used to describe what was then the recent real estate crisis. In this *ad hoc* piece, the artist documented the meaningful case of a new development on the southern fringes of the Ensanche de Vallecas, to the south of Madrid, which had been abandoned in the midst of construction and that, perhaps, hoped to become, just like the Barrio de las Letras in the center of town, a kind of Neighborhood of the Arts. This enclave, left unfinished at the beginning of its development, like so many others at the time, reached another level of meaning because of the name used for its streets, each one of which designated a contemporary art movement.

That plan, with the name of each of those streets, was an arbitrary cartography of twentieth-century century art history. It combined global movements with national artists, an interesting concoction we could play around with, like the surrealists did, imagining who lived next to whom, or making up a game of postal art, like Alighiero Boetti's experiment which consisted in sending letters to Marcel Duchamp using fictional addresses crossed out over and over again when they were returned to him. It is fun to imagine children reciting the names of these streets when asked, a way of learning by heart, at an early age, the enigmas of recent art. Smithson often recalled the sign that fascinated him as a boy at the Museum of Natural History: an arrow in one direction pointed to the "Solar System," and in the opposite direction it pointed to the "Toilets." Figurative Art Street, Hyperrealist Art Street, Minimal Art Street, Conceptual Art Street, Pop Art Street, Eduardo Chillida Street, School of Vallecas Street; the taxonomy, which in itself had something of a conceptual installation to it, was left in absurd question when one checked that, in truth, the plan drawing had barely begun to become reality. One could think of the daunting responsibility that any sensible architect would face when designing a project in accordance with the name of the streets of this unique neighborhood.

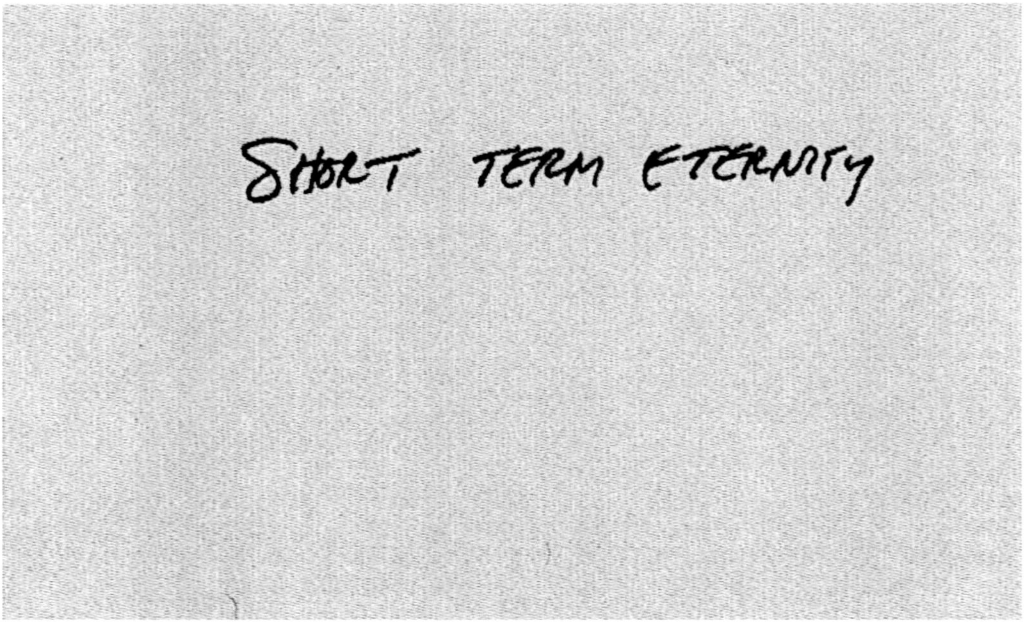

Gordon Matta-Clark. "Short Term Eternity." *Anarchitecture Notes*. Estate of Gordon Matta-Clark.

Gordon Matta-Clark. *Bingo/Ninths*. Niagara Falls, New York, 1974. Estate of Gordon Matta-Clark.

Moreover, we could even say that that layout with its air of names on a game board—the whim of a developer with cultural interests or the capacity to choose good excuses—seemed to be waiting for an artist such as Haacke. Let us recall how, in pieces such as *Shapolsky et al. Manhattan Real Estate Holdings* from 1971, he had tried to untangle the real estate market's network of invisible forces. Perhaps, after all, the artist managed, with his Madrid piece, to make sense out of that nonsensical case, by using art as a value to exorcise, as we have been invoking in this writing. I also remembered this piece by Haacke when the theme of the Spanish Pavilion was made public, as if the curators' proposal hoped to make sense out of a certain inherited situation, one that in some cases was insane, by establishing a conceptual basis that allowed the dissemination of projects that had also done something similar, each at their own scale. That is, to give a new and positive meaning to something that, without an architectural project, would have been worthy of regret. All in all, architecture, or art, as a proactive mechanism to find solutions.

The content of the Spanish Pavilion confirms the fact that, as time goes by, the work of architects consists less in creating new forms and more in altering those that already exist, all while accepting the unfinished nature of all work. Architecture, like all other creative expressions in time, is temporary, perishable; when it is written it turns into the dust the moment it is put on paper. To raise buildings, to discover buried ones, to contemplate some in intermediate states—in truth, all are intermediate—to study structures under construction or their skeletal ruin, are all ways of consuming time, paying tribute to it as it deserves, swimming in any direction along its course. Let us recall Yourcenar's quote, time as sculptor, until matter returns once again to the inert state its creators extracted to give it shape. In the book mentioned above dedicated to Sisyphus, Albert Camus resorted to Pindar's famous verse as the opening quote: "O my soul, do not aspire to immortal life but exhaust the limits of the possible." Architecture dreams of perpetual permanence, but knows that it has its limits and that it is mortal: our function is to attempt to retain something, to leave a trace, or to find an imprint; architecture also dreams of altering things for an instant with our stroke, an a binding course.

"So we beat on, boats against the current, borne back ceaselessly into the past." This is the last line of *The Great Gatsby*, a story about characters who leave the world of the concrete to take refuge in imaginary castles. It seems like all accounts are, in reality, about time, and that this implies nostalgia and loss. However we must not believe what Augusto Monterroso said, that all great stories are sad, that they all have the same ending. Of all possible times, we only have one, now, "short-term eternity," as a note states in Matta-Clark's booklet *Anarchitectures*. The present is the time that never ceases to pass. Nostalgia is sadness for what has been lost, but we still have the present and architecture as a conjuration, a vehicle to skip to other times and other places. As in Eliot's quote at the beginning I understand the architectural project as a projection toward the future, as a strategy that allows us to overcome the weight of the past through architectural creation, to feign that the past never existed even though architecture, like life itself, is also a demolition process. "Energy cannot be created or destroyed, it can only be changed from one form to another." Borges thought that we could recognize art's perfection without taking into account its date. We think of a story in which, through architecture, humankind's progress can be traced. In *The Notebooks of Malte Laurids Brigge*, Rilke evoked the images of a past life that had taken place within a house that had been torn down through the marks left behind on the walls of a neighboring house. Our attraction toward buildings that are somewhere between the unfinished and their path to ruin has to do with our interest in literature, a succession of spaces in which to place life itself, which, while it lasts, will, hence wise, remain unfinished.

VISIONS

CARLOS QUINTÁNS EIRAS

Photography is a documentation system that fixes time and permits us to share things that we find or that occur around us. Photographs retain the vision of the photographer, showing the captured image while timidly hiding how it was made.

Photography brought to art the fullness of the concrete, converting the commonplace into something memorable. The first photographic images were of static scenes, objects that had to remain completely still in order to be captured with the long exposures of the first cameras. From the very beginning architecture stood out as an object to be photographed. The view out the window in Le Gras was the first photograph made by Nicéphore Niépce in 1826; a screen in his house in Leacock, Wiltshire by William Henry Fox Talbot, from 1835; and a panorama of the Louvre from the left bank of the Seine, by Jacques Louis Mandé Daguerre from 1839, are some of the best-known photographs from the beginning of this new world.

In 1851 the Commission des monuments historiques, an agency of the French government, created the Mission héliographique, to carry out the first important photographic survey to document the nation's architectural heritage. Other documentary projects include William Notman's photography of Canada, which he began in 1860, compiling an important archive of some 200,000 negatives. Later, William Eugene Smith developed a project documenting Pittsburgh that contained 11,000 photographs.

Many photographers consider their work to be a labor of documentation, while others consider it artistic expression. At the end of the nineteenth and beginning of the twentieth centuries Eugéne Atget (1857-1927) brought an auteur's vision to his documentation work. Another of photography's great masters, Walker Evans, expressed with great precision Atget's achievement: "It is characterized by a lyric understanding of the street, trained observation, a special taste for patina and an eye for detail. And, above all, the reign of poetry that isn't 'the poetry of the street' or 'the poetry of Paris,' but a projection of the self." Atget took photographs of daily life in the city at the beginning of the twentieth century, concentrating on urban neighborhoods trades or ways of life that were starting to disappear. Man Ray tried to increase the awareness of his work, but Atget always repeated the same phrase: "They are documents, just documents." Atget's only objective was to capture images that would serve as the starting point for the work of others.

Gerry Badger wrote: "Atget is at the heart of what we know as photography. He is a bridge between the photography of the nineteenth and twentieth centuries, between the documentary discipline and modern artistic photography, between partially vernacular and fully conscious photography."

Many photographers have shown us places where we have never been and let us experience events that we didn't live through. We understand the Far East a little better through the images taken by John Thomson between 1862 and 1872. Between 1909 and 1915 Sergei Mijáilovich Prokudin-Gorsky had an entire train car equipped for the important task of documenting Russia at that moment in time.

Edward Sheriff Curtis worked for more than thirty years in the United States trying to document the life, customs, myths, habits, religion, language constructions, etc. of dozens of Native American tribes that were in the process of disappearing. A few years later Walker Evans left us many images documenting the 1929 economic crisis. Many other photographers have added to our visual memory of other places: Felice Beato photographed the Middle and Far East; John Murray, P.A. Johnston, Samuel Burne and Linnaeus Tripe travelled all over India, and we could continue with a long, nearly endless list. Even though we may not be conscious of it, each and every one of us retains photographs in our memory that have broadened our perspective and allowed us to perceive the world differently.

The ease with which photographs can be taken has permitted a progressive increase in the number of graphic documents, particularly in recent years. The quantity of images became overwhelming even before the popularization of the internet and the possibility of sharing digital documents.

As architects, we use images not only to prepare what we want to do, but also to explain what we have already done. Le Corbusier started along many of the photographic paths we continue to follow today, including the possibilities of printing photographs in widely-circulated publications and the great changes that would occur in architectural photography. To Le Corbusier we owe not only the books that document his buildings through photography, but also the album format that included abundant photographic documentation destined to formulate new directions and interests in architecture. From the concrete territory of the photographers we also learned lessons from Albert Renger-Patzsch when he photographed the work of Gropius and Ezra Stoller when he documented the work of Saarinen, Mies, Aalto, Le Corbusier, Breuer, etc. Julius Schulman enriched our universe of references with a wide range of California architecture, Marcel Gautherot with his images of Brasilia and Català-Roca with the buildings of Coderch. For many years architectural photography focused on recently finished buildings, often unused, and sometimes still under construction.

The International Photography Museum in Rochester, New York held an exhibition in 1975 entitled "The New Topographics, Photographs of a Man-Altered Landscape" that gathered the work of young photographers who focused on the urban landscape of industrial cities: Robert Adams, Lewis Baltz, Joe Deal, Frank Gohlke, John Schott, Bernd and Hilla Becher, Henry Wessel Jr., Nicholas Nixon and Stephen Shore; photographers who shaped the practice of photography in relation to landscape all over the world. Also influential were Ed Ruscha's *Twenty-Six Gasoline Stations,* 1962, Some *Los Angeles Apartments,* 1965 and, above all, *Every Building on the Sunset Strip,* 1966. "The images were stripped of their artistic flourishes and reduced to an essentially topographic state, transmitting large quantities of visual information, but completely avoiding aspects of beauty, emotion or opinion." Only exceptionally did architectural publications include photographs with characteristics similar to the New Topographics photographs. Normally, the images that appeared showed perfectly finished, clean, neat and generally unused architecture; any other photographs were merely anecdotal.

A series of photographs of the Villa Savoye taken by Victor Gubbins were accompanied by a short text explaining how they were taken: "We entered in the abandoned property and approached a ruin, gray and stained. Still standing respectably, but a ruin, slender and present . . . It is emotional to confront a ruin, stained and intervened, without the makeup of the stucco." These photographs made us question all of the images showing the house without alterations. Only the images published by Le Corbusier of the construction process served as a link, but in that case due to the clarity with which the process was explained and not the results of the passage of time and abandonment. Gubbins's photographs included his companions, whose positions and clothes revealed them to be visitors. With a little imagination the people in these images could be transformed into characters using the Villa Savoye in spite of its ruined state. In 1959 G. E. Kidder Smith and René Burri photographed a decadent Villa Savoye that had not yet reached the state of destruction that Gubbins would find.

With the fall of the iron curtain we gained access to architectural publications that previously had been inaccessible. The Tugendhat House appeared with new photos of a space that was used as a dance school and later as a rehabilitation center for a children's hospital. This space was referenced as Mies van der Rohe's Villa Tugendhat, although it was necessary to look very carefully to recognize the completely transformed house in these photos. Shortly thereafter more photographs appeared showing the house's different uses over the years: anything from a stable to a small industrial space. Photographs taken by the family showed the house as it was lived in before it was abandoned and before its change of use. This group of photos, never used by Mies, changed the pure perception of the house, which represents one of architecture's most intense moments. Mies had finished a house in which each fragment had been specifically designed and built. A house into which it would seem difficult to insert the life of a family, but which nevertheless succeeded comfortably. The photographs of these two houses, symbolizing the high points of twentieth-century architecture, let us understand how built spaces can undergo transformations which, in some cases, enrich the design.

Since the publication of their first projects, Lacaton & Vassal have shown little concern for tidiness in the images depicting their architecture, unlike typical architectural photography, thus allowing us to see how people actually live in their buildings, without preparing them for a visit.

Much has been written about Spain's problems during recent years. Many articles, books, movies, and programs have been produced that complement the constant flow of information in the news media; information that can only be made sense of through economic, political or social analyses. However, only the images let us fully comprehend the magnitude and proximity of the problem. Distance is an obstacle for the consciousness of reality and especially for the awareness of problems.

We are left with the remains of the constructed presence and the inconclusive residue of what was the largest building enterprise in the history of Spanish territory. The fast, insensitive and clumsy construction sought quick profits at any cost and has left a built footprint that will not be easily assimilated by this or future generations. The end of this overwhelming growth, due to the bursting of the real estate bubble, has left a fabric of partially-built and unconsolidated volumes that will be difficult to integrate. This situation is revealed in seven photographic series which make visible a reality that could have remained hidden, while also showing processes that have been interrupted for periods of time much longer than normal or changing scales of work in architectural endeavors.

"The Physical Impossibility of Life in the Mind of Someone Dead," by Alfonso Batalla, shows digitally reconstructed spaces that don't exist in reality.

"Spanish Dream," by Cadelasverdes, intervenes in ruins, simulating fictitious uses by recreating familiar scenes in unfinished buildings to demonstrate the situation of so many people that were expecting to own their home as a compensation for their work.

"Architecture and Resistance," by Nicolás Combarro, looks at spontaneous construction forms; a free architecture.

"Landscapes under 30: Transitional Space," by Miguel Fernández-Galiano, are profile images of projects by architects around thirty years old and consist of small interventions in already built structures.

"Re-Edificatoria" is a series by Adrià Goula in which buildings are shown under construction, revealing their slow speed, far removed from the velocities that were reached at the moment of the greatest constructive impact. The same occurs with "Standstill Architecture" by Iñaki Bergera.

"Roundabout Nation" by Miguel Álvarez, Esteban García, Guillermo Trapiello and Rafael Trapiello is a documentary project in which the roundabout is the central element of an absurd urban design that has left without justification some of these elements designed for vehicular circulation; a study of roundabouts as an exaggerated element in urban plans that were never built or not completed.

Extremely interesting photography has been produced in recent years, which helps us to place this

THE PHYSICAL IMPOSSIBILITY OF LIFE IN THE MIND OF SOMEONE DEAD

ALFONSO BATALLA

Photography was born with the purpose of capturing reality. It seems to fulfill this task: we think that what we see in these pictures is real. However, none of these spaces exist in the real world, or at least in the way they are shown here. Some have been digitally reconstructed from their own parts. In others, shiny elements of our everyday life have been inserted into decaying locations. But even if none of this had happened, these works would have never been able to reflect reality. The freezing of time, the flattening of three dimensions into two, the artist's conscious decisions in the instant composition, lens and any other technical elements of the photographic work, generate a specific, voluntary , fragmented and altered perception of reality. Therefore, to show this ambiguity, these photographs contain a metaphor about the device and photographic language.

19: 14

Bowling Green
Subway Station

ling Green
way Station
4 5

STANDSTILL ARCHITECTURE

IÑAKI BERGERA

The economic crisis in Spain resulted in the stoppage and abandonment of aspiring and outstanding facilities conceived to provide luxury amusements during those happy years of well-being and abundance. The proposed restoration of the old Balneario of Panticosa, located in the heart of the Spanish Pyrenees, and its transformation into a luxurious and modern tourist resort was suddenly halted, producing the closure of the Gran Hotel designed by Rafael Moneo, the cessation of the construction—at its very ending stage—of the High-Performance Sports Center designed by Alvaro Siza and the abandonment of an impressive parking structure anchored to the mountain. The images of this last facility selected for the Venice exhibition faithfully depict this sad reality and suggest a totally different visual narrative of the architectural space and its unexpected ruinous condition.

78

SPANISH DREAM

CADELASVERDES

Spanish Dream proposes a critical approach to the economic crisis and its consequences, referring to the American Dream as a symbol of identity of a country through its collective desire: to achieve homeownership, in the Spanish case. This dream shattered and, as a legacy, we have a country invaded by unfinished buildings, premature ruins that are part of our landscape, like symbols of an individual and collective drama. Spanish Dream refers especially to the emotional, creating family scenes in unfinished buildings. The setting is far from a domestic place and contrasts with the normality of the daily scenes, looking for a reflection of a society that, following the desire of becoming homeowners forgot the real sense of inhabiting.

iittala

3

IBERDROLA
CAMPEONES
DEL MUNDO

ARCHITECTURE AND RESISTANCE

NICOLÁS COMBARRO

Architecture and Resistance looks at spontaneous forms of construction, where structural logic is mixed with cultural inheritance. This architecture is free and represents a form of resistance to economic, social and political constraints. It also refers to traditional or vernacular construction that continues to be valid in spite of being forgotten or maligned. Investigating, locating and documenting this type of construction helps us to understand other ways of building, far removed from grand architecture and urban planning, where the emphasis is on the creator's resources and intentions. These are buildings with a personal aesthetic that assert their existence and push us to look at, understand and assimilate them, breaking down an increasingly uniform and monumental vision of architecture.

VOTA PREPAL
L3

VOTA

LANDSCAPES UNDER 30: TRANSITIONAL SPACE

MIGUEL FERNÁNDEZ-GALIANO

This is demolition journalism: breaking up with the previous, portraying new possibilities. Eight photographs show moments in the transformation, carried out by architects under 30, of several dwellings. Individually, each image freezes an instant of the process revealing an invisible reality; together, they reflect the work of this generation: refurbishments and renovations. In tune with the theme of the Biennale, the series implicitly defends destruction over construction, or refurbishing instead of building from scratch. Demolishing means breaking with a previous state that unveils the invisible qualities, and alters the original work plans. The photographs don't show the finished objects but rather the processes that describe them and the virtues found in them. Faced with the uncertainty of the finished, the unknown comes to the fore, the fragility of the processes. The unfinished.

RE-
EDIFICATORIA

ADRIÀ GOULA

Re-build, build on what already exists, pick a project and redo it from top to bottom. The intersection of two eras, two architects, two different construction techniques: an explosive encounter. A crossing in the same space and time of destruction and construction, demolition and installation. The two worlds intermingle in a temporary chaos. The guts of the work, imperfect, brutal, complex, unpredictable, are scattered throughout the slit open building. New interventions overlap multiple layers that they did not even know existed forming a sandwich of the building's history. A catalog of impure solutions gradually portions are removed, others sewn, capped, and in the end there are no traces of drastic intervention. Having seen the building inside shows its true interior beyond its final appearance.

tuaris

ESCO STRUCCIÓ DE
bcn.cat/
habitaturba
Ajuntament de
Barcelona

Accés
tancat
Sortida
OBRES TRANSFORMACIÓ DE LES GLÒRIES

ROUNDABOUT NATION

MIGUEL ÁLVAREZ,
ESTEBAN GARCÍA,
GUILLERMO TRAPIELLO,
RAFAEL TRAPIELLO

Designed on the draftsman's screen and on the councilman's desk, the true shape of the Roundabout Nation comes to life when we travel around it with the same point of view that was used to create it. Flying over it in different years and at different heights, stopping here and there along the way, you are invited to walk the nation as we have done for the past two years: without really knowing what we were seeing, in disbelief and amazement. We wondered at every step if it is true that when you gaze long into an abyss, the abyss will also gaze into you.

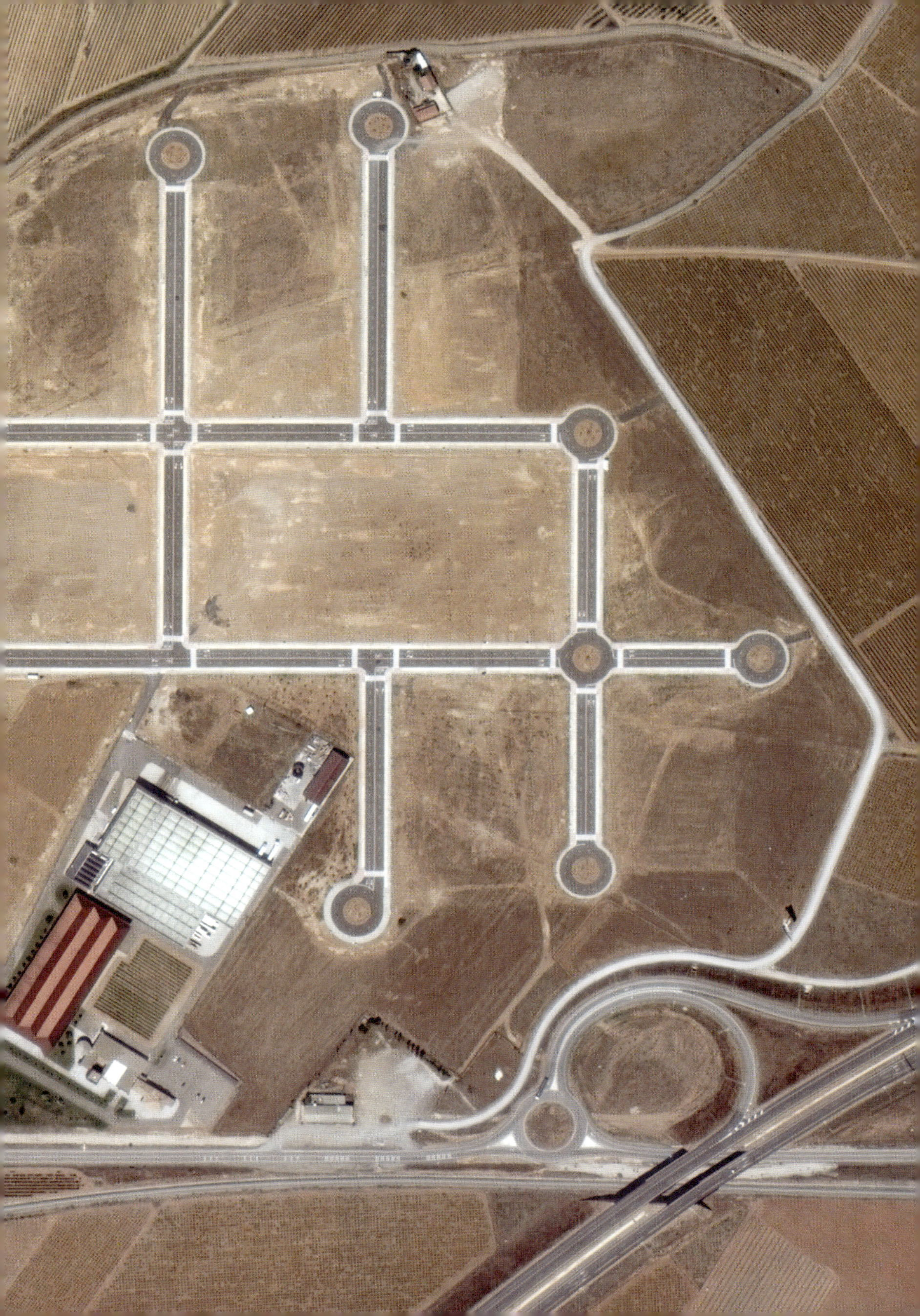

INTERVIEWS

AMALE ANDRAOS	Dean, Columbia University Graduate School of Architecture, Planning and Preservation
BARRY BERGDOLL	Meyer Schapiro Professor of Art History and Archaeology, Columbia University Department of Art History and Archaeology
KENNETH FRAMPTON	Ware Professor of Architecture, Columbia University Graduate School of Architecture, Planning and Preservation
SOU FUJIMOTO	Sou Fujimoto Architects
JORGE SILVETTI	Nelson Robinson, Jr. Professor of Architecture, Harvard University Graduate School of Design
ANDREA SIMITCH	Associate Professor of Architecture, Cornell University College of Architecture, Art, and Planning
MARTINO STIERLI	Philip Johnson Chief Curator of Architecture and Design, the Museum of Modern Art
NADER TEHRANI	Dean, Irwin S. Chanin School of Architecture, the Cooper Union
VAL WARKE	Associate Professor of Architecture, Cornell University College of Architecture, Art, and Planning
SARAH WHITING	Dean and William Ward Watkin Professor, Rice University School of Architecture
MEEJIN YOON	Professor and Head of the Department of Architecture, Massachusetts Institute of Technology Department of Architecture

AMALE ANDRAOS

Rem Koolhaas presented the exhibition "Elements of Architecture" at the 2014 Architecture Biennale with the intention of reexamining the fundamentals of buildings, analyzing the evolution of design in different contexts and different periods of time. This year, Alejandro Aravena will lead an investigation into the role of architects in the "battle" to improve living conditions for people all over the world with the exhibition "Reporting from the Front." What do you think of this more social perspective on the role of the architect?

That's an important question. Throughout his career, Rem Koolhaas has, in a way, expanded the field of architecture. It was a kind of reactionary moment for me, however, when he used the term "fundamentals" and "elements." And even though it's obvious that you can't reduce architecture to its elements alone, it was an interesting and provocative kind of ground zero. I do think that the theme of this Biennale is important. For me, architecture doesn't exist autonomously and without context—it's always engaged in social and environmental concerns. But it's also engaged in knowledge. My interest is not so much how we can save the world, because architects have frequently failed to save the world, but how we can engage critically with real-world problems and move knowledge forward. I think it's not just about practice, but also about forms of practice and of discourse—rethinking the relationship between scales of environment, rethinking the global and what it means for architecture, and thinking about technology and the flow of information across scales. I think that the social can't be reduced to just one type of action.

The Spanish Pavilion responds to Aravena's call to speculate on the major architectural issues of the last ten years. After a building boom driven by a period of high economic growth, steep economic decline resulted in a lack of demand and resources needed to maintain many unfinished constructions. This [situation] rendered a collection of contemporary ruins and neglected spaces across Spain.

Do you think this consideration of time is present in contemporary architecture? Should architects be responsible for dealing with the fact that social and economic contexts and the functional needs of new construction may change over time?

You are describing a great moment—we are in a post-growth moment, right? Faced with climate change, the idea that we can just continue to build new is problematic, and the idea that Spanish architects are now looking at contemporary ruins, the ruins of excess, and trying to find ways to reinvent them is really fascinating. One of the most interesting aspects of contemporary architecture is the question of preservation—the question of contemporary cultural heritage. I think that how we reinvent and reuse is really fundamental. In the same way that we propose concepts for tactical urbanism, we can produce tactical architecture. That is quite exciting. Consider modernism and maintenance, the first proposes a very abstract idea of life and the other is the reality of what it takes to maintain modernist buildings. This is something that Hilary Sample is writing about as a way to reread modernism. It's important not only to think about time and the image of a building, but also to think about what happens as it transforms materially—even as we continue to think about flexibility, event, and program.

Titled "Unfinished," the exhibition in the Spanish Pavilion draws attention to these contemporary ruins in order to discover principles for design strategies. "Unfinished" promotes creative speculation about how to subvert the past through [positive] contemporary action, exhibiting architecture developed in Spain during the last seven years. In these projects, design emerges as a response to preexisting conditions while remaining open to evolution over time. The speed with which we commonly evaluate society's developments and the urge to constantly reinvent affect our perceptions of architecture. How do you position yourself with regards to the contradiction that exists between the architecture commonly presented by the media as finished forms frozen in time and architecture that has the capacity to evolve, adapt, and transform?

It's time to fight against the rendering and to reengage with drawing, with making, with the reality of material and decay, and the transformation of systems. The idea that there is either no context or that we are always starting anew is not true: there is always a context—a desert is a context. Engaging with the complexity of what we inherit—for example those ruins, some of them are real ruins, some of them are the ruins of utopia—and advancing architecture as a body of knowledge is something that we are constantly reconsidering and reworking. I think the opportunity to rework it materially as well is really important and exciting.

Robert Venturi recalls Paul Rudolph in *Complexity and Contradiction* in Architecture saying: "All problems can never be solved.... Indeed it is a characteristic of the twentieth century that architects are highly selective in determining which problems they want to solve. Mies, for instance, makes wonderful buildings only because he ignores many aspects of a building. If he solved more problems, his buildings would be far less potent."

When you look at architects succeeding in the international scene, do you think their success is a consequence of being very selective in terms of which problems to solve and which to ignore? Do you think architects should be selective according to their own approach or according to society's needs?

I believe we need to move beyond this "either/or"condition. If you think about it, architecture at its best is a synthetic discipline. We are integrating many diverse forces, intentions, ideas, representations, and realities. Some architects are better synthesizers than others—some dial up certain things and dial down others. Today we are certainly working with many more flows of information than ever before, even if we need to edit and draw the line at some point. But there's room to become better synthesizers, and we can't edit in the same way that we edited before. There are pressures to address more concerns simultaneously. This may be an invitation to move away from the complicated and toward the complex. Maybe we need to simplify, maybe it's a question of scale. If we address the question of scale beyond Bigness and return to a scale at which we can actually engage more ingredients and synthesize better, rather than rely on an array of consultants and diverse expertise that we have very little control over, then we could start to regain control and engage more issues. What we dial up and what we dial down in order to address a broader range of concerns is an important question for architects.

Intending to remove certain architectural elements from the equation, the Spanish Pavilion announced a call for projects looking at buildings and structures developed under the constraints of the economic recession—architecture without a site, without cladding, without new materials, without new space. The result has been quite unique, defining a new spectrum of innovative design strategies developed under constraint. How can we evaluate the quantity and quality of new versus existing architecture?

It seems that we could move beyond this notion that there is something new and that there is something existing, and instead reimagine the existing as new. The challenge is to reframe the question rather than agree with what we inherited as oppositions. Once we reframe this question, then there is no difference between existing and new. It's how we look at things and how we intervene within them.

What draws you most to Spanish architecture? What aspects of Spanish architecture do you consider to be most unique? And the weakest?

It's interesting you should say "Spanish architecture" because I never think of architecture with a qualifier in front of it in terms of ethnicity or nationality. I remember seeing Terence Riley's exhibition at the Museum of Modern Art in New York while I was still working in Rotterdam—I had a sense of Dutch architecture and I thought that with Spanish architecture there was a different, more Mediterranean, sensuality. But still, I don't think about architecture as Spanish or Dutch even though I think architects such as Iñaki Ábalos and Juan Herreros, now separately in their practices, have been instrumental in reclaiming questions of typology, the generic, and a kind of strategic, tactical intervention that moved away from architecture of spectacle. There is an intelligence and a sensuality that are operating at the same time.

Does it make sense in the globalized world to talk about architecture in national terms? What does the term "Spanish architecture" mean to you?

I don't really consider myself a Lebanese architect in the sense that a lot of the work I've done on the Arab city is precisely to undermine the notion that there is such a thing as an Arab city. And yet, it can be strategic and productive to posit a perspective other than the normalizing, Western viewpoint. I think that's a problem with the Architecture Biennale, that the work is still organized into national pavilions around a "Central" pavilion, where national differences are supposed to be highlighted. That was very clear in 2014 when many of the pavilions were in fact making similar claims in terms of how they engaged modernity and how modernism was hybridized and absorbed locally. Looking at concerns and ideas across national boundaries is more interesting. I consider whatever I bring as a Lebanese architect as a sense of otherness and I try to use this perspective to look at questions from differing perspectives.

What are Spanish architects contributing to American academia?

I think we should talk about shared concerns. Questions of global organization, questions of technology, questions of climate change, the question of modernity, how we understand and teach history, these are all important questions that cut across national boundaries. In Venice, I always find the spaces and conversations between the pavilions more interesting than the pavilions themselves. I understand that it's one way to organize the event, but I think we should organize ourselves transnationally and in much more radical ways given the complex issues that we're facing today. It would be interesting if the Architecture Biennale became more radical.

What would you say to young, recently graduated architects struggling to find a footing in a troubled economy and architectural landscape?

Whether you're "at home" or "abroad,", you want to position yourself both on the inside and on the outside at the same time. We need to think relationally today—it's a privilege to travel and work around the world, and that privilege shouldn't be abused. At the same time, there is a productive naïveté of looking at things from the outside. I think one can use that position to project alternative ideas that may be more difficult to propose when you are really embedded within. Constantly stepping inside and outside of one's own knowledge and experience is quite productive and can be liberating. So be fearless—that would be my recommendation. Be fearless and humble at the same time.

BARRY BERGDOLL

Rem Koolhaas presented the exhibition "Elements of Architecture" at the 2014 Architecture Biennale with the intention of reexamining the fundamentals of buildings, analyzing the evolution of design in different contexts and different periods of time. This year, Alejandro Aravena will lead an investigation into the role of architects in the "battle" to improve living conditions for people all over the world with the exhibition "Reporting from the Front." What do you think of this more social perspective on the role of the architect?

The Architecture Biennale is always a bit of a pendulum. Not only does the dialogue inevitably shift, but each Biennale is a strong reaction to the previous one. This year, it is going to be extremely interesting because there are certain paradoxical situations. The Koolhaas Biennale was largely a historical exhibition: it was about digesting modernity, but also about closing a century and being on the other side of it. Aravena's proposal—to go out in the world and see what is going on *now*—does two things that people are really talking about. First, it has a social agenda. That is interesting, but the main thing it does is return to practice. Except for a few outliers that didn't follow the brief two years ago, practice was largely absent from the last Biennale. It was a century-long historical reflection on how we got to where we are. There was even some ambiguity between the exhibition and the book, which shifted from elements to fundamentals. These are two different things. Aravena is going into the "trenches" to see what is happening in a world that has changed drastically in the last two years. Rather than create some partisan warfare between aesthetics and social purpose, it is interesting to ask to what extent Aravena is reactivating the modernist project of the social commitment of architecture. This social purpose is as historical as the last one. It asks a lot of questions about the role of the architect, from the Modern Movement to today. I don't think it represents, as some have said, only a small segment of the architectural profession who put a social agenda before an aesthetic one.

The Spanish Pavilion responds to Aravena's call to speculate on the major architectural issues of the last ten years. After a building boom driven by a period of high economic growth, steep economic decline resulted in a lack of demand and resources needed to maintain many unfinished constructions. This [situation] rendered a collection of contemporary ruins and neglected spaces across Spain.

Do you think this consideration of time is present in contemporary architecture? Should architects be responsible for dealing with the fact that social and economic contexts and the functional needs of new construction may change over time?

I think that Spain is an interesting case, because there is hardly another country in the world that has gone so dramatically from an architectural boom to a collapse. It raises all sorts of questions: What do you do with the architecture of the boom when all the financial structures that gave rise to it are in crisis, political power shifts, and the entire infrastructure of the infrastructure is no longer there? I don't think that there is another place in the world where we have ruins of the boom. We have ruins of the communist experiment; we have ruins of empires. It is very rare to have ruins that were never occupied. The idea of the never-occupied ruin is something that Spain gave us. Historically there are examples of new towns that were built and never occupied, but they are very rare. As a national condition, this makes Spain an absolute hyperbolic expression of the globalization of capital and the globalization of architecture. And that, ironically enough, makes this problem specific to Spain. Nowhere else do you have young architects and photographers making repertoires or reportages on airports that were never opened, highways that were never driven on, and subdivisions that were never occupied. It is a very interesting situation. But as hyperbolic as it is in Spain, it is not unique. In 2011 we did a workshop exhibition at the Museum of Modern Art called "Foreclosed: Rehousing the American Dream," and we invited architects to look at the suburban fringe of various US cities where the mortgage crisis started in the same global configurations as the Spanish crisis. Depending on the age of the city, it hit nearer or further from the epicenter of the historic downtown. One project in particular is very relevant to the theme of the Spanish Pavilion and Aravena's Biennale in general: a project by Andrew Zago looked at an abandoned subdivision of so-called McMansions in ex-urban Los Angeles. This is a reminder that while the Spanish case is across the entire territory of Spain, there are many ruins of architecture as the product of economic boom that raise questions about the relationship of architecture to time. What do you do when you have a brand-new building whose very existence represents a time that suddenly evaporated?

Titled "Unfinished," the exhibition in the Spanish Pavilion draws attention to these contemporary ruins in order to discover principles for design strategies. "Unfinished" promotes creative speculation about how to subvert the past through [positive] contemporary action, exhibiting architecture developed in Spain during the last seven years. In these projects, design emerges as a response to preexisting conditions while remaining open to evolution over time. The speed with which we commonly evaluate society's developments and the urge to constantly reinvent affect our perceptions of architecture. How do you position yourself with regards to the contradiction that exists between the architecture commonly presented by the media as finished forms frozen in time and architecture that has the capacity to evolve, adapt, and transform?

The issue of time is fascinating particularly in a media culture. Andy Warhol's notion that we will all be famous for fifteen minutes now seems hopelessly outdated; fifteen minutes is an incredibly long time. Today the media moment is so ephemeral and short, and newness is seizing the headlines. The problem of how to reconcile that with the unfinished projects of the economic boom is fascinating. Do you start over with [a] tabula rasa and try to rapidly make new things that respond to the new situation [or lack thereof]? Buildings evolve over time and changing circumstances: How do you respond to that? The theme "Unfinished" is very potent because unfinished in architecture is usually perceived as a negative quality. It raises the question, In what way can you make it whole; do you complete it as originally intended? You can achieve the dream of architecture, that it will be assimilated into the world of art and become an autonomous, perfect object. This has been one of the great fictions of architecture since it entered the Renaissance academies. Paradoxically, the Metropolitan Museum of Art just reopened the Breuer building abandoned by the Whitney Museum with an exhibition titled "Unfinished." The concept of unfinished in works of art is nonfinite. The *non finito* is open to a world of possibilities that inspire imagination: whether to imagine what Michelangelo was going to draw next in an incomplete drawing, or to imagine the possibilities of an unfinished piece of literature. The opportunity to take on the unfinished as a positive, creative project rather than a reluctant necessity of the ruins of a more "go-go" moment is really exciting. The economic crisis of 2008, which is ongoing in many places, is nothing compared to the global climate crisis. Architecture will need to recalibrate and rethink how to work within the existing and the unfinished—unfinished as a larger metaphor for the world. Whether we want to call modernity an unfinished project or we want to think about our cities and landscapes as perpetually unfinished, the production of [wholly] new projects is less and less the role of architecture. Our understanding of what architecture is is out of sync within the reality of what an architect does on a daily basis.

Robert Venturi recalls Paul Rudolph in *Complexity and Contradiction in Architecture* saying: "All problems can never be solved.... Indeed it is a characteristic of the twentieth century that architects are highly selective in determining which problems they want to solve. Mies, for instance, makes wonderful buildings only because he ignores many aspects of a building. If he solved more problems, his buildings would be far less potent."

When you look at architects succeeding in the international scene, do you think their success is a consequence of being very selective in terms of which problems to solve and which to ignore? Do you think architects should be selective according to their own approach or according to society's needs?

This is a very ambiguous, complex, and contradictory assessment of Mies seen from fifty years later. It reminds us that Mies had a certain renaissance that coincided with the reconstruction of the Barcelona Pavilion in 1986 and [influenced] new ways of thinking about Miesian space. The Barcelona Pavilion is a building that solves very few problems. It had an absolutely minimal program: to create an architecturally rich space in which the King and Queen of Spain could sit down for a couple of minutes and be photographed by the press. Otherwise, there was nothing on display other than the building itself. It is no wonder it gave rise to such rich reflection on the very nature of architecture; it is nearly void of program. What Venturi is hinting at here, and what scholars of Mies began to think after the Barcelona Pavilion reconstruction, is what Detlef Mertins called "Miesian event space": space with the potential for the unexpected, the unprogrammed, to happen. Mies's buildings were often unspecific in the relationship between form and program. Ironically, they are some of the most flexible buildings that the masters of the Modern Movement left us. The lesson is to question how literally and point-by-point one should respond to program in the pursuit of form. If we were to do an extended exegesis of Venturi's now fifty-year-old quote, which is a quote of a quote of a quote, we might arrive at the paradoxical hypothesis that Mies van der Rohe and Alejandro Aravena, who also sometimes gives his clients [only] half of a building, are not that far apart—that the perfectly-finished-but-not-fully-programmed and the deliberately-unfinished may find some common ground.

Intending to remove certain architectural elements from the equation, the Spanish Pavilion announced a call for projects looking at buildings and structures developed under the constraints of the economic recession—architecture without a site, without cladding, without new materials, without new space. The result has been quite unique, defining a new spectrum of innovative design strategies developed under constraint. How can we evaluate the quantity and quality of new versus existing architecture?

This was a question that came up in the Dutch Pavilion a few Biennales ago. Instead of presenting current [architectural] work from the Netherlands, the pavilion presented a scaled representation of all of the empty space, all of the unused space in the Netherlands, in blue foam core: a provocative invitation for architects *not* to build. The institution of architecture is in a very paradoxical situation, and I think that Alejandro Aravena has raised that paradox and framed a new level of awareness with his invitation to reflect on the social responsibility of architects: architecture as the vanguard of social thinking. Market forces shape architecture, and the role of the architect as a consultant—on the proper use of terrain, on the proper deployment of resources, on all sorts of things that involve the questioning of many programs—is clearly, from a business point of view, professional suicide. It raises an interesting question about the relationship of architects' ethos to the hazards of the marketplace. Whether commissions come from the state or the private market, architects work on a delicate tightrope between taking what's going to happen and discovering how the process of design and discussion with the client might lead to a result that is not embedded in the initial request. One of the great paradoxes and tensions in architecture is how to develop a critical architectural project in a global marketplace, and the invitation this year is to take it on, *from the front.*

What draws you most to Spanish architecture? What aspects of Spanish architecture do you consider to be most unique? And the weakest?

It is very difficult for outsiders to speak of Spanish architecture today, which is not paradoxical because in the last ten years it was very difficult not to speak about Spanish architecture: Spanish architecture created a sense of euphoria. Spain itself felt a euphoria that was reflected in the ambitions of architectural projects and the ambitions of municipalities and other commission-givers. A very old culture was changing rapidly; the whole world was invited to the party and paying attention to it. My predecessor at the Museum of Modern Art in New York, Terence Riley, put on an exhibition celebrating Spanish architecture and it turned out to be his last great undertaking at MoMA before he left. Little did he know that in two years this perception would be challenged by events. At one point, after I took over his position at the museum, I thought that one could go back and revisit those sites and think about them—that would make an interesting exhibition. I suppose the approach of the Spanish Pavilion fills that difficult bill, but it means that our thoughts on Spanish architecture are half a generation out of date.

Many of the most interesting Spanish architects have become more international perforce, and they have moved on to other activities, installations, curatorial work, and writing for the obvious reason that the economy has become so weak. Spanish architects, thinking about architecture in general, have infused more into the world. The influence has changed very fundamentally. It is difficult to characterize Spanish architecture in 2016, but it would be very easy for me to characterize it in 2006. Not that there was one unified practice, but there were a number of interesting regional trends in Spain: very distinctive architecture in Barcelona versus Madrid versus Andalucía. One thing that has been maintained in Spanish architecture is an attention to the urban situation of buildings, to the idea of an intervention as a complex layering of what's inherited. This has been carried into the pedagogical project that Spanish architects teach internationally. I think it is something that Spanish architects still struggle with. One of the very few silver linings of the Iberian economic crisis is that, before, Spain was beginning to go the route of the rest of the world and allow a non-urbanistic guerrilla to invade its territory. Both Ireland and Spain, poised to destroy themselves through ill-considered development, achieved this state of arrested development. It was an extremely painful situation, but one from which we can learn a great deal. To ask: What were the weak points of Spanish architecture? is very tough, because it would demand that there is such a thing as "Spanish architecture." There are many trends, many tendencies and approaches, that have had a long history in Spain. I don't think that one can address a collective weakness. There are certain weaknesses in certain projects in Spain that are a matter of taste, ideology, and opinion. My personal taste leads to a more understated, austere and materially conditioned architecture. I am less attracted to an architecture of willful fantasy. I liked the Sagrada Família more when it was unfinished than today as a to-be-finished project. Those elements of fantasy, no matter how rational to Gaudí, are not the creative aspects of Spanish architecture that I am most drawn to, even though they have managed to survive for over a century. I don't think that they are problematic in any fundamental way. It is ultimately a question of something that no one talks about anymore: taste.

What do you think are the main challenges Spanish architecture will encounter in the future?

One of the main challenges Spanish architecture and Spanish architects face now, and will continue to face, is the justification of developing new buildings in relatively undeveloped territories: the remnants of a generation of excess. This is not unique, but exists in an exaggerated form in Spain. This excess is about as appealing, in many situations, as week-old leftover food. It was a great dinner, but the last thing you want is old leftovers. You want something exciting and new. Even if you want to create something new out of the old, you want something that has a certain cachet or heritage to it rather than something that has fallen into such disfavor. The real challenge as we deal with the fallout of the last adventure of global capitalism is how to deal with its more compromised, sometimes even noxious, products in a productive way. In that sense, it is ironic that there are places in Spain and in other countries that suffered from a fall, from a boom, to a really dramatic financial crisis: a situation not unlike certain regions of conflict.

Does it make sense in the globalized world to talk about architecture in national terms? What does the term "Spanish architecture" mean to you?

One of the ironies of the Giardini is that we are invited back [every other year] to think about architecture in national terms in a set of pavilions that were constructed [beginning] in the late nineteenth century, representing the high points of construction in the European nations in particular, but also the beginning of decolonization. It was a time of nation building and national consciousness [building]. Today, we have all the benefits and disadvantages of globalization, and the category of nation is in flux in an enormous way. To speak about Spanish architecture—in the case of our commissioner this year, for Alejandro Aravena to speak about Chilean architecture—is often to speak the language of the ministry of commerce or the ministry of tourism. There is a financial investment in the notion of nationality. The evidence of global financial and intellectual interconnectedness raises serious questions about what it means to speak of a French architecture, a British architecture, a Spanish architecture, an American architecture, and so on.

There are certain traditions, to be sure, that continue, because different territories were marked in different ways during moments when the world was less globalized. I am not sure how useful the category of nation is for us to construct the questions about architecture that really matter today. Thinking about architecture as preserving qualities of daily life, but also taking on enormous challenges like climate change, some have called this question of the nation a "migration crisis." Others have encouraged us to think of it as a migration opportunity, but all of their suggestions are engaged with the complex issue of how to define what it means to have a particular passport.

What are Spanish architects contributing to American academia?

This question of nationality and national architecture also deals with migration out of the country. There was a huge professional exodus of Spanish architects; that may start to change in the coming years. This is not without precedent: the history of the United States, where I am from, had similar moments. American architecture was marked by the revolutions in Europe in 1848 and 1849, in particular by the large migration of young German and Central European professionals. It was a very formative moment in [the history of] American architectural education. Inevitably, it had an enormous impact, diffused as part of a complex melting pot, that can be traced in many different venues. For several decades, there has been a lot of back-and-forth between Spanish academia and academia [in particular in architectural training]. American schools are often well set up to receive new blood, to receive people from outside, and to integrate them in a very open way. It is what makes many architecture schools so exciting. They are places open to new ideas, new people, and continuous debate. They always want more voices in the debate so that it is meaningful in educating young architects, but also in the role schools play helping define architectural discourse in general. I am avoiding citing a roster of Spaniards who have contributed to American schools of architecture. I think that it comes from a country of immigrants. I like to think of people as individuals rather than as their nationality.

What would you say to young, recently graduated architects struggling to find a footing in a troubled economy and architectural landscape?

It is a tough time to be a young architect, and yet as far as I know, there hasn't been a massive decline in the number of students who go to architecture schools. I think that architecture is a very interesting way to think through issues. If one is trained as an architect, practicing related professions instead of architecture is not necessarily a failure. Many people go to law school, for example, to learn a type of legal thinking and bring it to the world of politics and policymaking. I think it would be interesting to think about architecture school as a way of thinking that is every bit as rich, from policymaking to territorial planning. Instead of seeing the glass as half empty, we should see it as half full and celebrate architecture as a type of visual training that can address the social and political challenges that we face across the planet.

My concern, and it is somewhat ironic to express in an interview for a Biennale, is that there has been a proliferation in recent years of installations in museums and biennials by young architects that diverge from the thinking that is so valuable in training architects to shape the social and infrastructural spheres. Most of these are good fun, so there is no sense in finding them dangerous. I worry about a short-term economy of cool objects. That is a kind of dead end. One of the roles of exhibition venues exposing the work of young architects is to change the political landscape and broaden the role of the architect. The architect is not necessarily the single practitioner on the cover of *Time* Magazine; there are many venues in which an architectural training can be taken. That doesn't mean simply telling young architects that there are many things they can do with their training. It involves a collective project of training and administration to understand that you don't just call in an architect when you need to beautify a project; you call in an architect when you want to think about a set of issues in which design intelligence can be an integral part of the solution from the beginning. We have to maintain architecture as an attractive prospect for students and work to broaden the scope of architecture across public administrations and civic organizations. We don't just need to design a new architect; we also need to design a new client and a new situation. Easier said than done.

KENNETH FRAMPTON

Rem Koolhaas presented the exhibition "Elements of Architecture" at the 2014 Architecture Biennale with the intention of reexamining the fundamentals of buildings, analyzing the evolution of design in different contexts and different periods of time. This year, Alejandro Aravena will lead an investigation into the role of architects in the "battle" to improve living conditions for people all over the world with the exhibition "Reporting from the Front." What do you think of this more social perspective on the role of the architect?

The social perspective of the architect isn't entirely new, but we live in a somewhat dark period of history, I think. Since the 1960s, we have dedicated the first semester of the second year at Columbia to a housing studio. It's a tradition that no one can quite explain, but I suppose there's a certain pride in this anachronism because in New York, as in many large cities, there is one high-rise after another full of extremely expensive apartments selling for 15, 20, 30 million dollars apiece. They are mostly bought by rather wealthy figures from outside the country—they are stockpiling both apartments and money, I suppose. And at the same time, there is no housing of any consequence being built in the United States. In the early 1970s, I was involved in the Museum of Modern Art exhibition "Another Chance for Housing: Low-rise Alternatives." As part of the Institute of Architecture and Urban Studies, we managed to realize some low-rise, low-density housing in Brooklyn—but that's the last moment of housing in the United States of any consequence other than private middle-class or upper middle-class housing. There is no larger project in the United States and, of course, in other countries there are other dimensions. I think it's a weak field in the Americas.

The Spanish Pavilion responds to Aravena's call to speculate on the major architectural issues of the last ten years. After a building boom driven by a period of high economic growth, steep economic decline resulted in a lack of demand and resources needed to maintain many unfinished constructions. This [situation] rendered a collection of contemporary ruins and neglected spaces across Spain.

Do you think this consideration of time is present in contemporary architecture? Should architects be responsible for dealing with the fact that social and economic contexts and the functional needs of new construction may change over time?

It is a long story. Mies van der Rohe had this idea of flexibility, of a universal flexible space that would be large enough for the user to occupy in different ways. The responsibility of the architect is also a question of society. It reminds me of Giancarlo De Carlo who, during the 1968 student protests, wrote an essay in which he puts forward the ironic hypothesis that although we always talk about cheap housing, on the contrary, housing should be expensive. This implies that we build durable housing. The issue of durability, in a way, is what you are raising. And the issue of adaptation and how open buildings are to adaptation—these are the issues, right? Durability and adaptation: sustainability in the broader sense.

There is always a certain tension, it seems to me, between designing a building for a specific institution or use and designing the degree to which it can be adapted. This arises with 19th-century buildings; I have in mind factories or railway stations or quasi-utilitarian nineteenth-century buildings. There was a period, for example, of endless museums—this, that, and the other—and one had the feeling it couldn't go on endlessly. We don't have an infinite need for museums. It's a kind of non sequitur. Beginning in the nineteenth and twentieth centuries, there is the specificity of a response to a brief, to create a building for a specific purpose. I don't see anything wrong with that, but it contradicts the idea that a building should be infinitely adaptable. You seem to bring up the question of the responsibility of the architect, but I think the architect can only be as responsible as the client allows him or her to be.

Titled "Unfinished," the exhibition in the Spanish Pavilion draws attention to these contemporary ruins in order to discover principles for design strategies. "Unfinished" promotes creative speculation about how to subvert the past through [positive] contemporary action, exhibiting architecture developed in Spain during the last seven years. In these projects, design emerges as a response to preexisting conditions while remaining open to evolution over time. The speed with which we commonly evaluate society's developments and the urge to constantly reinvent affect our perceptions of architecture. How do you position yourself with regards to the contradiction that exists between the architecture commonly presented by the media as finished forms frozen in time and architecture that has the capacity to evolve, adapt, and transform?

It's a complex issue. I don't know how it works in Spanish, but the term "building," for example, is a gerund and implies process. In that sense, it is open to mutation: to changes in its form and changes in its use. This is rather general if we refer to unfinished work. I am not really familiar with what you are talking about, but I suppose it's a 2008 bubble and many of those unfinished ruins were housing. It depends on how unfinished they are and how long they remain unfinished. Building materials can't be expected to survive changes in climate, and so on and so forth—if they're left unfinished for too long, they become real ruins. Then all you can do is watch them.

Robert Venturi recalls Paul Rudolph in *Complexity and Contradiction in Architecture* saying: "All problems can never be solved.... Indeed it is a characteristic of the twentieth century that architects are highly selective in determining which problems they want to solve. Mies, for instance, makes wonderful buildings only because he ignores many aspects of a building. If he solved more problems, his buildings would be far less potent."

I think it's very interesting to compare Alvar Aalto and Mies van der Rohe. It seems to me that Mies's work was oriented toward the fundamental technological changes that had taken place in society and was an attempt to come to terms with those changes while still recognizing that technology is to some extent a kind of threat—not only a benefit, but also a danger. I think it's very interesting because when one looks at the work of

When you look at architects succeeding in the international scene, do you think their success is a consequence of being very selective in terms of which problems to solve and which to ignore? Do you think architects should be selective according to their own approach or according to society's needs?

Mies—and we know that he was very influenced by the priest-philosopher Romano Guardini—it is a kind of a Degree Zero approach to the problem of building architecture that seeks to overcome the crisis induced by technology through technology. But if we come back to the figure of Alvar Aalto, it seems to me that Aalto had a concept of the built environment that was more organic, more durable, and more open to appropriation by society in different ways. So whether or not Aalto solved all the problems—Rudolph's statement is very ambiguous in a way—I think the tradition that Aalto demonstrated was one in which a solution synthesizes many different aspects to a problem, and it is this synthesis that is really of consequence. It is this synthesis that is also rendered accessible to society, not just functionally accessible, but also psychologically. I think this is the legacy of Aalto. With regard to today's spectacular architecture and invention and its relationship to media, I think much of it is simply spectacle. It enjoys a certain kind of success, but it's not directly oriented toward the more fundamental reasons for society.

Intending to remove certain architectural elements from the equation, the Spanish Pavilion announced a call for projects looking at buildings and structures developed under the constraints of the economic recession—architecture without a site, without cladding, without new materials, without new space. The result has been quite unique, defining a new spectrum of innovative design strategies developed under constraint. How can we evaluate the quantity and quality of new versus existing architecture?

I'm not sure what the Spanish experience has been like after the crash. However, I recently encountered a movement on the part of young Chinese architects, for example, to return to a kind of "repetitive difference"—to balance the relationship between innovation and tradition in a more subtle and accessible way. I think this tension between innovation and tradition is fundamental and in a society dominated by technical science, it is more and more difficult under the realities of late capitalism. It is very difficult for societies and for the agencies that design and realize buildings for those societies to find shared objectives and applications that are relevant and can be realized.

What draws you most to Spanish architecture? What aspects of Spanish architecture do you consider to be most unique? And the weakest?

If you compare Spanish architecture, say in the last thirty years, to architecture in France or in Italy, or for that matter in England, the range of Spanish architecture—the cultivation, the realization, and the refinement of the architecture—is striking. It is curious, there was a sort of retardation of Spanish society under Franco. And once the Francoist period was over, there was an enormous demand for public building all over Spain. The Spanish city-state played an enormous role, and the Colegio de Arquitectos played a very important cultural and political role in a period of a sudden spanish Renaissance. The quality of the public building in Spain is quite exceptional in my opinion, and there are certain architects who stand out during this period, like Rafael Moneo and Alejandro de la Sota. The consistency of their work, in many ways, is unparalleled in Europe in the same period.

What do you think are the main challenges Spanish architecture will encounter in the future?

I don't know if it has already arrived in Spain, but there is this system called BIM, which I think means Building Industry Management [Building Information Modeling] or something like that. The promise, but also the threat of industrialization and digital management is that theoretically one could optimize production, lower the cost of production, and increase the resolution and precision of building to a much higher level. This system promises to transform the building industry altogether. In a recent issue of *AV (Arquitectura Viva)*, there is a short discussion about this possibility. In the article, the author writes, "but of course this is not culture." That is a big dilemma: Increase production and make it more economic in relation to what? In relation to a larger vision of society? The problem with late capitalism is that there is no vision. A long time ago I wrote to Álvaro Siza, who is not Spanish but Portuguese, to say, "I hear you have many projects. You must be happy about that," or something like that. He wrote back: "Yes, I have many projects. But I am not happy. How can one be happy when Europe has no project?" This is the problem of late capitalism: it doesn't have a project other than globalization and sudden economic rapacity. Basically it doesn't have a project.

Does it make sense in the globalized world to talk about architecture in national terms? What does the term "Spanish architecture" mean to you?

One of the anachronisms and virtues of building culture, and therefore architecture, is that it is site specific. The issue of place always arises, which is determined by climate, by topography, by available materials, by sustainability, and so on. Maybe we shouldn't think in terms of abstract national bodies. Site is not abstract: it is specific. It is still the ground. We could say that the profession of architecture has an anachronistic dimension and at its best it is dedicated to small interventions. I have often talked about this—the idea of sites of resistance. When you think about the city, for example, it is clear that the city has escaped. It is an interesting question, Can we still talk about cities at all? When historic cities still exist, or at least small historic cities in the case of Italian and Spanish city-states, it is possible to have a reliable sociocultural reference. But once you have cities of 20 to 30 million people—once you have these huge economic explosions in Dubai, Shanghai, Beijing, or Mexico City, for example—can we still talk about the city at all? It's assuming an apocalyptical dimension.

What would you say to young, recently graduated architects struggling to find a footing in a troubled economy and architectural landscape?

It is not only the young architects who are having trouble finding their footings. The fast-moving economic opacity of late capitalism is indifferent to the future fortunes of individuals. I am referring, of course, to unemployment and to a kind of Rupertized economy that is always volatile in both the macro and the micro sense. Employment is very vulnerable under this system. An extremely realistic person wouldn't go into architecture in the first place because it's a precarious métier in our society. Of course, I am a little old fashioned. I was born in a European welfare state of the 1950s and 1960s. That began to change in England with Margaret Thatcher and the rise of neoliberalism. This is still the primary force today—What can we say?

SOU FUJIMOTO

Rem Koolhaas presented the exhibition "Elements of Architecture" at the 2014 Architecture Biennale with the intention of reexamining the fundamentals of buildings, analyzing the evolution of design in different contexts and different periods of time. This year, Alejandro Aravena will lead an investigation into the role of architects in the "battle" to improve living conditions for people all over the world with the exhibition "Reporting from the Front." What do you think of this more social perspective on the role of the architect?

I would say that the meaning of architecture is to create another environment. Of course, we have some part [in that]. For example, we can say, "We are satisfied with this [or that]," but we can also invent something new—invent more and more. In different climate conditions, in different economic conditions, and in different [social] situations, we can find many different opportunities to create new proposals for a better living environment. So this [proposal for the Architecture Biennale] is quite creative. Of course it's social[ly responsive], but it's also creative at the same time. The integration is quite interesting.

The Spanish Pavilion responds to Aravena's call to speculate on the major architectural issues of the last ten years. After a building boom driven by a period of high economic growth, steep economic decline resulted in a lack of demand and resources needed to maintain many unfinished constructions. This [situation] rendered a collection of contemporary ruins and neglected spaces across Spain.

Do you think this consideration of time is present in contemporary architecture? Should architects be responsible for dealing with the fact that social and economic contexts and the functional needs of new construction may change over time?

Sometimes after designing [architecture] for a specific function, the functions or programs change. But the unique design and character of the space remain. Interpretation must occur [in order] to invent different ways to use that kind of strange space. We must always think about space beyond the current or required programs. We must be more generous, or create an open field, or propose different types of flexibilities. Specific, unique spaces can also be flexible and have the potential to be re-templated. I am so impressed by the term "contemporary ruin." Of course, it has a positive meaning. Many people would understand that if we had nice contemporary ruins. It requires finding different ways to use these ruins and to maximize the different [qualities and] characters of these spaces. Thinking about current programs and future programs is a creative process. We must [constantly] rethink what we have now and what we could have in the future. The flexibility to enjoy and to play with that is quite exciting.

Titled "Unfinished," the exhibition in the Spanish Pavilion draws attention to these contemporary ruins in order to discover principles for design strategies. "Unfinished" promotes creative speculation about how to subvert the past through [positive] contemporary action, exhibiting architecture developed in Spain during the last seven years. In these projects, design emerges as a response to preexisting conditions while remaining open to evolution over time. The speed with which we commonly evaluate society's developments and the urge to constantly reinvent affect our perceptions of architecture. How do you position yourself with regards to the contradiction that exists between the architecture commonly presented by the media as finished forms frozen in time and architecture that has the capacity to evolve, adapt, and transform?

Of course we have these contradictions, and I see them in a positive way. Finished architecture clearly shows its concept and everything is very clean. But after ten years, whether because of life or different [events and] activities, the relationships between people's behaviors, people's activities, and the potential of the space is much more exciting. Often we discover unexpected potentials of a space after many years. We can't say the definite concept or the definite meaning of architecture is "this" and that's it. We can only say that it has potential. It could have the potential to be a contemporary ruin. Then, in a positive way, it would have more diverse meanings and interpretations. That is a really powerful and rich aspect of architecture.

Robert Venturi recalls Paul Rudolph in *Complexity and Contradiction in Architecture* saying: "All problems can never be solved.... Indeed it is a characteristic of the twentieth century that architects are highly selective in determining which problems they want to solve. Mies, for instance, makes wonderful buildings only because he ignores many aspects of a building. If he solved more problems, his buildings would be far less potent."

When you look at architects succeeding in the international scene, do you think their success is a consequence of being very selective in terms of which problems to solve and which to ignore? Do you think architects should be selective according to their own approach or according to society's needs?

Society's needs reveal very powerful and very interesting things—not only the opportunities to solve problems, but also to engage in real social situations. Architecture's creativities, behaviors, and responses to social needs are like conversations. It is not about pushing [or forcing] something on society or getting something from society. It is like a conversation. Through these conversations, we change and society also changes. When architects build, we find a nice, unexpected matching or merging of the two. When we try to make something really good for our [living] environment, sometimes we are successful and sometimes we fail. But future people can chose to make reinterpretations and improvements. I am very optimistic about these kinds of conversations between society and architecture. We should do our best to create and allow the future to do more.

Intending to remove certain architectural elements from the equation, the Spanish Pavilion announced a call for projects looking at buildings and structures developed under the constraints of the economic recession—architecture without a site, without cladding, without new materials, without new space. The result has been quite unique, defining a new spectrum of innovative design strategies developed under constraint. How can we evaluate the quantity and quality of new versus existing architecture?

For me, the existing and the new are not quite opposites. Existing architecture is like an existing site condition. Here at Cornell, in Ithaca, New York, the landscape is hilly and we can't make it flat. So we have to start with the hilly landscape and the unique climate in this area. Then we can start to think about new architectures. If we have existing architecture, it is a given condition just like a hilly landscape. Of course, it is a structure, but we can reinterpret what it is. We must be creative and rethink what it is and before finding solutions and making interventions. Designing new architecture is different than doing something with existing architecture, but at a fundamental level it is almost the same as making an intervention in an existing site or making an intervention in an existing building. The site and the buildings are almost the same—maybe not the same, but equal. If you think about this equality between site, climate, and existing structures, it is more flexible and open.

What draws you most to Spanish architecture? What aspects of Spanish architecture do you consider to be most unique? And the weakest?

I don't know what generic Spanish architecture is, but for me and some of my friends, Spanish architecture has a pureness of materials, a nice relationship to context, and a character that is quite special.

What would you say to young, recently graduated architects struggling to find a footing in a troubled economy and architectural landscape?

I didn't have any projects for about ten years after school. I didn't work for anybody. I didn't go to architectural offices. But it was very nice because I spent that time thinking about architecture for myself—thinking about [the] future [of] architecture and asking, What is architecture? It is such an abstract and real question. I was not pressured by others. I didn't have budget limitations. It was a limitless expansion of the thinking. And it was really exciting. I did competitions. But those competitions, and even the competitions I do now, are not about winning but about thinking. I didn't make anything—as in, I didn't build any real architecture—but I produced very, very precious ideas. We should be very patient, but not isolated and patient. We do not instantly become architects. Time spent thinking is work for your future.

JORGE SILVETTI

Rem Koolhaas presented the exhibition "Elements of Architecture" at the 2014 Architecture Biennale with the intention of reexamining the fundamentals of buildings, analyzing the evolution of design in different contexts and different periods of time. This year, Alejandro Aravena will lead an investigation into the role of architects in the "battle" to improve living conditions for people all over the world with the exhibition "Reporting from the Front." What do you think of this more social perspective on the role of the architect?

The last Biennale was heavily debated and I think that this one will be too. There was a lot of discussion about Rem's Biennale, about the "Elements [of Architecture]." Frankly, there was a lot of praise for the richness and the recovery of the idea of [architectural] elements—sometimes referencing traditional connotations, but also providing a healthy new look at the elements as inescapable in terms of the design process and architectural history. There was a lingering question that was expressed in many different ways, some complicated and others very clear: What do you do with the elements? It is not [only] an issue of exhaustively cataloguing the elements. I think that this Biennale is trying to ask how architecture can improve the living conditions of those that really need improvement rather than talk about the social role of architecture and architects as active members that change the social makeup of society. It is about what architects do and can do better, or worse, and how we can help with our tools. Does architecture have a social context that we can work with[in]? On one level, architecture is not autonomous. It is related to all the things that happen in a moment and to history itself. So it is dependent on infinite variables, many of which are social. At another level, the disciplinary level, architecture is autonomous. The discipline changes over time, at different speeds and for different reasons. If we articulate our discipline in response to social demands, we will be acting socially responsible. [Alejandro] Aravena is involved in this and came up with the theme for this Biennale, and ELEMENTAL is a very good example of this approach. He is not just another architect trying to deal with housing as a social issue, but [design housing] as a political action. He looks back at architecture that addressed these problems in the past and detects the failures: failures in financing as well as in the design of the units. As architects, we all have to work on those aspects. How can we use the process of financing differently to maximize what we can do as architects? How can housing provide a different kind of living experience in which the architecture becomes part of the people and they become their own authors?

The Spanish Pavilion responds to Aravena's call to speculate on the major architectural issues of the last ten years. After a building boom driven by a period of high economic growth, steep economic decline resulted in a lack of demand and resources needed to maintain many unfinished constructions. This [situation] rendered a collection of contemporary ruins and neglected spaces across Spain.

Do you think this consideration of time is present in contemporary architecture? Should architects be responsible for dealing with the fact that social and economic contexts and the functional needs of new construction may change over time?

I think conditions are changing and the problem is that the time[frame]s of architecture are still different: the cultural, social, and financial demands move. I think that we are going to face different kinds of crises because, in spite of all the technological advances, I am not convinced that the pace of architecture is going to change significantly. Talking about buildings, [and] not necessarily architecture, most building will continue to exist for a long time based on traditional technologies that do not coincide with the speed of things moving in a world that is operating globally: the time demand of processes are very difficult to coordinate.

Titled "Unfinished," the exhibition in the Spanish Pavilion draws attention to these contemporary ruins in order to discover principles for design strategies. "Unfinished" promotes creative speculation about how to subvert the past through [positive] contemporary action, exhibiting architecture developed in Spain during the last seven years. In these projects, design emerges as a response to preexisting conditions while remaining open to evolution over time. The speed with which we commonly evaluate society's developments and the urge to constantly reinvent affect our perceptions of architecture. How do you position yourself with regards to the contradiction that exists between the architecture commonly presented by the media as finished forms frozen in time and architecture that has the capacity to evolve, adapt, and transform?

I think that the architectural media, wherever it is now, is not addressing the reality of architecture. Period. I don't need to elaborate; I think any intelligent architect who understands the processes of design and construction and the life of buildings would agree with that. The idea that a building is an object frozen in time and in photography is absurd. It doesn't teach us anything. I have to congratulate the Spanish Pavilion for choosing the theme "Unfinished" and speaking about these constructions as ruins. Because if we look at the history of ruins in the Western tradition, which is very old, we can turn the dire economic situation of these unfinished buildings into something very productive. Most of the work that architects do continues to involve reusing old buildings, particularly in urban areas. There is nothing wrong with this and there are many cases that use unfinished buildings to produce something else. It is an amazing opportunity. I always like to establish dialogue with architecture, either with the [existing] architecture that is there, the architecture of another architect that is present in what I am doing, or with the history of architecture. The joining of new [architecture] with preexisting architecture is one of the most productive types of work that architects do. I think that is fantastic. Spain should be happy that it has all of these unfinished constructions. The bad moment has passed; now you have to do something great with them.

Robert Venturi recalls Paul Rudolph in *Complexity and Contradiction in Architecture* saying: "All problems can never be solved.... Indeed it is a

I entirely agree with Paul Rudolph. I don't think Venturi meant choosing something *instead* of dealing with society's problems, because

characteristic of the twentieth century that architects are highly selective in determining which problems they want to solve. Mies, for instance, makes wonderful buildings only because he ignores many aspects of a building. If he solved more problems, his buildings would be far less potent."

When you look at architects succeeding in the international scene, do you think their success is a consequence of being very selective in terms of which problems to solve and which to ignore? Do you think architects should be selective according to their own approach or according to society's needs?

architectural problems are not total problems. Architectural problems are predetermined by many factors that ignore many things: how the client determines what the problem is or what society, politics, the economy, ideology, and the side guys do at a given time. Of course, no architect and no design can solve all the problems because all the problems are, by definition, undefinable. The architectural design process always involves a selection of things to solve. That is inescapable. Architecture should not only be judged on how it looks but on the intelligence of the problems the architect selected to solve. How we select problems, [including] our priorities and hierarchies, is part of our work. Of course, problems may be defined for us by someone else: a client or a group of people. But then it is a matter of determining what the problem really is and what we [as architects] choose to emphasize. The beauty of architecture and other design processes is that, in prioritizing certain problems versus others, you discover and invent new problems. The ingenuity and genius of architects are in discovering problems that weren't apparent at the beginning. I am not concerned with the totality of problems because they are undefinable.

What draws you most to Spanish architecture? What aspects of Spanish architecture do you consider to be most unique? And the weakest?

I think that there was a time when Spanish architecture was very clear in terms of what it was; let's say the 1980s and 1990s. This isn't the case anymore. The architecture of the 1980s emerged at the beginning of an [economic] boom due to very unique [historical] circumstances in Spain. It produced an architecture that was very distinctive, and it had a tremendous impact on the culture of architecture. I think it changed as Spain became part of the larger, [globalized] world. As it became part of the more general discussion of global crisis, for better or worse, I think it has also became less distinctive. Now it is more about the individual [architect], as it is everywhere. There is an unusual number of incredibly good architects in Spain. Before, one saw a mass of production and shared qualities. Now I tend to look for individual signatures and [characteristic] ways of designing.

Does it make sense in the globalized world to talk about architecture in national terms? What does the term "Spanish architecture" mean to you?

Not as much as it used to. There is always an ambivalence about national architecture: there will always be something admirable about work that has to do with place and local history. I think that the evolution of Europe has produced an architectural discourse at the global level; I am more inclined to speak about a certain European architecture than a Spanish architecture. I am not sure if the term ["Spanish architecture"] is as precise and informative as it used to be. Last year, there was an exhibition at the Museum of Modern Art of Latin American architecture ["Latin America in Construction: Architecture 1955-1980"] which discussed whether a Latin American architecture exists or not. I don't think it exists, but sometimes it is good to talk about it. For two years, for example, the Mies van der Rohe Award for Latin American Architecture was awarded, but it was stopped because there was such a polemic of whether a Latin American architecture exists. I am not sure why it stopped, but certainly the polemic was in parallel. It benefited from a strong craft tradition [in architecture] that had [more or less] disappeared in other countries in Europe and had [all but] completely disappeared in this country. And then the coincidence of political change, economic boom, and what we call postmodernism—wrongly, I think—questioned what architecture should be after modernism, at the end of the twentieth century. I remember that I had a very clear idea of how to continue modernism and [how to] be disciplinary and look at architecture as a culture related to its past. No other architecture had all of that. I think it is comparable to the Neo-Rationalists and the Tendenza who were much more narrow-minded, much more fixed on vocabulary, than the Spanish. I think that the discourse at that time, when postmodernism was raging in America and in Europe, made Spanish architecture very distinctive and very clear and paradigmatic. One way to look at this moment is as a critique of modernism—looking back at history, but also moving forward with a new, contemporary architecture. It was very intense and dissipated gradually as things changed.

What are Spanish architects contributing to American academia?

I don't think Spanish architects have contributed to American academia to the same extent as they had in the 1980s and 1990s. Spanish architecture isn't definable anymore. I cannot say that there is a Spanish architecture. The impact that Rafael Moneo had at Harvard, the way he understood what he could accomplish and his seriousness and commitment to the job, was tremendous. The school evolved and became more influential as a result of his sporadic but very important relationship with the Institute of Architecture and Urban Studies in New York and many other individuals and institutions in the United States. In my opinion, that is the best example.

What would you say to young, recently graduated architects struggling to find a footing in a troubled economy and architectural landscape?

It is a troubled economy, but if you look at the indexes, statistics, and numbers, the American economy is doing well. The world has changed. There is a lot of money, but the boom is not going to happen again. And that is probably good. The profession is what is in trouble now; it is in flux. It is not [a matter of] what architects should or should not do. We need to practice in a way that makes architecture viable. We are beginning to see practices that are evolving [and operating] in ways that used to be common. I have seen this in my office. The office is very different than the way it was twenty years ago. We have adapted slowly by reacting to change. New offices are trying to think of new and different ways to practice. Buildings will always be built—we know that. Someone has to think about how they are inserted into culture, into society, into history, and into place. If architects continue to do this, I think there will be a lot of work for young architects. But it is difficult to articulate this demand, this necessity, in a way that is part of the practices of society. I don't have any advice [for young architects] other than to rethink practice itself. New models are beginning to emerge. The large corporate office that used to be anathema to young architects is becoming quite an attractive place. Today, design research is probably more advanced in large corporate offices than in academia. I think you probably have a better opportunity to investigate and test ideas in large offices that have research groups and laboratories than you do in academia. On the other hand, the floating, independent architect that works electronically, moves around the world, and creates ad hoc teams to work on individual jobs is the beginning of a new model of practice. It is inevitable.

ANDREA SIMITCH

Rem Koolhaas presented the exhibition "Elements of Architecture" at the 2014 Architecture Biennale with the intention of reexamining the fundamentals of buildings, analyzing the evolution of design in different contexts and different periods of time. This year, Alejandro Aravena will lead an investigation into the role of architects in the "battle" to improve living conditions for people all over the world with the exhibition "Reporting from the Front." What do you think of this more social perspective on the role of the architect?

What I find interesting about the theme is the refocus, the reformulation of the role of architecture, shifting from architecture as spectacle and architecture as brand toward the more prosaic—calling attention to the potential of the everyday, things that are on the edge, that are more liminal, and finding the beauty in them. I'm less interested in the metaphor of battle and of war, even though I understand the urgency of the moment. What's more interesting to me is the notion that architects need to pay more attention to the discarded, the traditionally insignificant role of architecture, as an opportunity to solve certain kinds of problems. Recently, architecture has emerged as a brand. I think in the hands of good architects, that's not so bad. But in the hands of the less talented, architecture has been reduced to a series of quick one-liners that are detrimental to the contexts in which we live.

The Spanish Pavilion responds to Aravena's call to speculate on the major architectural issues of the last ten years. After a building boom driven by a period of high economic growth, steep economic decline resulted in a lack of demand and resources needed to maintain many unfinished constructions. This [situation] rendered a collection of contemporary ruins and neglected spaces across Spain.

Do you think this consideration of time is present in contemporary architecture? Should architects be responsible for dealing with the fact that social and economic contexts and the functional needs of new construction may change over time?

I believe that architecture that doesn't change and evolve has no life beyond itself. I think the ability for architecture to be incomplete, to be unstable, is a necessity, not just in terms of being able to be occupied or reoccupied in multiple ways but in its ability to change its meaning and respond to changing contexts—cultural or physical. So this notion of a failed or a weak architecture, I believe, is its potential strength. It's not fixed. One of the most fundamental aspects of architecture is its ability to transform and to change over time, perhaps not literally but certainly culturally, physically, and programmatically. What the economic devastation precipitated is, in fact, an incredible opportunity for architecture to learn its lesson. As a theme for the Architecture Biennale, I think it's incredible.

Titled "Unfinished," the exhibition in the Spanish Pavilion draws attention to these contemporary ruins in order to discover principles for design strategies. "Unfinished" promotes creative speculation about how to subvert the past through [positive] contemporary action, exhibiting architecture developed in Spain during the last seven years. In these projects, design emerges as a response to preexisting conditions while remaining open to evolution over time. The speed with which we commonly evaluate society's developments and the urge to constantly reinvent affect our perceptions of architecture. How do you position yourself with regards to the contradiction that exists between the architecture commonly presented by the media as finished forms frozen in time and architecture that has the capacity to evolve, adapt, and transform?

Architecture is firmly based on dialogue. There is always a dialogue between itself and others, whether it's between the site and the architecture or among the occupants. The ability to constantly shift and adapt its references is very important. When one doesn't begin with a clean slate, which I don't think ever really exists, then architecture's ability to engage in multiple forms of dialogue is crucial to its continued existence. There are many architects that we can think of—Carlo Scarpa, Sverre Fehn, Rafael Moneo—who really embraced the idea of the ruin not only as a given condition associated with a very specific context, but as the ability of architecture to continuously engage its context, to evolve. These changing conditions in Spain are creating a very explicit notion of dialogue in architecture.

Robert Venturi recalls Paul Rudolph in *Complexity and Contradiction in Architecture* saying: "All problems can never be solved.... Indeed it is a characteristic of the twentieth century that architects are highly selective in determining which problems they want to solve. Mies, for instance, makes wonderful buildings only because he ignores many aspects of a building. If he solved more problems, his buildings would be far less potent."

When you look at architects succeeding in the international scene, do you think their success is a consequence of being very selective in terms of which problems to solve and which to ignore? Do you think architects should be selective according to their own approach or according to society's needs?

I think the term "society's needs" is so generic and enormous. One can never solve everything—if you try, you end up with nothing. "Selective" is not a very positive term either. Establishing constraints—parameters to prioritize the design process—is crucial. The idea of the Architecture Biennale is to propose a series of constraints that actually expand what we traditionally think of in relationship to architecture—to go beyond the spectacular to establish constraints that are more broadly defined by the everyday or the prosaic—and in so doing to instigate astonishing invention that is not outside of the solutions it's proposing, but that is creating a much broader audience, a more accessible architecture. I firmly believe in constraints: parameters are very important.

Intending to remove certain architectural elements from the equation, the Spanish Pavilion announced a call for projects looking at buildings and structures developed under the constraints of the economic recession—architecture without a site, without cladding, without new materials, without new space. The result has been quite unique, defining a new spectrum of innovative design strategies developed under constraint. How can we evaluate the quantity and quality of new versus existing architecture?

We have to evaluate the existing; we can't say that everything existing is good and valuable. But we can't say that we need a blank slate every time. Part of the architect's role is to examine and evaluate the existing: the physical condition, the cultural condition, the context over time, and certainly the economic condition. If you start off with a blank canvas, it's often debilitating and paralyzing. Yet if you narrow the parameters meaningful creativity can occur as it rubs up against and works to expand familiar territories. Working within the existing context is very positive, but one has to evaluate the strength and potential of the existing, the '"fragment." The question is: In which ways can the architectural fragment, regardless of scale, become a significant part of the DNA of the project?

What draws you most to Spanish architecture? What aspects of Spanish architecture do you consider to be most unique? And the weakest?

I was thinking about this recently, about what is so powerful about Spanish architecture. I think that it has established a series of dichotomies or opposites; it's interested in pragmatics and in problem-solving, yet it transcends those and becomes magical. It's all about structure, gravity, mass, and material, yet it becomes ephemeral, weightless, and light. It has a sort of contradictory internal dialogue that makes it very rich. The word "attractive" often emerges, perhaps not in the Spanish language, but in its translation, and I've been thinking about this recently. I think Spanish architecture is either very attractive or it tries to be very attractive. On one hand, I think it's a beautiful term. It suggests an architecture that is meant to be experienced sensually and that is about the poetics of space. On the other hand, could this relentless beauty of the object sacrifice other, perhaps equally important, responsibilities of architecture?

What do you think are the main challenges Spanish architecture will encounter in the future?

Spanish architecture is facing a challenge, and it's something that Francisco "Patxi" Mangado talked about a year ago here in Ithaca, New York. He talked about the diaspora of the economic crisis—the departure from Spain of a whole generation of Spanish architects seeking work elsewhere. Today, the younger generation doesn't have the mentoring opportunities that were so important in establishing the 35- to 50-year-old architects, who are just now coming into their own—who are beginning to define themselves, getting interesting commissions, etc. and yet they're not there as mentors for this younger generation. In my opinion, that's going to be one of the biggest challenges of Spanish architecture. Of course, there are going to be new, previously unimagined forms of practices that will emerge as a result of this "gap": global practices, hybrid practices, etc.

Does it make sense in the globalized world to talk about architecture in national terms? What does the term "Spanish architecture" mean to you?

The term "national" makes me a little uncomfortable, to be honest with you. I would prefer to use the word context. It's absolutely important that architecture has a context and defines that context and how it relates to it. Whether it's a kind of local or cultural context, a craft context, a series of rituals, or even a psychological context, I think it's a crucial aspect of architecture. Of course, a good building can associate itself simultaneously with multiple contexts and can be reread again and again. It questions a fixed, finalized architecture and instead proposes one that is more fluid or more transformative. The ability of a project to mine several different kinds of context is really important, as simply defining a single context is detrimental to the work—it makes it into caricature or something of a cartoon.

What would you say to young, recently graduated architects struggling to find a footing in a troubled economy and architectural landscape?

I'm going to refer to a comment that Rem Koolhaas made at a lecture several years ago here at Cornell. I found it really profound because most of our students rush off to work for the same ten architects when they graduate. Rem encouraged young graduates, young architects, to spend time *building knowledge*—in different contexts and unfamiliar worlds, sometimes counterintuitive—in other words not to practice architecture with a capital A immediately, but to instead sense what is important to them in the world and how they might begin to define their own forms of practice. And it might not always begin as an apprentice working for another architect.

MARTINO STIERLI

Rem Koolhaas presented the exhibition "Elements of Architecture" at the 2014 Architecture Biennale with the intention of reexamining the fundamentals of buildings, analyzing the evolution of design in different contexts and different periods of time. This year, Alejandro Aravena will lead an investigation into the role of architects in the "battle" to improve living conditions for people all over the world with the exhibition "Reporting from the Front." What do you think of this more social perspective on the role of the architect?

I would say that this shift represents a dilemma in architecture generally: on the one hand the search for autonomy and the definition of architecture as an autonomous discipline, on the other hand its deep entanglement in social, political, economic, and environmental issues. In a certain way, this is a welcome shift from Koolhaas's Bienniale. Koolhaas was not merely looking for autonomy. It was also a historical project looking at the history of modernism in the past hundred years, which was, of course, very much entangled in the political, social, and economic aspects of life.

The Spanish Pavilion responds to Aravena's call to speculate on the major architectural issues of the last ten years. After a building boom driven by a period of high economic growth, steep economic decline resulted in a lack of demand and resources needed to maintain many unfinished constructions. This [situation] rendered a collection of contemporary ruins and neglected spaces across Spain.

Do you think this consideration of time is present in contemporary architecture? Should architects be responsible for dealing with the fact that social and economic contexts and the functional needs of new construction may change over time?

I think your analysis is from a distinctly Spanish perspective. It is a condition that is not necessarily true in other parts of the world. New York, for example, is experiencing an ongoing, unbelievable building boom. I agree with your assessment that contemporary architecture is too obsessed with product as opposed to process. The question of reuse and adaptability over time—of different occupants and their behaviors in space—is not given the attention it deserves. In a way, as horrible as the situation in Spain was and perhaps still is, it created an opportunity for some intelligent and productive projects moving forward.

Titled "Unfinished," the exhibition in the Spanish Pavilion draws attention to these contemporary ruins in order to discover principles for design strategies. "Unfinished" promotes creative speculation about how to subvert the past through [positive] contemporary action, exhibiting architecture developed in Spain during the last seven years. In these projects, design emerges as a response to preexisting conditions while remaining open to evolution over time. The speed with which we commonly evaluate society's developments and the urge to constantly reinvent affect our perceptions of architecture. How do you position yourself with regards to the contradiction that exists between the architecture commonly presented by the media as finished forms frozen in time and architecture that has the capacity to evolve, adapt, and transform?

I find the category of the unfinished quite interesting. I think it is important to differentiate this from the unfinished as a deliberate aesthetic concept in the Renaissance when sculptors left their work intentionally unfinished in order to invite the viewer to imagine its potentialities, in the sense of Umberto Eco's "open work." Then there's the other unfinished: the accidental unfinished, which the Spanish Pavilion is addressing. This is an unwanted condition resulting from external parameters that do not work as intended. It is perhaps helpful to look at Aldo Rossi's writings, which postulate typologies of buildings that survive and are adapted over many centuries, changing function and use without changing form. This becomes increasingly relevant in highly urbanized environments. It is important to think about how program can change and how form can remain, and how form can take on a new meaning and a new program. Obviously the media is obsessed with final results, presenting architecture as frozen images, as icons. But that is probably not the most productive way to think about buildings.

Robert Venturi recalls Paul Rudolph in *Complexity and Contradiction in Architecture* saying: "All problems can never be solved.... Indeed it is a characteristic of the twentieth century that architects are highly selective in determining which problems they want to solve. Mies, for instance, makes wonderful buildings only because he ignores many aspects of a building. If he solved more problems, his buildings would be far less potent."

When you look at architects succeeding in the international scene, do you think their success is a consequence of being very selective in terms of which problems to solve and which to ignore? Do you think architects should be selective according to their own approach or according to society's needs?

The pessimistic answer is that in contemporary architectural discourse, success is very much defined by a star system. I am not sure if many of the products of so-called star architecture solve problems or if they actually create more problems. They cater to a very narrow definition of what architecture should do—it should catch attention. The beginnings were promising for sure. Frank Gehry's Guggenheim Museum Bilbao, for example, successfully transformed the economics of a whole region. People tried to copy it, but that doesn't work if you don't think of architecture as part of a much larger issue. History has proven that the example of the Guggenheim Bilbao cannot be copied successfully ad infinitum. That said, the Rudolph quote is very abstract. I think that architects by necessity have to define some parameters that they are interested in while leaving others out. Differentiating in an intelligent way what is essential and what is accidental is key to a successful project.

Intending to remove certain architectural elements from the equation, the Spanish Pavilion announced a call for projects looking at buildings and structures developed under the constraints of the economic recession—architecture without a site, without cladding, without new materials, without new space. The result has been quite unique, defining a new spectrum of innovative design strategies developed under constraint. How can we evaluate the quantity and quality of new versus existing architecture?

The question is very timely. It relates to the problem of mass urbanization that we are facing and increasing land scarcity. We have to find ways to creatively deal with what we already have. In a postmodern vocabulary, you would say adaptive reuse is like a palimpsest: superimposing a new onto an existing function. I think architecture is strongest when it is faced with a very strong initial assertion. As an architect, it is not very interesting or challenging if you are operating in a field that is totally undefined. The modernist project basically began with the idea of the tabula rasa and starting anew. However, not even Le Corbusier's Plan Voisin cleared away the center of Paris; it was an insertion into a well-defined urban landscape. Most of the urban fabric was removed, but many of the key monuments were preserved. I think these kinds of restrictions are a very important starting point for creative work. They don't have to be historical monuments. They can be ruins that never lived up to their potential. I think that these unfinished structures, or these ruins, are not actually ruins. They are building sites that have been left behind. I think that it is very interesting to realize the potentialities of these unfinished projects. And I have to say that when I look around New York, I find the end product of contemporary architecture here oftentimes very disappointing. I'm being polemical, but what I find more interesting are constructions that are in the process of going up. This moment of unfinished is extremely exciting and suggests the potential of architecture.

What draws you most to Spanish architecture? What aspects of Spanish architecture do you consider to be most unique? And the weakest?

I'm not sure that there is such a thing as "Spanish architecture." Speaking as an architectural historian, what is fascinating about Spanish architecture is its inherent hybridity. The cathedral in Córdoba is an amazing clash of Islamic architecture and a Catholic cathedral. The university buildings in Salamanca show the influence of the Spanish colonial empire over many centuries. This aspect of hybridity is very interesting and I think that it is very relevant in an increasingly globalized world. I also think that the Spanish (if there is such a thing) is defined to some degree by a fascination with the excessive and with a will to test what is permissible and what goes beyond established limits and norms. That said, in 1992, the Universal Exposition in Seville and the Summer Olympic Games in Barcelona really set a standard for international architecture and demonstrated that architects can change entire cities and regions. Those were not nationalistic endeavors; they were radically open. Spain has many extremely talented architects, which is obviously a reflection of a very good educational system. After the economic crash in 2008, many good Spanish architects are now in diaspora, living overseas. I think that this is to the benefit of architecture in general, and to Spanish architecture in particular.

What do you think are the main challenges Spanish architecture will encounter in the future?

Spain is looking at a project of "restoration," and I think that it's good to start by taking stock. As a political person, I would say that the refugee crisis is really changing the sociopolitical landscape of Europe, and sooner or later that will have a significant impact on Spain. This is a challenge, but it is also a great opportunity for architecture—not only for architecture, but for society in general. Europeans tend to forget, but Europe is really facing an age problem. Being more open to immigrants will rejuvenate society and make it sustainable for the future.

Does it make sense in the globalized world to talk about architecture in national terms? What does the term "Spanish architecture" mean to you?

I am not sure there such a thing as a "Spanish architecture." I am also not sure there is a Swiss architecture or an American architecture. How do you define Spanish architecture? Is it everything that happens in the Spanish territory? Or is it everything that is built by architects of Spanish nationality, or is it only things built on the Spanish mainland by Spanish architects? Is Basque architecture Spanish? Is Catalonian architecture Spanish? I don't think it's a very useful category. I think it is more productive to talk about architecture in Spain as opposed to Spanish architecture, which opens up all these questions of context.

What are Spanish architects contributing to American academia?

I think that the situation of the migrant or of the diaspora is more normal than exotic today. The experience of in-betweenness or hybridity can be a very important resource to enrich a new environment or a new field in which you find yourself operating in by drawing from that background, and by inserting it into that new place where you're living. Spanish architects have an extraordinarily good education. I think they can contribute in many ways, wherever they find themselves. There is nothing for them to be ashamed of: quite the contrary.

NADER TEHRANI

Rem Koolhaas presented the exhibition "Elements of Architecture" at the 2014 Architecture Biennale with the intention of reexamining the fundamentals of buildings, analyzing the evolution of design in different contexts and different periods of time. This year, Alejandro Aravena will lead an investigation into the role of architects in the "battle" to improve living conditions for people all over the world with the exhibition "Reporting from the Front." What do you think of this more social perspective on the role of the architect?

The social function of architecture is inevitable because it is the foundation from which our work as architects has always evolved. That it has become the focus of this particular Architecture Biennale is probably the result of the need to re-examine the agency of the discipline and its impact on the world, but also a reaction to the many prior Biennale's eclipsing of these very issues in lieu of disciplinary arenas of advancement, whether they be technological, formal, or material. The irony is that the "social" is often used as a euphemism for the lack of a design agenda in architecture; certainly this is not the case for Alejandro Aravena. If anything, he is actually the most guilty of all the architects out there, with "designerly" impulses that consistently generate a form of surplus from within the discipline; his dexterity with form, tectonic systems and even iconographic play bear witness to the kinds of architectural motivations that cannot be reduced to social responses if seen from a reductive point of view. Maybe it is Aravena's delicate dance between his political activism and his architectural ingenuity that makes this theme so poignant: he has managed to seamlessly align these two poles into conversation. Thus, for all the press that claims social priorities, they often miss the actual instrumentality of the design work he brings into focus; conversely, for all the press that has questioned his elimination of relevant design agendas, I think that Aravena, the curator, did try to articulate this point, underlining where design matters and how its devices are instrumental to a larger social function.

The Spanish Pavilion responds to Aravena's call to speculate on the major architectural issues of the last ten years. After a building boom driven by a period of high economic growth, steep economic decline resulted in a lack of demand and resources needed to maintain many unfinished constructions. This [situation] rendered a collection of contemporary ruins and neglected spaces across Spain.

Do you think this consideration of time is present in contemporary architecture? Should architects be responsible for dealing with the fact that social and economic contexts and the functional needs of new construction may change over time?

Notions of time and incompletion in architecture tap into two interrelated themes in which I am interested. The first is about designing for expansion, and the second is the idea of flexibility, something that was latent in historic typologies, but that was also expanded on in the 1960s in a more self-conscious way.

The first goes back centuries, but takes on a different charge with the invention of steel and reinforced concrete structures. Much of the modern and contemporary construction in developing countries, from Iran to South America, is premised on the fabrication of "incomplete" structures—anticipatory buildings that are over-structured knowingly to expand from single-story structure to two-, three-, or four-story buildings. These structures anticipate growth as families increase in size, see generations grow within a common structure and even incorporate their business and other sources of livelihood within them. This perpetual state of incompletion is often a central part of the identity of certain cities; as such, they cannot be seen as incomplete cities per se, but rather cities conceived in evolution. They look provisional because they are designed to be flexible.

The idea of flexibility is not necessarily about the urgencies of the economic moment, even if it has the power to respond to them, but the persistent anticipation of what will happen next. It reflects the inevitability of growth. It reflects the promise of financial wealth or even its loss. For architects, this is interesting because typologically flexibility resides in many aspects of our discipline.

Tensions between the fixed and the mobile, the permanent and the impermanent, are part of a much larger historical trajectory that, because of the forces and speed of modernization, is accelerating. Consider the rate of growth of cities in China, for instance, where rural cultures have been supplanted by megacities in less than twenty years: how do these cities imagine their own transformation as they foresee transformations in their economy, needs and fluctuations? How would an economic crash at the scale that Spain has recently seen impact these new cities?

Understanding the poignancy of the question of time in Spain, especially as materialized in the work displayed at the Biennale, one can measure it in various scales. It is certainly not only registered in the projects that succumbed to the economic crash, even when their architecture was able to deftly navigate an apt response through austere measures. It was also in the way in which the *longue durée* was implicated by historic structures that are repurposed toward new uses and cultural mandates. Within this process, the nuances of preservation, renovation and intervention have played themselves out in complex and inventive ways, often showing how the constraints of the economy might offer even more powerful alibis for ingenuity than the frictionless alternative of opulence.

Titled "Unfinished," the exhibition in the Spanish Pavilion draws attention to these contemporary ruins in order to discover principles for design strategies. "Unfinished" promotes creative speculation about how to subvert the past through [positive] contemporary action, exhibiting architecture developed in Spain during the last seven years. In these projects, design emerges as a response to preexisting conditions while remaining open to evolution over time. The speed with which we commonly evaluate society's developments and the urge to constantly reinvent affect our perceptions of architecture. How do you position yourself with regards to the contradiction that exists between the architecture commonly presented by the media as finished forms frozen in time and architecture that has the capacity to evolve, adapt, and transform?

The idea of the unfinished is invariably also associated with scarcity. When resources are limited, when you know that the fundamental structure of a building may cost more than 60 percent of the budget, or when you know that the mechanical systems are going to drive the form of the building, it suggests radically different approaches in building priorities. If you have no control over the architectural assemblage of parts, you may elect to decorate the surface as a last resort—what many do as the main project of architecture in this day and age. Or alternatively though inelegant as it may seem, you may invest in the building's infrastructure, raw and unfinished as its results may be. The latter offers the possibility of an eventual process that may yet complete, evolve, or transform its state, while the former mummifies it, rendering it into earlier obsolescence.

It is interesting that this is all being discussed in relationship to the "social," because I relate to it from a completely different perspective: the "value engineering" process very common in the United States that often drives a wedge between designers, fabricators and the clients/users. While its intentions are to optimize resources, to protect design intent, and to build collaboration between the various players in the design process, it is more often than not also a vehicle that separates the architect further from the means and methods of construction. Often, outside consultants are brought in to evaluate the design, and from a different mindset than that which formed the priorities of the project in the programming and design process. The disparity in mentalities often results in "design features" being seen as a surplus, as unnecessary, or as frivolities. In this sense, it overlays performance criteria that only underline the bottom line—not the cultural values that drive the design as a more cohesive project.

What would it mean to undertake an "intellectual value engineering" process at the beginning of a design, such that there is no need for architectural finishes? The finished project as unfinished! What mechanical model would you arrive at in order to complete a building in a state of incompletion? I think that is something that is provoked not only by your question, but by the theme of the Architecture Biennale in general. There is, of course, an implicit metaphor in the question. In architecture, there is a concept called "finish": the project's finishing veneers, and that which gives it character. The plaster, the wood sheathing, the stone, for example—if you like, the skin of the building. The assumption in most construction today is that it is composed of a system of frames and veneers, building up walls as composites of layers, among which the finish is but one element. This also means that if one were able to dispense with certain layers, or those found to be redundant or extraneous, then we would focus on that which is irreducible. Any attempt to find the fundamentals of the necessary are also in vain, since the current legal and technological requirements for insulation, and energy control, not to mention waterproofing and other elements, such as vapor barriers, are at odds with the notion of a raw or unfinished building. For this reason, the impulse to drive the building back to a state of the indispensable is, in many ways, diametrically opposed to the evolution of contemporary technologies. I think that we are at an interesting moment, balancing the urge to look forward to the future while also looking back to the elements. If we think about the range of responsibilities we are confronted with, whether for a client in a state of wealth or a nation in a state of poverty, architects deal with the ethics of spending resources as a critical part of their design strategy, and effectively the state of incompletion can be seen as a proactive strategy, rather than de facto liability. That is a critical question about the indispensability of design: What is the least action we can take to yield the maximum payback?

Robert Venturi recalls Paul Rudolph in *Complexity and Contradiction in Architecture* saying: "All problems can never be solved.... Indeed it is a characteristic of the twentieth century that architects are

The assumption that architects exclusively solve problems is a huge missed opportunity. It is, in part, how we pose questions and how we reformulate problems. If we are only to respond to

highly selective in determining which problems they want to solve. Mies, for instance, makes wonderful buildings only because he ignores many aspects of a building. If he solved more problems, his buildings would be far less potent."

When you look at architects succeeding in the international scene, do you think their success is a consequence of being very selective in terms of which problems to solve and which to ignore? Do you think architects should be selective according to their own approach or according to society's needs?

society's problems as they are delivered to us, then the questions are already formed. We should ask: What questions should architects ask about society such that they transform society in the process? In doing so we are not solving problems that are assumed to exist, but we are creating new questions that pose the possibility of generating new forms of inhabitation, new forms of economics, new spatial and social relationships, and new ways of inserting architecture into the world.

I am thinking about how Edward Said talks about "worldliness" here and how architecture is invariably a social and political instrument. What is architecture's agency? We should to be able to clearly describe how our use of form, space, materiality, and organizational systems impacts the types of questions we pose, such that these problems are transformed through our instruments.

I suspect Aravena might reinforce this view; he looks at the world, and imagines what architecture can do through its techniques. Accordingly, he formulates new questions, but through architecture. He is not an innocent problem-solver either; he is much more strategic in the way he reformulates questions. Beyond the lure of positivism, his questions are not reducible to the determinism of simple responses or the linearity of thought that evades the complexity of multiple narratives.

I think that the richness of architecture has more to do with its speculative possibilities, its iterative nature, and its multiple interpretations. What is beautiful about the Paul Rudolph quote is that it underscores the bias that we each bring to our architecture. There is no architecture of perfect proportion. The only time we have architecture is when something is too big, too small, too bare, or too excessive.

Intending to remove certain architectural elements from the equation, the Spanish Pavilion announced a call for projects looking at buildings and structures developed under the constraints of the economic recession—architecture without a site, without cladding, without new materials, without new space. The result has been quite unique, defining a new spectrum of innovative design strategies developed under constraint. How can we evaluate the quantity and quality of new versus existing architecture?

The tension between new and old buildings, and how we reconstitute the city in terms of deploying resources, is instrumental; buildings have been used, reused, and programmatically redefined for centuries. Consider Aldo Rossi's use of the Piazza del Anfiteatro in Lucca, Italy and how it transformed over centuries, from a public arena to residential units, adopting the radial structural system of the arena as party walls for the houses. Great organizational systems and potent typologies have this resilient ability to take on multiple lives, and somehow withstand the cycle of obsolescence that comes with technological accessories.

But this question also addresses the broader relationship between preservation, renovation and intervention, and the varied ethics involved in negotiating them. Sometimes, in the process of preservation, we have to rediscover techniques of construction that are long gone and obsolete—in effect giving life and continuity to certain trades. At the same time, most historic buildings are led slowly into obsolescence if only because they are drawn out of compliance with new fire and egress laws; finding creative ways in which to insert these requirements into old buildings requires a nuanced ethic of renovation that might produce a more stealth approach—again, giving new life to the building. Naturally, there are also moments when new interventions are necessary, without which new missions, programs and requirements simply cannot work; as such, a clear attitude is also required to articulate the insertion. Consider the canonical work of Scarpa in Castelvecchio, and how the project objectifies the new insertions within a historical carcass, respecting both the new and the old. These three modalities of thinking all offer ways of engaging the culture of preservation as animate, alive, and progressive. It is another lens into the idea of the unfinished project, in perpetuity.

What draws you most to Spanish architecture? What aspects of Spanish architecture do you consider to be most unique? And the weakest?

There is an aspect of Spanish architecture that fascinates me, especially in the more speculative works as characterized by figures such as Antoni Gaudi, Miguel Fisac, and more recently Anton Garcia Abril and Debora Mesa. In this tradition, architecture is conceptualized through its material agency with the idea that it might advance the discipline in unanticipated ways. At once experimental, and materially inventive, it was also an architecture that delves into engineering sciences while expanding the way we can think about the discipline.

There is also another tradition of modernism in Spain that is maybe more orthodox. Whether this set of values was planted early in the twentieth century or whether it was well-guarded by the relative isolation that Spain experienced in Franco's years, it also has its revival in the post-Franco years with the re-inauguration of the Barcelona Pavilion by Mies van der Rohe. Whatever are the circumstances that produce such cultural consensus, it is also something that gives light to the level of consistency that we see in the selected projects for the Biennale: How cansuch a vast array of architects achieve such unity and excellence, given their diversity? Within this tradition, invention happens within a more well-established forum, where certain values are assumed, a common language is spoken and the architecture speaks to other architectures as a basis for both confirmation and critique.

There is, also, of course the new generation of Spanish architects, and they are looking at the history of both the Spanish peninsula and modern architecture more broadly and challenging it from many perspectives: technological, organizational and environmental. Thinking just of a few, from Selgascano to Andres Jaques, and from RCR to Ecosystema Urbano, all somehow educated under the rigors of classical modernism and yet all in their own way overturning the very orthodoxies in their own manner, challenging not only the questions posed by the previous generation, but also the unity of expression they offered. It would seem that this generation benefited from the closure of a well-disciplined tradition, while also falling into practice at the critical moment when the Internet gave way to global communication that unleashed a wider and more panoramic theoretical field for them. What is clear though, is that despite the more recent adventures in global discourses, the virtuality of space and the reliance on the Internet, that these architects are still somehow deeply invested in the physicality of architecture, the materiality of its specification and the discipline of its commitments.

What do you think are the main challenges Spanish architecture will encounter in the future?

If I am not wrong, Spain has an institution called the Colegio de Arquitectos. As an instrument of power, it maintains legal jurisdiction over what the profession can do, and though it functions in part like the AIA in the United States, it seems to offer much more power, consistency and advocacy for architects. In this sense, the AIA is effectively very weak.

In the USA, much of practice is organized around the idea of risk; many cannot gain access to work, because they cannot afford the right level of insurance. The idea of a lawsuit is not the exception, but a rule even. This often inhibits the speculative potential of architecture, how it can contribute to society, and more importantly how it can produce new forms of knowledge. That is the risk that Spain faces as its economy becomes more globalized—if that is, the power of the United States and some of the more conservative tendencies of the EU come to bear their weight on the profession in Spain. For this reason, I continue to be fascinated by the relationship between progressive institutions in economies that are less developed, as was the case in Spain some years ago. They are able to build in much more speculative ways and yet rely on a framework that is at once powerful, yet permissive.

Does it make sense in the globalized world to talk about architecture in national terms? What does the term "Spanish architecture" mean to you?

Our conversations have been global for many years. I can hardly say that I come from one country: my parents are from Iran, I grew up in South Africa, I was educated in the United States, and my professors were Argentinian. We speak many languages and the work we produce is a response to our hybrid cultures.

The coherence of Spanish culture, as a peninsular nation, is unique. The Pyrenees and Franco helped to separate Spain from very close neighbors in curious ways. At the same time, Spanish architecture references traditions beyond its borders. In that sense, we don't need to dichotomize between the local and the global. These realms permeate each other in quite complex yet concrete ways. As we reconstitute ourselves in relation to global challenges, we also realize the degree to which our politics only gain traction at very local levels, and this tension between the two is certainly playing itself out in Spain also. In this sense, talking about architecture in national terms seems somewhat out of focus, despite the wealth of consistency that Spain has offered.

What are Spanish architects contributing to American academia?

Beyond their leadership in our schools of architecture over the years, the new generation of Spanish architects is already changing the face of architecture in the United States. You have already seen them winning the PS1 competition and on the cover of *Architectural Record* magazines, and these are but a couple of random examples within the new generation. Many of them, young as they are, have had a good deal more experience in building, and this has had an impact on the way in which it is impacting both faculty and students in the American scene—not simply to build, but to pose questions through building, to experiment through it and to produce new forms of knowledge through it.

It should be underlined, however, that this new generation is anything but monolithic. Instead, we are witnessing many voices and it is impacting not only design culture, but research and history and theory alike.

What would you say to young, recently graduated architects struggling to find a footing in a troubled economy and architectural landscape?

What distinguishes this era from the generation prior is the role of communication and technology in the education and worldliness of architecture students. This agency has afforded many young architects the power to transform practice from the bottom up, rather than work under somebody for twenty years. New partnerships are also forming across states and countries, giving young architects the agility and dexterity to react to site-specific and culturally remote areas in a more hands-on way. All in all, the ability to produce with an output that is unprecedented has catapulted the new generation to be able to take on an immense set of projects and challenges that would have been very unique in another age. My advice to the young graduate would be to look closely at these opportunities, since they afford them amazing access to an architectural practice that is more broad and diverse than ever before.

VAL WARKE

Rem Koolhaas presented the exhibition "Elements of Architecture" at the 2014 Architecture Biennale with the intention of reexamining the fundamentals of buildings, analyzing the evolution of design in different contexts and different periods of time. This year, Alejandro Aravena will lead an investigation into the role of architects in the "battle" to improve living conditions for people all over the world with the exhibition "Reporting from the Front." What do you think of this more social perspective on the role of the architect?

I think that it is important to separate the quality of life from social stability and from the social project of architecture in a larger sense. Architects have never been very good at social determinism. Being socially prescriptive is what got most of the twentieth-century architects into trouble: the idea that there were certain ideal ways to act in the environment, certain ideal situations, social organizations, and social structures that were very localized or strategically imposed. Architecture is best at improving the quality of life when it allows occupants to become architects themselves by producing forms that are not fixed and have a certain open-endedness. Children are great at that. They can use an empty field. They can use a parking lot—if the lines aren't exactly straight, especially—and can make amazing architecture. But when architects are prescriptive and say, "This is what you do here, this is just for parking,"

The Spanish Pavilion responds to Aravena's call to speculate on the major architectural issues of the last ten years. After a building boom driven by a period of high economic growth, steep economic decline resulted in a lack of demand and resources needed to maintain many unfinished constructions. This [situation] rendered a collection of contemporary ruins and neglected spaces across Spain.

Do you think this consideration of time is present in contemporary architecture? Should architects be responsible for dealing with the fact that social and economic contexts and the functional needs of new construction may change over time?

I don't think that time is considered very much in contemporary architecture even though many of us think that it is. The idea that a building will last through time by meeting its functional requirements and by using durable materials, that probably isn't good enough. Should architecture be responsible for dealing with socioeconomic context or functional needs? Yes, I think it has functional needs. But authoritarian functionalism never works. A building has to function: it has to be able to stand up, it has to have fire safety rules, and all of those kinds of things. I think that's where functionalism exists. We are notoriously bad at interpreting social needs. The last I knew, I thought there was a science they tried to make in the late nineteenth century to deal with social needs. While it may never have achieved true scientific status, today there are all of these sociologists who are notoriously bad at the predictive aspects of social interaction. So I don't think architects should do that. There is always an economic responsibility that architects have to make things affordable and functional. But in terms of actually being able to anticipate future economic contexts, economists—another branch of the social sciences—can't even do that. So I can't imagine how architects could. It seems to be out of our realm.

Titled "Unfinished," the exhibition in the Spanish Pavilion draws attention to these contemporary ruins in order to discover principles for design strategies. "Unfinished" promotes creative speculation about how to subvert the past through [positive] contemporary action, exhibiting architecture developed in Spain during the last seven years. In these projects, design emerges as a response to preexisting conditions while remaining open to evolution over time. The speed with which we commonly evaluate society's developments and the urge to constantly reinvent affect our perceptions of architecture. How do you position yourself with regards to the contradiction that exists between the architecture commonly presented by the media as finished forms frozen in time and architecture that has the capacity to evolve, adapt, and transform?

It is a tricky question. I think that the media that fixes these things the most are, of course, photography and archival drawing. Most architectural photography is probably consumed by architects. In a way, I think we are the most susceptible to seeing things as objects frozen in time and in an idealized condition. At the same time, the public is exceedingly fascinated with photographic images of so-called ruin porn—the pornography of ruins. People love to see old, dilapidated, modernist buildings. There seem to be more Pinterest sites that deal with this than ones that deal with brand-new, wonderful, isolated buildings. Strangely, it seems that mediated architectural images are the most effective in film, movies, TV commercials, and fashion shoots. In these media, architecture is often incidental—like the indirect views you see in relationship to some other activity in a film scene. Those are the types of representations where we see architecture changing in time. We see it evolving. We see it as a different phenomenon. Sometimes you can't even recognize a building in a film because all of a sudden there is graffiti all over it. You don't know until the end that it was a famous icon of modernism.

Robert Venturi recalls Paul Rudolph in *Complexity and Contradiction in Architecture* saying: "All problems can never be solved.... Indeed it is a characteristic of the twentieth century that architects are highly selective in determining which problems they want to solve. Mies, for instance, makes wonderful buildings only because he ignores many aspects of a building. If he solved more problems, his buildings would be far less potent."

When you look at architects succeeding in the international scene, do you think their success is a consequence of being very selective in terms of which problems to solve and which to ignore? Do you think architects should be selective according to their own approach or according to society's needs?

Architects definitely have to be selective not because they have to ignore problems, but because there are so many problems that no architect could anticipate or even identify. Architects have to be able to develop design strategies that are loose-fitting rather than tight. Rudolph's example with Mies is amazing. The Seagram Building is still amazing: the lobby is amazing, the restaurant was really amazing. Architects have to be selective because they don't know all the problems and because the people who are telling them what the problems are are often wrong. I always quote Ledoux at the beginning of his treatise. He writes: "The role of the client is to present his needs, often badly. And the role of the architect is to rectify those needs." I think that is what we're supposed to do. We are supposed to correct needs. The problem is the separation between client and occupant. As we are paid by clients and we often have to answer to government organizations for approval, it is so easy to ignore the occupant. In the end, we are often the only interpreters of the occupant. I think that is where the architect's strategies come in.

Intending to remove certain architectural elements from the equation, the Spanish Pavilion announced a call for projects looking at buildings and structures developed under the constraints of the economic recession—architecture without a site, without cladding, without new materials, without new space. The result has been quite unique, defining a new spectrum of innovative design strategies developed under constraint. How can we evaluate the quantity and quality of new versus existing architecture?

This is a very difficult question. The short answer is: I will do it. I will decide which buildings will be saved and which buildings shouldn't be. But, seriously, the issue is that you can't legislate it. You have to determine values—a building can have social value, it can have a nostalgic value, it can have monumental value. Even ugly buildings can have value. It might be the memorialization of something that is terrible. You can't erase every horrible development project in Spain, where sometimes banks and developers collaborated on a development that everybody knows is going to fail. There is no value in moving a project like that forward except as a monument to the greed that occurred during a certain period of time. We don't need many monuments like that. There is also aesthetic value, which is difficult to determine—I said I can do that! In terms of Spain, I think there is value in these monuments of undesirable architecture.

What draws you most to Spanish architecture? What aspects of Spanish architecture do you consider to be most unique? And the weakest?

It is funny that so many of us see a building and say, "Oh, that's a very Spanish building." It is usually a building that has a clear sense of mass. It could be that there is often a heaviness, but a heaviness that is made light. There is also often an amazing sense of site when, for example, a box is placed in just the right location to make everything around it work. Those are the things that one notices. There is also an attention and honor paid to material in the sense of how a building is put together and the materials that are available versus those that are exotic. I think there is a strong sense of color that is also unique—a lot of architecture still tends to be pretty blanched out—and especially the use of light both inside and outside. Buildings are often dampened on the exterior, but on the interior there is incredible vibrancy. This tradition recognizes the influence of twentieth-century artists like Jorge Oteiza and Eduardo Chillida on this sense of light and space, form and material that you don't see in many other places.

Now in terms of Spanish weaknesses: urban design, especially new communities. There is a strange fascination with the boulevard, which maybe is French, I don't know. Sometimes they are way too big, and that is why these ruined housing developments are ruined at a huge scale. Because they have massive boulevards that are totally uninhabited and empty. I think urban design in general has not caught up with architectural design. I think architects are so good at dealing with the incremental that when it comes to tabula rasa, design becomes overwhelming.

What do you think are the main challenges Spanish architecture will encounter in the future?

Spain is facing problems that are encountered everywhere. There are ecological problems, which will probably be the major ones. I am not sure whether that deals with the term sustainability, but certainly there is a notion of limited resources and those kinds of issues. Preservation is also very important. Of course, economic issues are always going to be there—they go up and they go down. The problem is long-term maintenance. It is ridiculous to construct so many buildings that require constant renewal and maintenance every other year. We also have to address more mobile populations with less fossil fuel because people are traveling further and further to work, or across borders dealing with unfamiliar cultures. The existing housing stock may be completely irrelevant for diverse cultural inhabitation, especially publicly sponsored housing.

Does it make sense in the globalized world to talk about architecture in national terms? What does the term "Spanish architecture" mean to you?

It makes sense to talk about it because there is a lot to be gained from sharing ideas. I think that there is always going to be a Spanish architecture because there is a base culture that is very unique and definable. Of course, there are many regions and climatic zones—I guess I have to say "Spanish architectures," not "Spanish architecture." In Spain, architects have a tendency to be very regional in certain ways. And it makes sense because there are so many climatological and topographic variations that are unique to these areas. People should understand that the most important things, things that have to do with regional material availability and regional construction crafts, suggest that architecture is never going to be fully global. There will always be an aspect that is regional. Making it global and forcing it into globalization is usually unproductive. Then you end up with buildings that age before their time.

What are Spanish architects contributing to American academia?

The American academic scene has benefited from Spanish architects. I think that it began when Rafael Moneo went to Harvard. There was a sense, at first a fear, that his emphasis on construction was going to become technocratic in American schools. But in the end, it was the idea that construction has a poetry to it—that there is a poetry to the idea of a building—that was achieved. And I think that this sensibility balances the technologies that we have today—the new technologies for representation, for construction, for engineering, and material technologies—with a sense of building and a sense of accommodation. There was also a kind of reintroduction on the theoretical side with people like Solà-Morales. I think that it has been really great for theoretical and critical dialogue. In general, I believe that a basic critical approach was introduced into American academia that is directly related to the Spanish sensibility. It's a more holistic sensibility. You can see this in relationship to a larger urban sensibility and a kind of infrastructural focus, and undoubtedly in developments in theater and in sculpture and in all of the other arts. In other words, now there is a larger sense of criticism in architecture that isn't simply responding to itself.

What would you say to young, recently graduated architects struggling to find a footing in a troubled economy and architectural landscape?

Ironically, it is lucky for current and future students of architecture that there are a lot of problems. Architects typically have to be selective in terms of what problems they address. It is amazing how many people are graduating from architecture schools today. An architectural education is a very valuable education because it is a form of problem-solving, typically through making. I would suggest that young architects find regional problems, local to whatever they are doing, and just start working. Investigate the issues of a problem and then, perhaps, move on to a second problem. It is amazing how young architects are developing intelligent and strategic ways of solving problems that we never considered before, precisely because they are not prejudiced by the standard operations of architectural practice.

SARAH WHITING

Rem Koolhaas presented the exhibition "Elements of Architecture" at the 2014 Architecture Biennale with the intention of reexamining the fundamentals of buildings, analyzing the evolution of design in different contexts and different periods of time. This year, Alejandro Aravena will lead an investigation into the role of architects in the "battle" to improve living conditions for people all over the world with the exhibition "Reporting from the Front." What do you think of this more social perspective on the role of the architect?

I assume the question is: "What do you think of this more social role in comparison to the Koolhaas call for a return to the 'fundamentals' of architecture?" One of the big problems in our field is the artificial division of social questions, cultural questions, and architectural questions. We do ourselves a disservice by putting "X" into one camp and "Y" into another camp. With any of these exhibitions, there has to be a theme. I think both themes are really well-timed; doing the social on the heels of Rem's "Fundamentals" is very smart. It shouldn't be posited as a contradiction of the previous Architecture Biennale, but rather as an expansion of that topic. Ideally, this exhibition will look at questions of the social thorough the very specifics, or "fundamentals," of architecture.

The Spanish Pavilion responds to Aravena's call to speculate on the major architectural issues of the last ten years. After a building boom driven by a period of high economic growth, steep economic decline resulted in a lack of demand and resources needed to maintain many unfinished constructions. This [situation] rendered a collection of contemporary ruins and neglected spaces across Spain.

Do you think this consideration of time is present in contemporary architecture? Should architects be responsible for dealing with the fact that social and economic contexts and the functional needs of new construction may change over time?

Today, I would argue that *time* is a key topic—perhaps *the* key topic—of contemporary society. I was just in a discussion two days ago where I suggested that sabbaticals be inserted in every career—everyone has a real need for time. We all want more of it. *Engaging with time in today's world* is a great theme. The idea that it is specific to Spain is key to these unfinished "contemporary ruins," as you put it. How you deal with these unfinished works is a real issue. It would be interesting to find out if a parallel exists in other places. If you look at the housing crisis in the United States, Chicago, for example, had a large number of empty condos and probably still does. Strategic architects would think about how these buildings could be reused and about how to insert new projects into existing shells. That is something that we should do anyway. The majority of what architects do is essentially build onto something that already exists, rather than build works *ex novo*. The ruins you're focusing upon in Spain are different only because they are new and incomplete, as opposed to complete and transformed. Architects should anticipate the possibility that their work will be utterly transformed (stopped, redefined, modified ...) because of conditions out of their control. But I don't think that you can design an utterly adaptable, flexible space from the get-go. Maybe have it in mind, but design intentionally for future transformation? No, I don't think so.

Titled "Unfinished," the exhibition in the Spanish Pavilion draws attention to these contemporary ruins in order to discover principles for design strategies. "Unfinished" promotes creative speculation about how to subvert the past through [positive] contemporary action, exhibiting architecture developed in Spain during the last seven years. In these projects, design emerges as a response to preexisting conditions while remaining open to evolution over time. The speed with which we commonly evaluate society's developments and the urge to constantly reinvent affect our perceptions of architecture. How do you position yourself with regards to the contradiction that exists between the architecture commonly presented by the media as finished forms frozen in time and architecture that has the capacity to evolve, adapt, and transform?

I'd argue that the media is catching up. It is not unusual to present projects as living—the way that they affect living. It is far more interesting to focus on how architecture influences life in a building and how it can advance that life. It is a very conservative, retrograde notion to say that architecture should be presented or discussed as a finished form that is a frozen moment in time. I find that utterly boring as a possibility and I am trying to think if I would pay attention to media that does that. It behooves us to really pay attention to how we present a project. It isn't a question of saying, "Oh! I'm going to present my project and give the impression that anything can happen or anything goes in." The possibility of a project to produce specific effects is critical. At the same time, the possibility of a project to generate things that we *can't* anticipate is also critical. If effects change over time because of changing living conditions, that's great. That's how architecture exists in the world.

Robert Venturi recalls Paul Rudolph in *Complexity and Contradiction in Architecture* saying: "All problems can never be solved.... Indeed it is a characteristic of the twentieth century that architects are highly selective in determining which problems they want to solve. Mies, for instance, makes wonderful buildings only because he ignores many aspects of a building. If he solved more problems, his buildings would be far less potent."

When you look at architects succeeding in the international scene, do you think their success is a consequence of being very selective in terms of which problems to solve and which to ignore? Do you think architects should be selective according to their own approach or according to society's needs?

The most successful architecture doesn't—I wouldn't put it in the category of *you solve something and ignore everything else.* But architects definitely create a hierarchy. There should always be a hierarchy and certain ambitions should be prioritized. Whether or not those ambitions are always social is an interesting question. Frankly, architecture is inevitably social and cultural. Again, I find that the separation is quite artificial. I'd prefer to see a variety of projects, ambitions, and directions on the table—that are very clear, that have a hierarchy, that have a project—and then make decisions to articulate what the social repercussions, impacts, and effects are. My priority would be projects that at first have clear formal and spatial ambitions, and then have clear social ambitions. The most successful projects, as Paul Rudolph pointed out, are those that are very clear about what the ambition is and that always tie that ambition to their cultural effect. And I like that use of the term "cultural" more than "social" because I think that it is a term that is less frequently opposed to the formal or the architectural. Somehow, "social" has become only about people using architecture as opposed to the architecture itself, so "cultural" is a broader term that helps to avoid that ridiculous tendency.

Intending to remove certain architectural elements from the equation, the Spanish Pavilion announced a call for projects looking at buildings and structures developed under the constraints of the economic recession—architecture without a site, without cladding, without new materials, without new space. The result has been quite unique, defining a new spectrum of innovative design strategies developed under constraint. How can we evaluate the quantity and quality of new versus existing architecture?

It is interesting to think about when certain things are taken off the table—that is, become impossible to achieve, either because of economic constraints or because the project needs to be more focused and honed. It's okay to have constraints, but you have to be willing to work to push those constraints. If you say that a project should already be framed or focused in a [certain] way, it makes it easier when some of that framing is done for you. Think about previous moments, the 1970s for example, when there was an economic crisis and the term "cardboard architecture" emerged as a response. Paper projects were one way of responding: drawings and projects that anticipate another world. The same thing happened during the Second World War, when architects forcibly had time to think. Many important ideas come out of that kind of constraint. Today, it is not a question of opposing paper architecture to construction—what if instead we do something that falls in between those two ends of the spectrum? As I mentioned above, the majority of what architects do is add onto something or rebuild an interior. Acknowledging that and making it part of a discussion is starting to happen more with radical and contemporary preservationists. Projects and writing by people like Bryony Roberts and others who are looking at these issues, for example. Contemporary preservation is becoming a common topic for us, and I think that is terrific.

What draws you most to Spanish architecture? What aspects of Spanish architecture do you consider to be most unique? And the weakest?

I think Americans envy Spanish architecture for their attention to and knowledge of construction. The relationship between architects and builders seems much stronger—or at least we assume it to be much stronger—and results in better buildings than we have here in the United States. It is that step between the design and the built that is more seamless. The danger is that this seamlessness between designing and building and the high quality of construction can actually limit a project to aspiring only to beauty. We see that in the sort of exquisiteness of a wall or when materials or details become a substitute for a project. But simple, beautiful examples are necessary and can advance the discussion of architecture, if their beauty is part of a larger ambition. And frankly, I would prefer even simple beauty to a lot of the crap that gets built here in the United States.

What do you think are the main challenges Spanish architecture will encounter in the future?

The fact that many Spaniards have had to leave because of the lack of work is the biggest challenge today for Spain, it seems to me: the exodus of talent from the country. Another challenge is the erasure of precisely the quality of building and of the building culture that is so strong. If Spain moves toward a culture that only favors efficiency and the bottom line, and loses its quality of labor and attention to construction, I think that would be a big challenge to the future legacy of architecture in Spain.

Does it make sense in the globalized world to talk about architecture in national terms? What does the term "Spanish architecture" mean to you?

This is a very good question, especially for the Architecture Biennale. It has already come up in several biennales: To what extent should we have these national pavilions, and is this really the right way to talk about architecture in a globalized society? I think there are still certain qualities that one retains as a nation, and then the question becomes: Do these exhibitions have to essentialize those qualities simply because of the national pavilions? I think there is indeed a quality of Spanish architecture in terms of the construction, in terms of the attention to detail. Every two years, at every Biennale, you see a response to this challenge. It would be very exciting to see one Biennale mix up the national pavilions in some way, but I also do not see that as obligatory. In fact, one could argue that maintaining the national pavilions, in light of growing nationalisms justly reflects our current moment.

What are Spanish architects contributing to American academia?

I am fascinated by the number of strong Spanish talents in the United States. Jesús Vassallo is an extraordinary addition to our faculty at Rice. Lluis Juan Liñán, who is also at Rice now as a Wortham Fellow, is another terrific presence. Young Spanish architects bring very clear training to the American academy in terms of how a building is both drawn and built; as a combination of very clear attention to representation, but also just knowing what a building is. They are very well trained. Combined with that, though, is a very strong thread of architecture culture and an ability to speak to a very sophisticated architectural discourse. At one point when I lost a faculty member, I actually called my friends in Spain and I said, "I need to find someone who is a good substitute and soon!" Three different people responded with Jesús's name—I didn't know him before. You can do that; you can have confidence that people in Spain are aware of up-and-coming talent. That talent has had a huge impact and offers a fantastic model for how one marries precisely the "fundamentals" of architecture, to evoke Rem's term, and cultural questions of architecture. Spanish architects have had the education to be able to make the connection between the two.

What would you say to young, recently graduated architects struggling to find a footing in a troubled economy and architectural landscape?

This is a question that speaks to how we should educate architects today. Is there a way young architects can learn a nimbleness of mind? How can their learning relate to many different things and be used in many different ways? How can they be trained in such a way that they actually find projects as opposed to assuming that one should train to do stand-alone projects on tabula rasa sites, as if we all get those opportunities. If that means that some projects in school are already constrained, I think that could be very helpful, as long as the constraints aren't writ in stone. For example, I don't think that it's fair to constrain a student project to a "real" developer budget, but I do think that it's important for students to realize how far their project might be from that budget. In other words, it's important to discuss the constraints of practice and discuss how one might practice in such a way as to push at those constraints, while recognizing that they are impossible to overcome entirely. To impose the constraints of reality in school tends to be the fastest way to ensure that culture will be taken off the table, which I think is disastrously wrong. Students need time (that perennial need) at school to gain a broad cultural knowledge of architecture and of the world. Architecture is hard, but it is still a great career. And no matter what career path you take, I think that an architectural education is still the best possible education for learning how to communicate both visually and verbally and for learning how the world is organized, and how that organization impacts how we live. What an amazing way to think. I am discouraged when people see a rift between architectural education and the reality that lies ahead for any student. Maybe I am just more optimistic about our abilities to push the world a little bit—to make practice culturally relevant rather than feel shackled by its constraints.

MEEJIN YOON

Rem Koolhaas presented the exhibition "Elements of Architecture" at the 2014 Architecture Biennale with the intention of reexamining the fundamentals of buildings, analyzing the evolution of design in different contexts and different periods of time. This year, Alejandro Aravena will lead an investigation into the role of architects in the "battle" to improve living conditions for people all over the world with the exhibition "Reporting from the Front." What do you think of this more social perspective on the role of the architect?

I think that the role of the architect has always had a social perspective. Social perspective has to be more pluralistic. "Reporting from the Front" is an interesting title because we don't necessarily think of this phrase in the way that Alejandro [Aravena] intends it to be perceived. We [usually] think of it as "reporting from the front" when you are in some sort of conflict. In a way, that is appropriate because there is a conflict between economic growth and capitalism and what is left behind. The mission [of this Biennale] is to return to thinking about the social role of architecture. It is [important and] commendable. But we also have to understand that economic and social inequities exist across all spectrums and are not always at the "front line."

The Spanish Pavilion responds to Aravena's call to speculate on the major architectural issues of the last ten years. After a building boom driven by a period of high economic growth, steep economic decline resulted in a lack of demand and resources needed to maintain many unfinished constructions. This [situation] rendered a collection of contemporary ruins and neglected spaces across Spain.

Do you think this consideration of time is present in contemporary architecture? Should architects be responsible for dealing with the fact that social and economic contexts and the functional needs of new construction may change over time?

Architects are [always responsible for dealing with time]. What is unique about our discipline—whether you consider it a practical discipline, an applied art, or a fine art—is that it requires work that takes a long time. It is not only the length of the design process; the construction process is long. [The time] from the initial brief to the end of construction is often two or three years, sometimes even longer. I would argue that a building is never really complete until it is used, adapted, hacked, and repurposed. That is the true testament to a work of architecture. Some buildings are so robust that they cannot be adapted; other buildings invite repurposing. Time is always an important dimension of architectural production.

Titled "Unfinished," the exhibition in the Spanish Pavilion draws attention to these contemporary ruins in order to discover principles for design strategies. "Unfinished" promotes creative speculation about how to subvert the past through [positive] contemporary action, exhibiting architecture developed in Spain during the last seven years. In these projects, design emerges as a response to preexisting conditions while remaining open to evolution over time. The speed with which we commonly evaluate society's developments and the urge to constantly reinvent affect our perceptions of architecture. How do you position yourself with regards to the contradiction that exists between the architecture commonly presented by the media as finished forms frozen in time and architecture that has the capacity to evolve, adapt, and transform?

While we feel that media try to freeze architecture in a perfect moment, similar to the way a rendering may be presented to a client, in fact, media have the capacity to document the life of architecture. From the initial design process all the way to the construction, use, and evolution of a building, I believe that a work of architecture is never complete. It is unfinished until it is used. The notion that unused architecture is a pre-ruin before it is used is very interesting. Architects tend to romanticize the ruin and the purity of architecture as a kind of sublime. I am also willing to engage in that appreciation of architecture as an art form, but I think that architecture needs a public to complete it. Actually, it needs multiple publics. It needs to be robust enough to have its own integrity, but also robust enough to respond to life inside and outside of it.

Robert Venturi recalls Paul Rudolph in *Complexity and Contradiction in Architecture* saying: "All problems can never be solved.... Indeed it is a characteristic of the twentieth century that architects are highly selective in determining which problems they want to solve. Mies, for instance, makes wonderful buildings only because he ignores many aspects of a building. If he solved more problems, his buildings would be far less potent."

When you look at architects succeeding in the international scene, do you think their success is a consequence of being very selective in terms of which problems to solve and which to ignore? Do you think architects should be selective according to their own approach or according to society's needs?

It is true that when we look back at who we might call the master architects, there seems to be a consistency in the work that comes from a thesis or a conviction of what architecture is or what architecture is not. I think that if you look at contemporary architects, you see a generation willing to take on programs traditionally excluded from the repertoire of the master architects; they are more willing to engage in hybrid, messy, conflicted programs. They are more optimistic about the potential of architecture to affect social change while still maintaining the high quality design you want to achieve in a work of architecture. They don't see these as exclusive—maybe the earlier generations did.

Intending to remove certain architectural elements from the equation, the Spanish Pavilion announced a call for projects looking at buildings and structures developed under the constraints of the economic recession—architecture without a site, without cladding, without new materials, without new space. The result has been quite unique, defining a new spectrum of innovative design strategies developed under constraint. How can we evaluate the quantity and quality of new versus existing architecture?

I think that different cultures have different expectations of the lifespan of a building. I don't want to stereotype, but there are cultures that expect buildings to be renewed in in ten-, twenty-, or thirty-year lifespans. I think that this is actually tied to markets, economics, financing, and so on. I believe that [the cultural legacy of] architecture should be of such quality that it lasts for a century or more. There are important works of architecture that transcend a decade or century and are of such societal and cultural value that we need to do our best to preserve them. But I would also say that there are many works of architecture, or many buildings, that do not have value after a certain lifespan. Whether it is an economic, social, academic, or cultural lifespan—I think those are all up for grabs. Actually, there is a certain pressure on architecture now to shorten its lifespan. The argument is that more specific use over a shorter period of time is more economical, but the counterargument is that designing a long-lasting building is the most sustainable strategy. I think that both [approaches] have value. We should appreciate the diversity of social, economic, and cultural perspectives as we weigh the old against the new.

What draws you most to Spanish architecture? What aspects of Spanish architecture do you consider to be most unique? And the weakest?

I think that Spanish architecture has a kind of religious quality in that it is deeply pure and poetic. Its strength comes from a purity and essentialism of form and space that I think we all recognize as Spanish. It is not particularly cerebral or technologically advanced. Its power comes from its purity. Form and space are the main ingredients of architecture—I think that is fundamental and true. I find that Spanish architecture filters out the noise of competing interests and refuses the notion that life complicates the purity of form and space, whether it is technological or intellectual and academic.

What do you think are the main challenges Spanish architecture will encounter in the future?

In the near future, we won't be able to label Spanish architecture as Spanish architecture. Globalization will begin to erode the clarity of [any] national style. I believe that culture is actually perpetuated by globalization. Thinking about architecture as form and space probably begins in the academy with the training of young architects. Maybe that is what I meant with the religious analogy. It is so deeply ingrained in young architects that it is hard to imagine that disappearing anytime soon.

Does it make sense in the globalized world to talk about architecture in national terms? What does the term "Spanish architecture" mean to you?

It is interesting to think about national architecture in global terms. We are thinking about national architectural styles from the 1980s and 1990s. If you were to ask me to differentiate between nationalities among the younger generation of architects, it would be difficult to distinguish Spanish from Argentinian from Dutch. There are traces that linger—your culture is in the foods you eat, in the landscapes you inhabit, and in your education. These things are always present. I think globalization has contaminated the purity of individual cultures in a good and useful way. You see a lot more hybrids that look like Moneo-meets-Koolhaas. That is a curious kind of architecture.

What are Spanish architects contributing to American academia?

Spanish architects are contributing a great deal to the American academy. Right now the United States is benefiting from many wonderful Spanish architects in leadership roles at their [respective] universities. They bring a new and different perspective to the educational system. My understanding of the Spanish system is [very much] "do or die": it is extremely competitive. Many students enter into architecture, and the education weeds them out. There seems to be a high demand for architectural education in Spain; there are more students than can be served by an academic institution. This produces a style of teaching, a value system and an approach to criticism, that is very different than in the United States where the numbers are a lot smaller. Having so many Spanish architects in American academia is very healthy and encourages us to think about and challenge the way we have traditionally done things in the US education system. It forces us, even at MIT, to think [critically] about the goal[s] of education and how to use our resources to meet the demands of many students. Hopefully we are innovating on that front.

What would you say to young, recently graduated architects struggling to find a footing in a troubled economy and architectural landscape?

Architecture as a field is much more diverse than one might initially perceive. The training you receive as an architect is fundamentally training as a designer, a thinker, a problem-solver, and a poet. It stretches across a wide spectrum [of expertise]. Many things are possible with a background in architecture. Working as a young architect in the current economy may be challenging, and the economic rewards may seem modest compared to many other fields. But I think of architecture as a long-term pursuit. Architecture takes time. It is a field that yields more the more you invest into it. To a young architect that truly loves architecture, I would say that there is a way that you can succeed if you are open to exploring many definitions of architecture.

UNFINISHED

CARLOS QUINTÁNS EIRAS

Many countries gambled on a model of construction-based growth. Cases such as Spain were extremely significant. The financial crisis paralyzed the real estate market and prevented the continuation of many already initiated construction processes, both in Spain as well as in other locations. Millions of square meters were finished with substandard construction or abandoned.

At this moment we have a built reality undergoing a process of assimilation; assimilation into the real estate market, and also assimilation of the excesses of *of* "starchitecture," the magnification of the egos of the architects and the politicians responsible for these projects.

At this point there are two very different problems we need to solve, one derived from negligence or a disproportionate thirst for profits, and the other caused by the obsessions of narcissists.

Current circumstances have left an overabundance of square meters built for profit and also an overabundance of those built as an exaltation of form. This leaves us to resolve two situations without any apparent relation. The two problems may be diametrically opposed, but they exist in the same reality. In both cases new buildings were hastily constructed without reflection or foresight and divorced from the reality of their surroundings.

The situation we have inherited cries out for rethinking everything and returning to an architecture of serenity and wisdom; architecture that can heal the excesses in both directions. Thoughtful and measured architecture existed before this and has always existed, but during the time in question it was obscured by the power of a new image on the one hand, and by the laws of a dehumanized economic market on the other. The lessons of these years teach us that architecture shouldn't be a haven for business or for facile gestures.

Architecture is usually hybrid because it is altered as it is used and as it wears it demands attention and adaptation to prolong its life as a useful building. Buildings must transform to adapt to inhabitants and uses. Architecture continually undergoes adjustments and is shaped into multiple realities in which different actors leave traces of their actions. Architecture can be a collage, capable of harmoniously integrating into a whole the history of each moment and every fragment of the process. We no longer expect a set of conditions that will yield a pure object, an object that satisfies only its creator or the expression of one's economic possibilities.

Architecture is continually changing its appearance, now and forever. Sometimes the change simply corresponds to an "aggiornamento" to erase the traces of the past, while at other times change is the result of more complex situations. The Romanesque was covered up by the Baroque in the Cathedral of Santiago de Compostela; the Renaissance was inserted into the Alhambra and the mosque of Córdoba. The Gothic was fitted into previous structures. Medieval structures were overlaid onto previous urban fabrics that were later cleared to create new urban spaces; boulevards, plazas, etc. Architecture has gradually followed a process of superposition, sometimes leading to densification and at others to the opening up of the urban fabric.

This succession of phases built up over time. The velocity of change began to accelerate until it reached the vertiginous speed of the end of the twentieth and beginning of the twenty-first century. At least we can now say that the time of this voracious appetite to change things quickly and at any price is past.

Architecture is an object that remains; it is the anchor of history, fossilized time to which layers are constantly being added. It is possible that a building's glory resides in its age, its walls and its contents. As Marguerite Yourcenar said, "That mighty sculptor, time."

It has always seemed to me extraordinary that one of the fundamental sculptures of the history of Western art was a fragment, which we cannot without some reservations imagine as a complete figure. This sculpture of a torso without extremities, awakening all kinds of speculation surrounding its provenance, has become a recognizable object, defined by what is missing, abiding parameters of beauty. Many other incomplete sculptures accompany the image of the Venus de Milo in our collective memory.

House in Patù, Salento. Photograph by Isabel Concheiro, 2016.

Giovanni Batista Piranesi, Theater of Marcellus.

Examples of mutilated or transformed works exist not only in architecture and sculpture. Recent analyses periodically reveal well-known paintings with concealed layers preceding the definitive painting. Artworks conceal previous works of lesser or greater worth than that which finally appears before our eyes. The layers and fragments have gradually revealed an engrossing story in these pieces, while in many others they remain hidden.

Deliberate or serendipitous occurrences. Among the serendipitous occurrences we can't forget *Le grand verre* by Duchamp and the broken glass which makes it different from any possible reproduction. Deliberate occurrences are not always ones that seek to improve or adapt found conditions. Renaissance paintings were routinely fragmented in order to satisfy the need of British aristocrats to take home souvenirs from their travels. In the nineteenth century paintings by Dutch masters were cut up, as well as other artworks whose value is unknown. The need to keep things to show or remember can alter existing logical conditions. Archaeology museums are actually nothing more than a collection of fragments that have been removed from their place of origin and are displayed according to different parameters from those that correspond to their original state. If the art world is sometimes affected by occurrences that alter the state of the art object, in architecture this is a regular occurrence.

We consider the finished artwork conserved in its pure state as the normal situation, when actually it is the rare exception. Many works of architecture cannot be finished and others are continually being modified. Throughout history travellers have described and drawn the progress of great works of architecture. There are numerous representations of the Cologne Cathedral, possibly the longest construction process in history, with cranes spanning various centuries; the shorter twenty-two years of construction for the Escorial, in Spain, is reflected in paintings by Luca Giordano and various engravings by travellers. The images of Le Corbusier's projects under construction also come to mind, showing as early as possible the good news of this architecture, trying to increase the velocity with which it would radically transform architecture. Enric Miralles also showed his projects under construction to help explain the materiality of his drawings. For one of his projects it was especially important; he saw the difficulties that would arise during its completion, as had already occurred in other larger projects. The photographs of the cemetery chapel show us the beauty of an incomplete work, full of energy and updating our vision and our reflections on the unfinished building.

Construction processes are documented, and processes of transformation, too. Piranesi left us with the vision of the Roman ruins that was available to him, which we contemplate today, but in another way.

"Unfinished" is a moment for reflection on recent Spanish architecture and its themes that can be extrapolated to other locations.

"Unfinished" postulates architecture that is created to be used and transformed, which is born and lives in a state of flux; architecture that doesn't renounce completing projects with high levels of coherence, but believes that the built project can also be a stage in this quest; architecture that solves real problems.

The project selection tries to discover and evoke the beauty of the collective. It attempts to blur the signature of the architect and transform the project into a collaboration. It tries to reclaim the urban environment as a source of guidelines; construction resulting from a succession of actions and the layers of time. Expansive urbanism no longer reigns; it is replaced by the inserting of elements into the existing fabric, consolidating disintegrated spaces and developing a sense of belonging and place. The exhibition also proposes the transformation and occupation of obsolete, abandoned or incomplete structures. It defends these parameters as strategies for adaptation, instead of other procedures. It features generic spaces suitable for a multiplicity or variety of uses over time; spaces that allow architecture to progressively adapt. "Unfinished" is searching for architecture that, although it needs to be built, also defends demolition, clearing and the regeneration of vegetation as architectural tools for intervening in inherited constructions.

Foundation, Temple of the Sun, Baalbek, 1915.

Today we are obliged to resolve many situations with basic, provisional and even precarious concepts. Provisional is often almost synonymous with precarious, as if being provisional was an exemption from all accepted requirements. If something doesn't have to last, it isn't necessary that it function properly during the period it is in use. The mass consumption of poor-quality, low-cost objects that abound in global commerce is changing our demands. *Provisional* should only mean the opposite of *definitive*, not of *correct*.

The works selected here call attention to the incomplete and the temporary or definitive expression of the material. We mustn't forget that in Spain our training focuses on the materialization of the design, without neglecting its expression, and is based on the sincerity of its construction.

Under the umbrella of the title "Unfinished" we proposed a sampling of an important number of architects, each represented by only one project. This exhibition could include many more architects or could use different projects. To talk about architecture as part of a continuous process, architecture that was always unfinished, we could analyze the projects of Spanish architects in other territories. Places with more developed economies or in situations of extreme necessity. In both cases there are projects that would permit and require a complete analysis and compilation to explain their processes, patterns and interests.

The projects are grouped into dominant or exemplary categories, but usually pertain to many of the other categories as well. Nine categories are defined through these projects, each of which is presented as a model or pattern, indicating a wide path in the direction toward mending the conditions we face today. We can follow this path by tending proactively to today's real opportunities and possibilities, while at the same time developing procedures that prevent new errors in the future.

In 1830 Sir John Soane held an exhibition of his work at the Royal Academy in London and he commissioned Joseph Michael Gandy to draw a perspective of the Bank of England building in ruins. A hypothetical state of the building to be exhibited: stable and abandoned. Soane must have wanted to demonstrate the validity and permanence that the tectonic part of his project would conserve even after it was abandoned and no longer used. A vision derived from the influence of Ruskin's ideas. But Soane, like Piranesi, shows us unusable spaces, while today we can't afford for existing constructions to remain vacant.

"Unfinished" is meant to be an inspirational reflection on how to intervene in a highly built-up territory.

The sociologist Niklas Luhmann insists in his book *Confidence* that the key to advancement in our societies is confidence, which permits the reduction of complexity. Confidence is necessary, as the rules will not allow us to operate easily in interventions on uneven terrain.

CONSOLIDATE

Consolidation is the first and most basic category, if we exclude emptying. Consolidation of that which we don't want to disappear. And once stability is achieved, uses must be found.

In some projects, the difficult economic situation hasn't permitted the construction process to continue beyond consolidation. Some of the projects, although unfinished, at least have structures that permit their use and have been converted into spaces for activities, instead of remaining romantic postcard images of unfinished ruins. It is necessary for all constructions to be used, even on a temporary basis.

Demolition of the obtrusive is necessary and helps to clarify or open up existing conditions; Teams like n'UNDO make subtraction and emptying their method. To quote Manuel Gallego: "Destruction is necessary before creation can begin."

Ciclopeenes/Dumas.

In the built fabric we want to conserve, the first thing we need to procure is stability. At least consolidating the structure. This approach is far removed from that of Viollet-le-Duc, who defended returning buildings to their completed state, an idealized state that might never have even existed; a state without the alterations that accompany the history of the building. Instead, we are defending the permanence of the traces left by what has happened to the building, to the extreme of imagining minimal interventions that only conserve the ruin, or exhibit without fear the degraded parts of the building that aren't problematic.

Looked at from this point of view, Piranesi's scenes of the Roman ruins need to demonstrate possibilities for use. It makes no sense to view the ruin as a beautiful object. Once stability is achieved, uses must be found. The conserved structure should develop procedures for its permanency, but also for its use.

Sometimes the disruptions involved in giving the building a use can be overcome with imagination. Ruins have been used as scenic backdrops. Good examples are the many Roman circuses and theaters that are converted into venues for activities during festival season. An example of a ruin serving as more than a decorative backdrop is the municipal theater of Lima after the fire of August 2, 1998. With only minimal cleaning, so that patrons wouldn't be soiled by the remains of the fire, the enormous open-air void was opened and continues to be used for theatrical representations. The theater could be used to accompany the play with its dramatic plasticity and a unique form that exceeded the expressive capacity of the building when it was complete. It took only one decision: its use and some minimal interventions to reveal the exceptional state of a space in which even the rubble could serve as a theatrical set.

At the end of the Second World War, the main tasks in Europe were emergency repairs, many to provide provisional housing and others for consolidation and demolition of ruins. We are reminded of the apparently temporary solutions in different buildings in Munich by Hans Döllgast, in which he intervened with fragility, clearly differentiating the found from the new and complementing it minimally or with something that respected the existing found element.

The selected consolidation projects show intermediate states, temporary solutions that permit a use and are revealed as a sufficient support for successive interventions. These projects are fruit of the scarcity of the moment and maintain a taste for the exhibition of traces, especially those that are constructed, even though they are dilapidated.

The Santa María de los Reyes Convent was in a partially ruined state when it was consolidated by Morales de Giles (MGM). New paths were introduced, enabling this project to be a suitable platform for new urban practices, which facilitate citizen participation and collaboration. MGM's design uncovers constructions that were concealed behind the walls of the convent, recovering and reactivating the resulting open spaces.

Re-Habitar, the house at Callejón de Menores 12, the site of an interesting collaborative process, initiated in the Toledo School of Architecture, which tries to demonstrate how to reactivate the residential urban fabric in the historic center of Toledo through the implantation of new uses. This project seeks the generation of new design methods, especially when it is necessary to assure stability. The house at Callejón de Menores 12 is stabilized with an exoskeleton, which supports all of the existing elements; none were dismantled.

In the Restoration of the Old Church of Corbera d'Ebre, it was necessary to preserve the memory of place, the location of the Battle of the Ebro during the Spanish Civil War. The intervention by Ferran Vizoso, Núria Bordas, Jordi Garriga and David Garcia strikes a subtle balance between nature and construction on one hand, and exterior and interior on the other, a combination that all ruins contain. Temporary use of the entire space is made possible here by the simple plastic roof.

The Intermediate House is more of a manifesto than a project. In this design Carmen Moreno raises the question of the frozen memory of an uninhabited place prior to the construction that will provide a new life for the building. The Intermediate House talks about stages and moments when spaces are normally vacant.

Temple of the Sun, Baalbek. Immense stones in foundation of the great temple, American Colony, Jerusalem.

REAPPROPRIATION

After consolidation, reappropriation. The reuse of abandoned buildings, obsolete industrial spaces, military or religious buildings that are no longer used, etc. These constructions are an exceptional heritage that can accommodate multiple uses. Buildings are abandoned when they cease to be profitable and efficient. It should be the public will that steps in to safeguard this heritage and ensure that it is used. However, private initiatives which use these spaces are also increasing.

Juan Domingo Santos occupies the former San Isidro Sugar Factory. His decision, made together with the factory owners, to convert a part of the factory into his architecture studio allowed him to develop a revitalization project for the entire complex. This project and the proposed activities increase the variety of possible uses and at the same time act as a safeguard against possible real estate speculation.

The Contemporary Art Space in Madre de Dios Convent designed by Sol 89 studio, could also be considered an example of consolidation if that was the only task they undertook in the convent. When the architects entered the convent they added something to its existing state, awaiting new actions in the future. They consider the architectural intervention as an installation in a found space, which permits its gradual execution over time.

In the Espacio Barberí in Olot, RCR obtains the space they need for their studio; an intervention that conserves the memory of the former foundry, in which they can make small incremental interventions that minimally create the conditions for a workplace in an atmosphere that conserves the aromas, colors and forms belonging to other moments.

Gaudí constructed the Rei Martí Water Reservoir which, until it was recently uncovered, had been hidden for many years. Its accidental discovery allowed for its reappropriation with a minimum of interventions, in the same way that Jordi Badía designed the provisional installation of the MUHBA (Barcelona History Museum) in the former Oliva Artés factory.

The Collage House by Bosch and Capdeferro is an intervention superimposed on a complex of dilapidated buildings that maintains the memory of the constructions as well as the traces of the family that are deposited like a collage. The Casa del Condestable is a public intervention by the studio of Tabuenca&Leache that develops the logical continuity between the old and the new with the use of original materials.

The Casal Balaguer is another public intervention by Flores & Prats where an aristocratic house from the fourteenth century is converted into a cultural center through the wide variety of resources wielded by its authors.

Manuel Gallego is charged with the elimination of the stigmas attached to the old Bank of Spain building in Santiago. This anomalous building in the urban fabric is converted into the Pilgrims' Museum at end of the Camino de Santiago. Victor López Cotelo designs the Granada School of Architecture through a long process that was drawn out over time. López Cotelo is a strategist who carefully fits together the different inherited fabrics with subtle and precise operations, converting this complex structure into a school.

Reappropriations also take place in empty spaces within the city, for instance, the construction of public parks in Amsterdam after the Second World War by Aldo van Eyck or the land occupations of the Guerrilla Gardens in New York, to name a few of the examples that are studied today. In Spain actions like *estonoesunsolar (this isn't an empty lot)* in Zaragoza and many others are raising consciousness about the city's latent possibilities. Of even greater relevance is the consolidation of platforms reclaiming the limits of uses and codes, especially the figure of Santiago Cirugeda and Recetas Urbanas, or interventions by Arquitectura expandida, etc.

Temple of Jupiter, Baalbek, Holy Land.

ADAPTABLE

Adaptability speaks to the capacity of buildings to modify the organizational schemes with which they were born. Many adaptive solutions have appeared after changes in use, some motivated simply by changes of ownership and others due to social or technological modifications. The decision to preserve our built heritage is a logical reaction against waste that leads to ingenious interventions to adapt existing spaces to new requirements. The adaptation of existing built spaces can be achieved with extremely limited budgets, wasting no unnecessary effort and taking advantage of the synergies that are encountered during the process.

The placement of cultural contents seems to work in almost any reappropriation, but it shouldn't become a universal solution. For this reason we also find subway stations, factories and churches that are converted into skating rinks, storefronts, discotheques or even sports facilities.

The Misericordia church in Venice was transformed into a gymnasium, others have been used as libraries, recently in the Netherlands and a century ago in Mexico. We also should remember appropriations like the amphitheater in Arles, the Theater of Marcellus in Rome or the vacant spaces in some of the aqueducts. We also have contemporary examples, more difficult to digest perhaps, like the non-residential uses of the Tugendhat House.

The Lidia Cinema by Nuria Salvadó and David Tapias speaks clearly about the adaptability of a space for conversion into housing. The Cultural Factory in Matadero in Madrid by Ángel Borrego also operates in this direction.

The Studio in Lacy Street by Sauquet is a minimal intervention to gain space, the Carreras-MúgicaGallery by Juan Herreros is an interior inserted into a dense urban fabric, and the Renovation and Adaptation of a Home-Studio by MAIO empties out part of the constructed volume to reduce its density and fill it with light, notably improving the quality of the space.

Many projects are developed taking advantage of part of an existing construction, like the House Inside a House by Josep Ferrando and the Luz House by Arquitectura-G.

Approaches that allow things to be moved, assembled and dismantled, folded, etc. Furniture as living space. One could almost say that the design of various of the selected projects is resolved exclusively with furniture. The New Space in Casa Nova by Toni Gelabert and Néstor Montenegro, the All I Own House by PKMN, San Jerónimo 17 by CUAC Arquitectura and the Susaloon by Uriel Fogué, Eva Gil and Carlos Palacios are all projects that are organized using minor elements, especially for storage, like the Put-Away House by Peter Smithson, 1993-2000.

INFILL

Insertions, elements that fill existing built spaces, appear more and more often and with greater intentionality. Insertions that complete, but don't hide, the existing built fabric; with smaller proportions in relation to the existing building, yet still notably changing the overall construction, achieving a reconfiguration of the original.

A large part of the selected projects could be placed in this category. These are elements without complete autonomy, which need the presence of other, already built constructions.

The Single-Family House in Tebra by Irisarri and Piñera completes the ruined walls with concrete volumes and the Two Houses in Oropesa by Paredes Pedrosa intertwine with the existing structures. Both projects are equally interested in the enclosed space and the interstitial spaces that occur between volumes. Fine Arts Museum of Asturias in Oviedo by Francisco Mangado is more ambitious, as it must resolve a complex, different-sized web. In addition, it must discover how to place the program behind the remnants of the facade, in order to conceal the direct presence of the new from the urban fabric surrounding the museum complex. The intervention around the Temple of Diana by José María Sánchez orders all of the irregularities of the site, at the same time as it tries to recover the Roman plan to the extent that is possible, and create a series of buildings for a variety of uses. The Denominación de Origen Ribera del Duero Headquarters by Barozzi and Veiga finds a way to suitably place itself within the historic remains. The Atrio Relais Châteaux project by Mansilla + Tuñón is an anti-modern building that distances itself from the expiration date of current architecture.

Joseph Michael Gandy, *A Bird's-eye View of the Bank of England,* 1830, showing Sir John Soane's design for the Bank of England in ruins.

REASSIGNMENTS

In Spain necessity has always forced us to modify conventional uses of materials and technologies. The scarcity of resources leads to inventions that breach established rules. Alejandro de la Sota played with these modifications, and before him Antoni Gaudi, Josep Maria Jujol and Antonio Palacios, among many others. A great number of the selected projects question the established uses of materials and alter their typical position, dimensions, connections and uses.

In Jordi and Africa's House, TEd'A arquitectes reuse the *marés* stone, revealing its imprint to give the building texture. In Matadero Madrid—Building 8B Arturo Franco uses abandoned clay roof tiles, converting them into a filter and a back-up for the structure. Suárez Santas, in the Auzo Factory Irazábal-Matiko, converts steel raceway channels into the building skin. In the House in Gaüses, Anna & Eugeni Bach use typical local construction solutions, but they then modify them, with a result that is notably different from the surrounding constructions. This also occurs in the Habitat Storehouse by Grau, Regusci and Bustos. HARQUITECTES works with brick in House 1014, as does Carles Enrich in the Cemetery of Gironella. In the Grao Cemetery Inés García Clariana designs an intervention with different shades of ceramic tiles, which completely changes the relationship of the wall to its surroundings.

NAKED

Nude architecture, unfinished and incomplete. The beauty of the unfinished work, which reveals its technology and materials that today aren't available. Architecture that shows the sincerity of its materials, which doesn't need to cover up everything in search of the clean lines that innocuously envelope all built forms. Architecture that has cleaner lines when its use or the climate permits.

The San Lucas Pavilion by FRPO and the Swimming Pool in Maceda by trespes take advantage of their summertime use to leave the buildings partially unenclosed. In the OE House by Fake Industries Architectural Agonism and Aixopluc, the use of the house is transferred depending on the mood of the occupants and climatic changes. The Glòries Information Point by peris+toral studio and the School in La Milagrosa by Pereda Pérez attempt to blur their presence in the space where they are sited.

This way of building is easier in other countries, outside of our territory. It appears in many projects by Spanish architects in Central and South America or Africa, such as those by José María Saez in Ecuador or Albert Faus in Burkina Faso.

PERCHING

Architecture sited on top of other architecture, built in unlikely places and permanently sitting on top of other constructions. This translated architecture doesn't present huge differences with the architecture into which it is inserted, it is no longer charged with references to a future that was represented by formal approximations of different types of vehicles. The translated architecture is more easily reconciled to the place where it is sited.

Projects can be permanently placed, like the Lude House by the Grupo Aranea, or temporarily, like the Pavilion for an Existing House designed in Barcelona by Flexo Arquitectura. The Cyclopean House by Antón García Abril and the Pier 57 Interim Project by Churtichaga and de la Quadra-Salcedo (CH+QS) are two projects that were built in Spain and transported to other locations, placed on top of, in the case of García Abril, or hung from, in the case of CH+QS.

Scuola grande della Misericordia, Salento. Photograph by Isabel Concheiro.

Scuola grande della Misericordia used as a sports palace.

GUIDES

Many of the projects propose guidelines, or design precepts. Many projects try to provide a solution that can serve as the seed for other constructions by establishing parameters that can be reproduced in other situations. These new projects tend to make spaces for possible transformations and develop patterns for evolution and changes that can enrich the design. They tend to let users add layers that adapt to the necessities and realities of the occupants.

Entresitio designed a health center in Madrid that has been used for three different sites, and could be used for more. The first project was designed with a clear program and budget, but then proposed as a solution that could be built on different sites.

Toni Gironés's project for 80 Houses in Salou is an apartment building that can be adapted to and by its users. Ease of modification using a clear set of rules is also characteristic of the 57 Housing Units on the ETSAV Campus by DATAAE+HARQUITECTES, but in this case using the tools of prefabrication.

PAVEMENTS

Finally, a category of projects for interventions in public space. Places without roofs that consist mainly of paving design. Pavements that define public space, as elements that connect to the history and the memory of a place. Pavements that don't completely occupy the space, that understand when there is a need for their presence and the advantages of their absence. Pavements that know to retract to allow the vegetation to appear and the direct contact with the ground, without unnecessary layers. Pavements that sometimes are just demolition; elimination of obsolete layers or interrupting elements.

The pavement is an element that connects with the history and memory of place in the project for Environs of the Born Market by Vora. And paving is used to create public space using a limitless sequence in the Renovation of Malpica Harbor by Creus and Carrasco.

Two projects that arise from demolition operations are the Pedra da Rá Overlook by Carlos Seoane and the Turó de la Rovira by Imma Jansana and Jordi Romero. In the first case, the demolition of a senseless structure built years ago permits the logical implantation of a public space, highlighting the force of the huge rocks. The second case is the recovery of a space of collective memory, which evokes the Civil War while adding references to the remains of a former shantytown, but avoiding any hint of excess.

PROJECTS

CONSOLIDATE	Santa María de los Reyes Convent, Re-Habitar, Restoration of the Old Church of Corbera d'Ebre, Intermediate House
REAPPROPRIATION	San Isidro Sugar Factory, Contemporary Art Space in Madre de Dios Convent, Espacio Barberí, Rei Martí Water Reservoir, Oliva Artés, Collage House, Casa del Condestable, Casal Balaguer Cultural Center, Pilgrims' Museum, Granada School of Architecture
ADAPTABLE	Lidia Cinema, Luz House, New Space in Casa Nova, All I Own House, Susaloon, House Inside a House, San Jerónimo 17, The Cultural Factory in Matadero, Renovation and Adaptation of a Home-Studio, Studio in Lacy Street, Carreras-Múgica Gallery of Contemporary Art
INFILL	Single-Family House in Tebra, Atrio Relais Châteaux, Denominación de Origen Ribera del Duero Headquarters, Two Houses in Oropesa, Fine Arts Museum of Asturias, Building and Urban Space Surrounding the Temple of Diana
NAKED	OE House, San Lucas Pavilion, Swimming Pool in Maceda, School in La Milagrosa, Glòries Information Point
PERCHING	Lude House, Pavilion for an Existing House, Cyclopean House, Pier 57 Interim Project
REASSIGNMENTS	House 1014, Matadero Madrid—Building 8BADD: New Access to the Historic Center of Gironella, Grao Cemetery, Jordi and Africa's House, House in Gaüses, Habitat Storehouse, Auzo Factory Irazábal-Matiko
GUIDES	3X1 / 3 Municipal Health Centers in Madrid, 80 Houses in Salou, 57 Housing Units on the ETSAV Campus
PAVEMENTS	Renovation of Malpica Harbor, Environs of the Born Market, Pedra da Rá Overlook, Turó de la Rovira

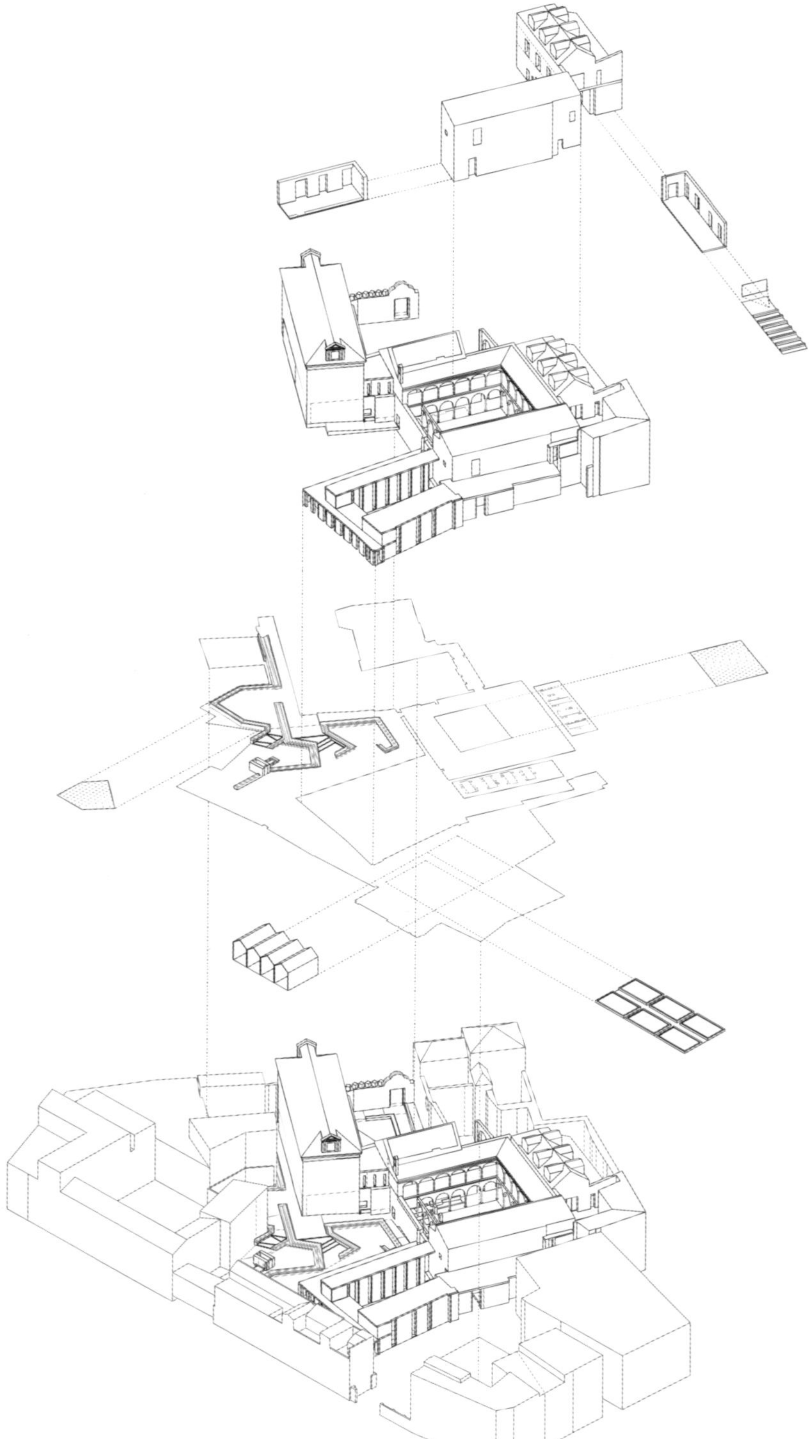

CONSOLIDATE

SANTA MARÍA DE LOS REYES CONVENT
MGM, Morales de Giles Arquitectos

The old Convent of Santa Maria de los Reyes is located within a built-up block in the historic center of Seville. It was abandoned and in a state of semi-ruin, except for the church, choirs and entry porch, which were used regularly for exhibitions and workshops. The old convent vegetable gardens had been converted into a large "vacant lot" concealed behind the walls of the old convent, waiting to be built on or rediscovered.

Due to the decrepit state of the historical complex (cloister, cells, rectory and old vegetable gardens) an urgent intervention was required. Given the scarcity of available funding and taking into account the requirements of the new urban partners in the historic center, it was decided to create installed consolidations; with new paths, consolidating urban practices and pre-inhabiting mechanisms for art installations.

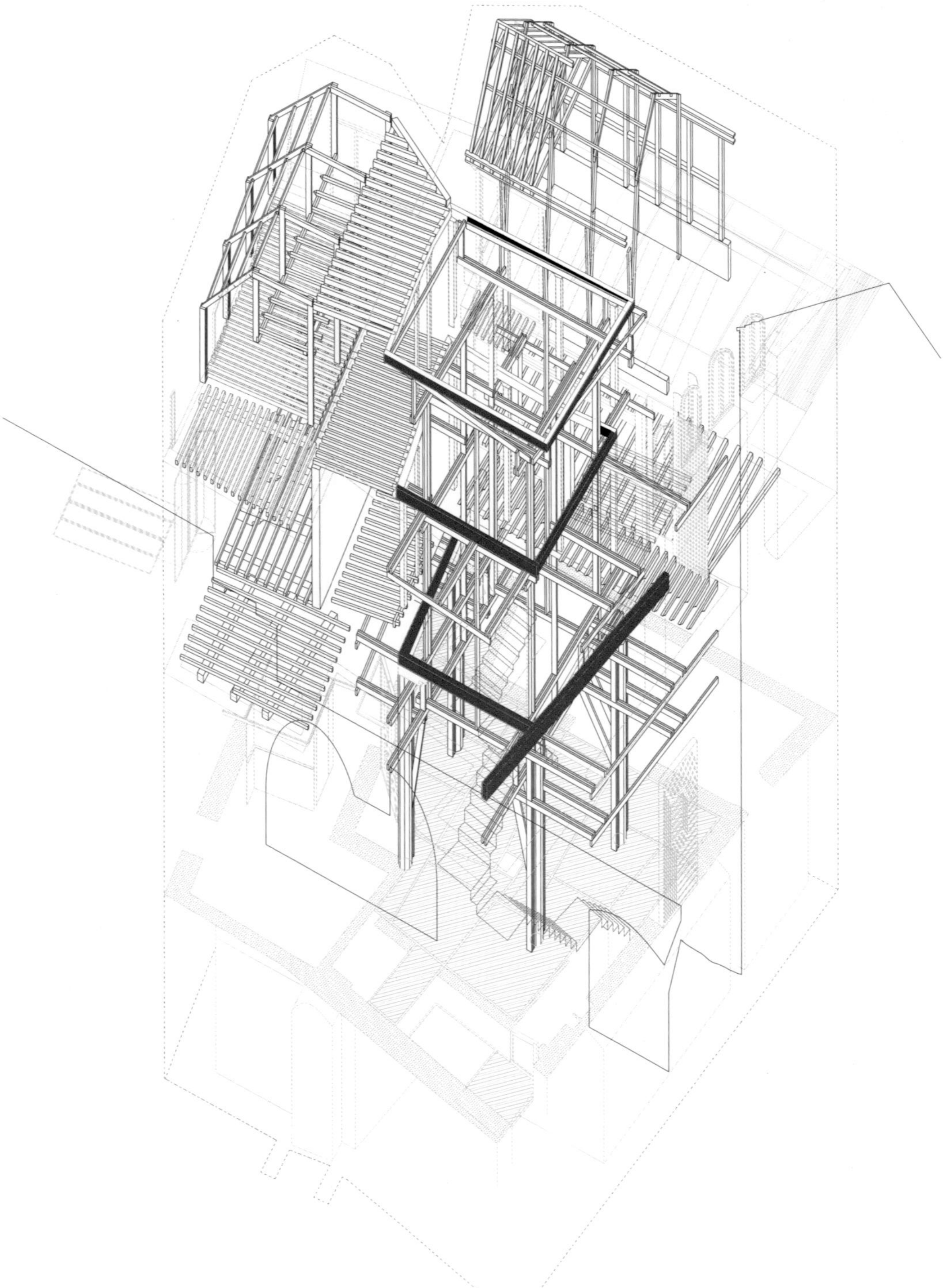

CONSOLIDATE

RE-HABITAR
Escuela Técnica Superior de Arquitectura de Toledo

The house at Callejón de Menores 12 is a courtyard house with many elements of interest, dating from the first through to the twentieth centuries. This project set out to establish innovative criteria for the renovation of historic buildings. The fundamental goal was to reactivate the residential fabric of the historic center with new uses: generate new design methods for historic buildings, transmit knowledge to the participating students and define other approaches to renovation ranging from project management to actual construction, which could be exported as models for other situations in the city. Regarding the interventions, the first was to ensure the stability of the structure by adding an exoskeleton that supports the existing structure, without removing anything. The intervention is accomplished while conserving the form and textures of the existing construction elements, maintaining the possibility of reading each moment of the house's history. Only reversible, dry-mounted construction systems are used.

CONSOLIDATE

RESTORATION OF THE OLD CHURCH OF CORBERA D'EBRE

Ferran Vizoso, Núria Bordas, Jordi Garriga, David Garcia

The objective of this intervention was to restore the ruins of the old church without drastically changing its identity as a symbol and expression of the Battle of the Ebro, a turning point in the Spanish Civil War. It was vital that the transformation of the church into a multipurpose hall be achieved without altering the memories it contained. The restoration called for the preservation of the subtle balance between nature and construction, exterior and interior, which is characteristic of all ruins. The perception that one is still "outside" even after entering "inside" had to be maintained. A transparent ETFE roof was installed, which prevents further deterioration of the building by atmospheric agents and notably improves interior comfort. The resulting space is halfway between inside and outside, thanks to the sunlight passing through the lightweight roof, the breeze, the sounds of the birds flying through the upper reaches of the aisles and the sand floors.

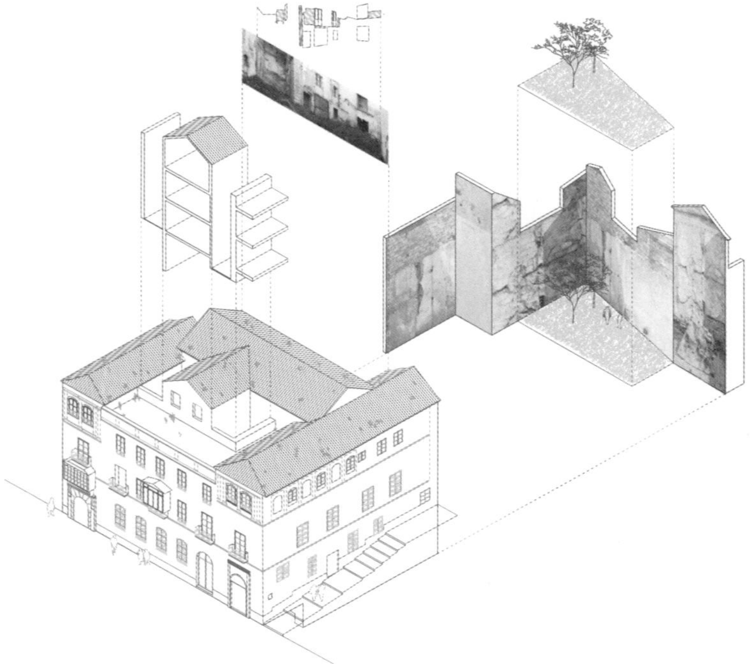

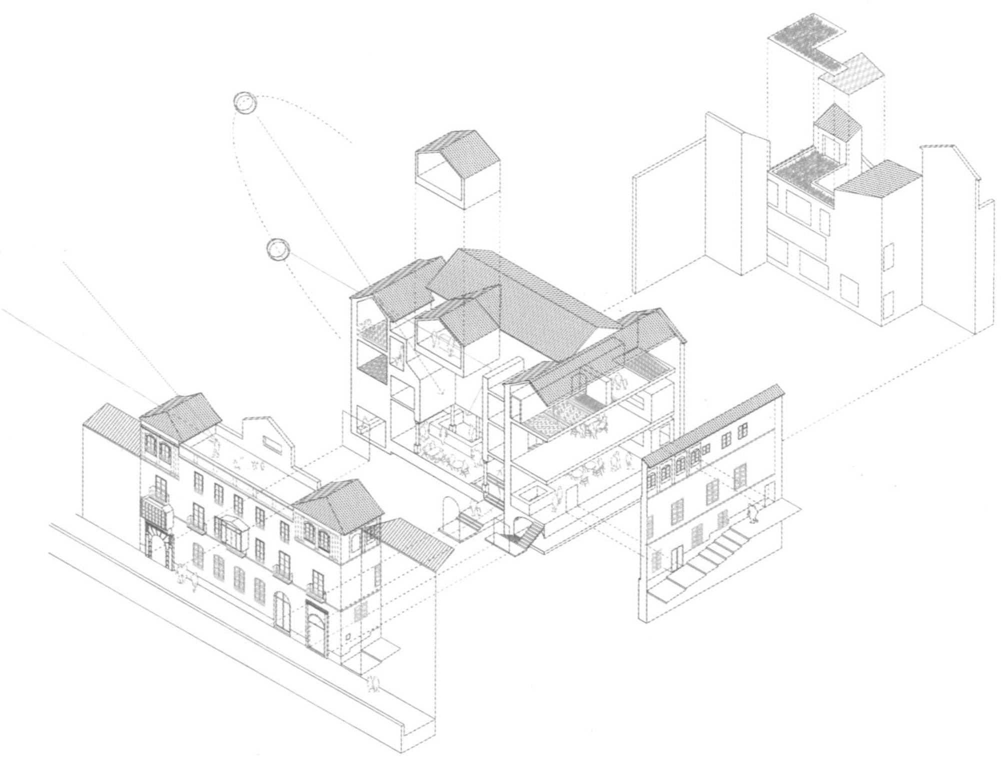

CONSOLIDATE

INTERMEDIATE HOUSE
Carmen Moreno Álvarez

The time that passed from the eviction of the tenants of this sixteenth-century palace and the commission to transform the building into a small hotel and restaurant resulted in an extremely suggestive and evocative intermediate landscape; somewhere between a ruin and a void, between existing conditions and archaeology, a window open onto history in which the marks of events and of our time are superimposed, like a palimpsest. It is an atlas of different undocumented materials, which registers the memories of the inhabitants and the history of the construction of the house and its transformations.

The Intermediate House is a place waiting for something to happen. An intervened space without intervention. It is the frozen memory of a place that at this moment is not inhabited. Containing the past, present and future simultaneously as a way to retain in memory this place and its origin.

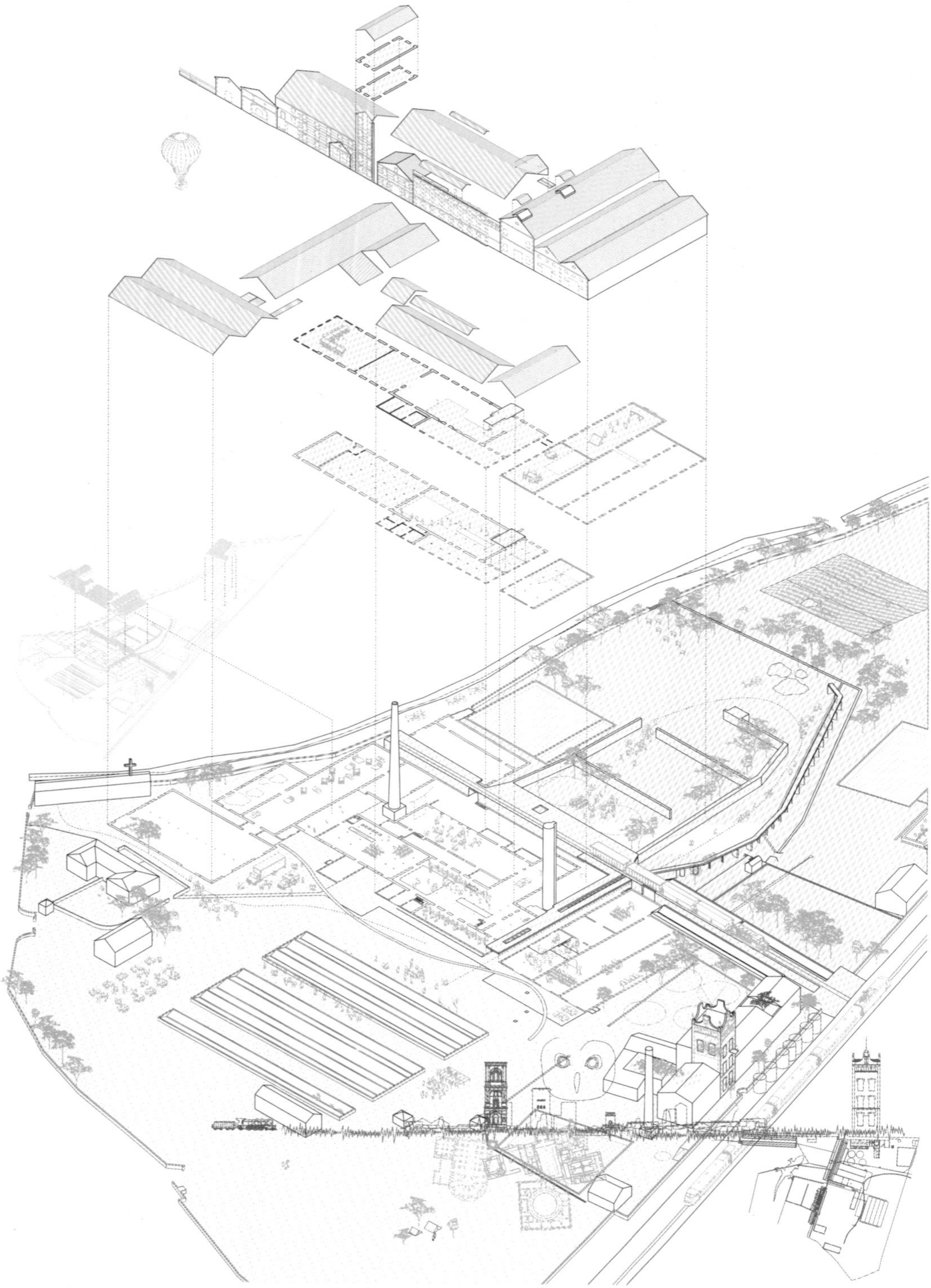

REAPPROPRIATION

SAN ISIDRO SUGAR FACTORY
Juan Domingo Santos

Juan Domingo had decided that he would convert the old, abandoned factory near the train tracks into his architecture studio. A desire that became stronger with the passing years. The factory quickly became a field for study and experimentation where he learned the importance of addressing history and its meaning in a more natural, relaxed and less dramatic way. He reconstructed his history by letting intuition lead him and through a series of experiences which let him decipher this mysterious place, until he had made a map of singular events, from its foundation up to his arrival. He remembers having made outings to the site and naming different places, relating the original toponymy of the spaces with possible or desired future activities. With the passing years the revitalization project and the activities that have been implemented can be recognized as a rescue mission for this industrial complex. The short film *An encounter*, produced together with cinema director Juan Bollaín, relates his experiences in the factory.

REAPPROPRIATION

CONTEMPORARY ART SPACE IN MADRE DE DIOS CONVENT
Sol 89
María González García, Juanjo López de la Cruz

This intervention interprets the building where the sixteenth-century convent is inserted as a context that over the centuries is continually being transformed. Beyond a historical interest, the succession of alterations suggests a metamorphosis; the approach to the building emerges from the search for its materiality, concealed by the cladding of the old university classrooms.

In this space that has been so dramatically altered, with an extremely limited budget, the project is activated by the action of discovery; converting destruction into something as natural as construction. After unmasking floors, walls and ceilings, the blurred openings between spaces were reinforced with steel jambs and lintels and new glazing was installed in the cloister to recover the transparent relationship with the courtyard that existed when it was an ambulatory. The result is a rough intervention that doesn't pretend to be conclusive, but offers an intermediate moment. From this point all options are possible; it is a space in an ellipsis, waiting expectantly for each artistic installation to complete it.

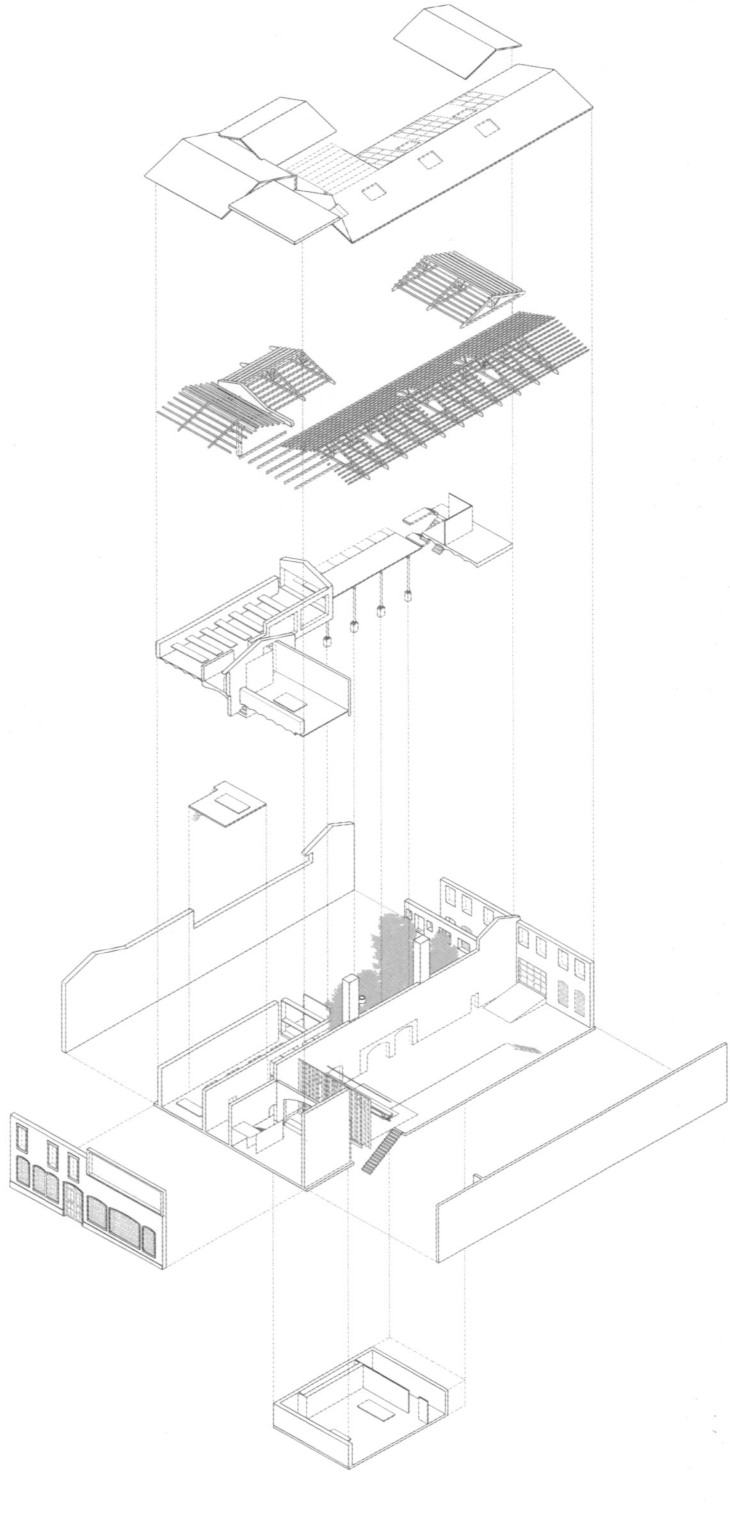

REAPPROPRIATION

ESPACIO BARBERÍ
RCR Arquitectes
Rafael Aranda, Carme Pigem, Ramon Vilalta

Acquired in 2004 in a state of ruin, over stages the old Barberí foundry has gradually become the studio of RCR Arquitectes. The past of this factory building, constructed at the beginning of the twentieth century, is evident everywhere and establishes a very close relationship with new interventions.

The connection between tradition and innovation, together with other core concepts of the RCR philosophy like relating to the outdoors and reflecting the passage of time, has given rise to an ensemble that combines different spaces and uses. The renovation work, which has been underway since 2006, consolidated the former complex and reorganized the existing industrial buildings, transforming them into a laboratory that meets their studio's various needs.

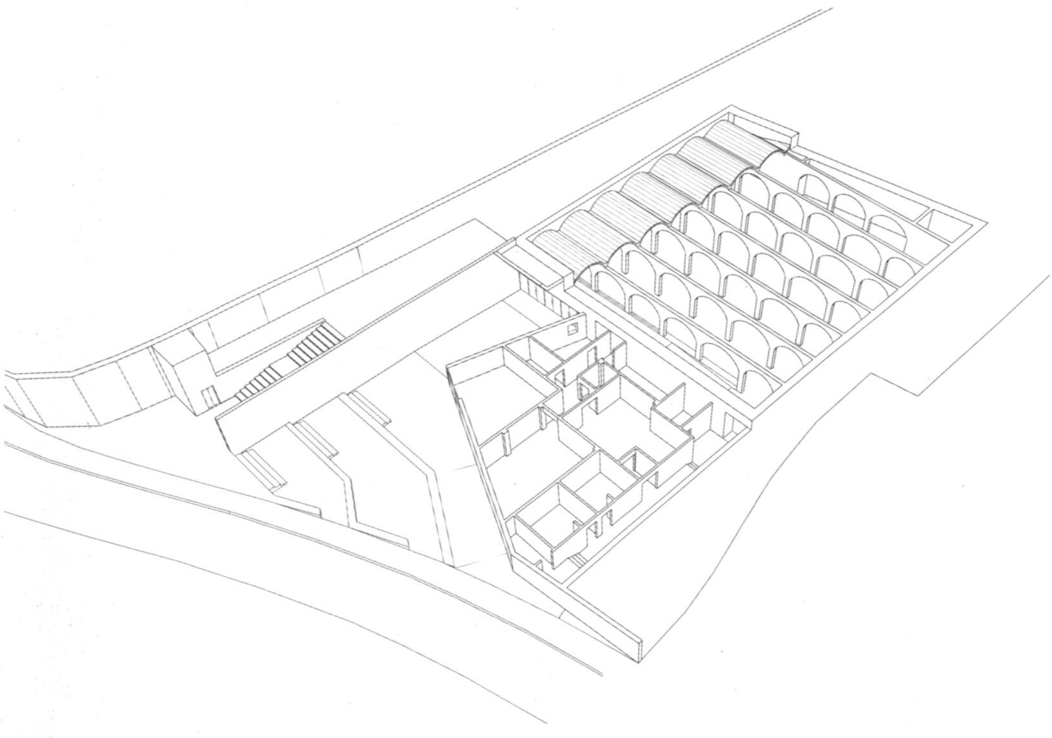

REAPPROPRIATION

REI MARTÍ WATER RESERVOIR

ARCHIKUBIK. Marc Chamalank, Miquel Lacasta, Carmen Santana + Enllaç arquitectònic Arc-Roig

It was the notion of discovery that occurred with the Rei Marti water reservoir, a former space for water storage of the Torre Bellesguard house in Barcelona, designed by Gaudi and located next to the viaduct that is also attributed to this iconic architect. This water reservoir had been concealed beneath a pine forest until twenty years ago, when during some minor maintenance work on the small part of the old-growth forest that still remained, a truck began to sink into the ground. Quickly it was confirmed to the amazement of all that a huge space of more than 600 square meters was crouching under the earth. It was decided to share the space, to invite the public to reclaim this stroke of luck, but, above all, share the emotion of the unexpected discovery. To this end the project had to be as faithful as possible to the space as it was originally encountered. The character, materiality, the force of a space with arches and vaults had to be valued, maintained and strengthened by the intervention.

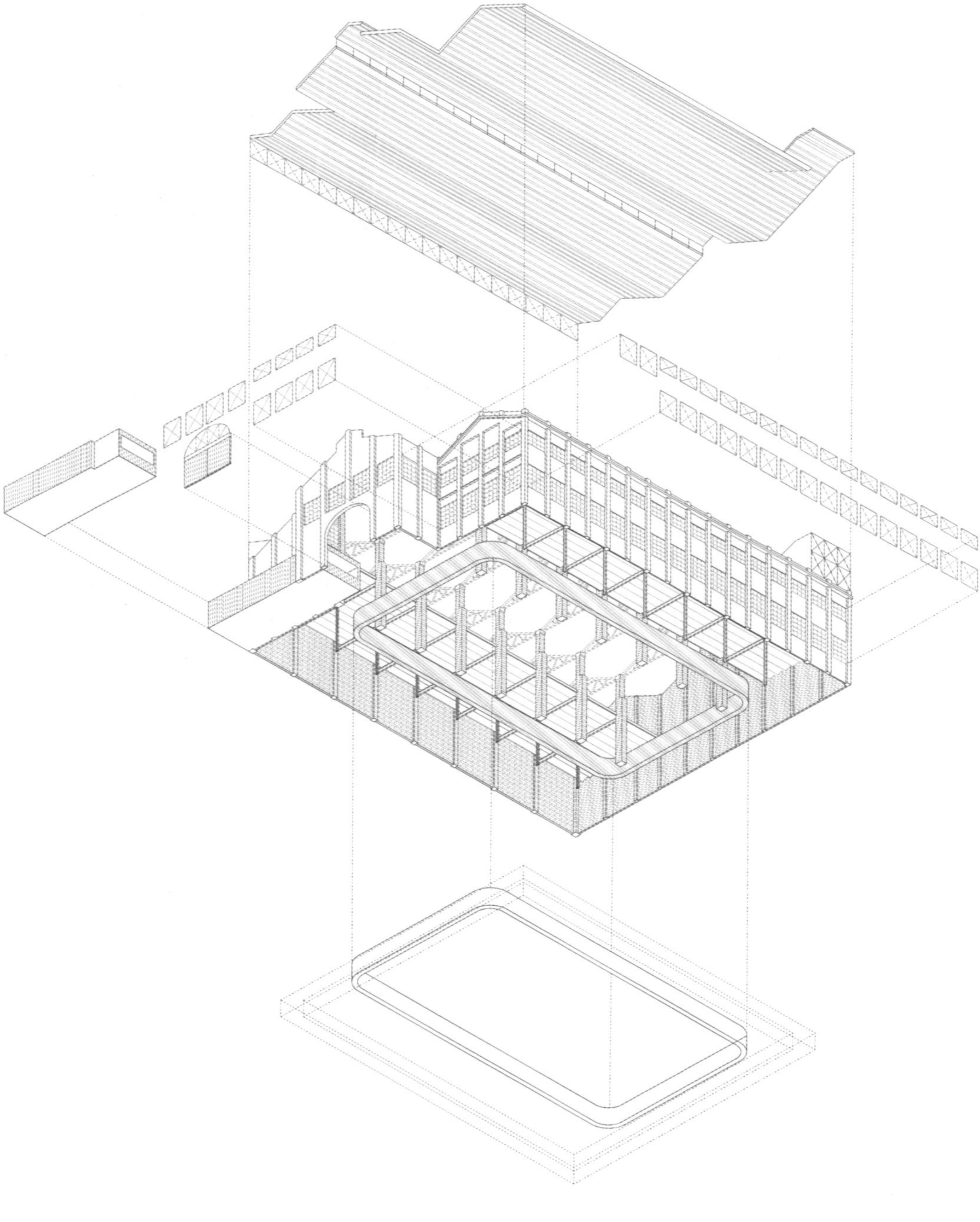

REAPPROPRIATION

OLIVA ARTÉS
BAAS
Jordi Badia

After the former industrial shed was consolidated and suitably protected, and while construction still hadn't started for the new MUHBA (Barcelona History Museum), it was decided that the complex would be opened to the public. First a minimum of strictly necessary construction had been carried out to protect the building from rain and wind: a new lightweight roof was built, supported on the existing structure, concrete paving was installed with an embedded raceway for future mechanical installation and the existing windows were protected with polycarbonate sheets. The objective of all the interventions was to affect as little as possible the interior atmosphere, in order to reflect the passage of time: the fire, the graffiti, etc. The design tried to define the intervention with a single gesture by proposing a huge lamp hung in the middle of the space, drawing a ring of light that separates the exterior perimeter, dedicated to housing a long-term exhibition about the city of Barcelona, from the interior which is to house temporary exhibitions and presentations.

REAPPROPRIATION

COLLAGE HOUSE
bosch.capdeferro arquitectures
Elisabet Capdeferro Pla, Ramon Bosch Pagès

Renovation always implies establishing a certain relationship with the past, or with the pasts that are accumulated in the space of the intervention. This residential project for the members of an extended family has as its point of departure the recovery and renovation of a complex of derelict buildings constructed over the course of centuries in the historic center of the city of Girona. The huge stone carcasses established an optimal relationship to the place in climatic terms. The project tried to discover, maintain and revitalize the different forms of intelligence deposited in these spaces over time. In terms of materials, we were able to work with a valuable inheritance: the house itself provided grates, mosaic tile and stone that could be reused in the construction. The project casually reveals the overlapping of old and new layers, depending on the state of conservation of each element, and the future use of each space. And, above all, the growing confidence in a design system that is necessarily open (in this case the collage) and capable of harmonically integrating into a whole all of the histories of each fragment of the process.

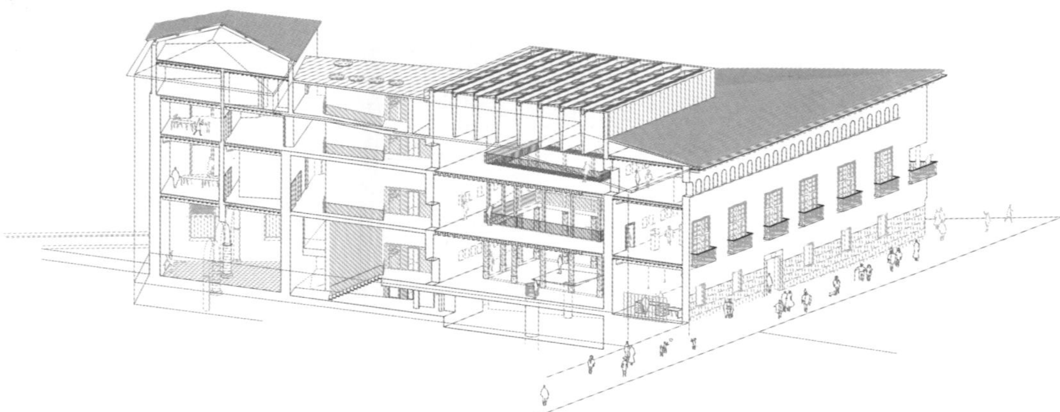

REAPPROPRIATION

CASA DEL CONDESTABLE
Tabuenca&Leache
Fernando Tabuenca, Jesús Leache

The Casa del Condestable is a sixteenth-century palace that had undergone sweeping renovations and alterations over the years, until finally the original building was unrecognizable and in a general state of ruin. The process of historical documentation, preparation of the design project and construction supervision of the building restoration and renovation lasted seven years. Original elements from the Renaissance building were uncovered, including almost 4,000 square meters of wood ceilings that had been hidden by suspended ceilings in the perimeter rooms. By removing the added ceilings and restoring the wood, these rooms recovered their original proportions and appearance. A major part of the architectural intervention centered around the recuperation of the central courtyard, of which only a few of the original columns remained. The project establishes a natural continuity between the old and the necessarily new, by using the original materials throughout: wood, terracotta, lime stuccoes and plaster.

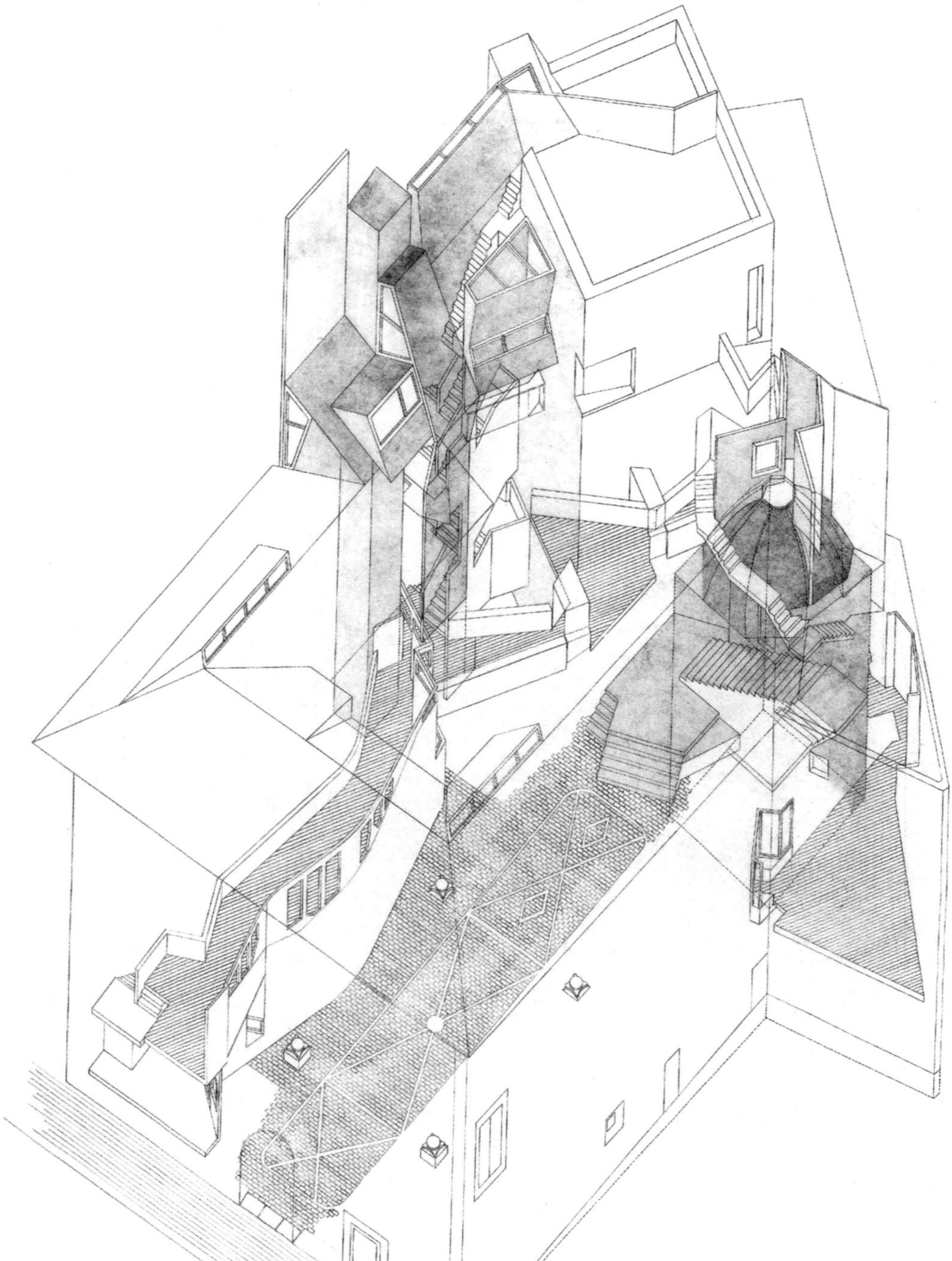

REAPPROPRIATION

CASAL BALAGUER CULTURAL CENTER
Flores & Prats + Duch-Pizá
Ricardo Flores, Eva Prats, Sé Duch, Xisco Pizá

The Casal Balaguer is a palace in the historic center of Palma. It was a grand aristocratic house with its origins in the fourteenth century renovated in the sixteenth century and enlarged in the eighteenth century. At the end of the last century the City of Palma decided to convert the building into a cultural center. The project signals a new era for the Casal, which will go from being a family home to a public building, open to the entire city. In the new program the ground floor contains the entry to the exhibition gallery and the cafeteria. The structural renovation on this floor made it possible to return the courtyard to its the original condition, with a complete view of the three arches that seem to support the suspended house. The main floor is dedicated to a museum about the house and the attic floor houses workshops for the fine arts circle and a lecture hall.

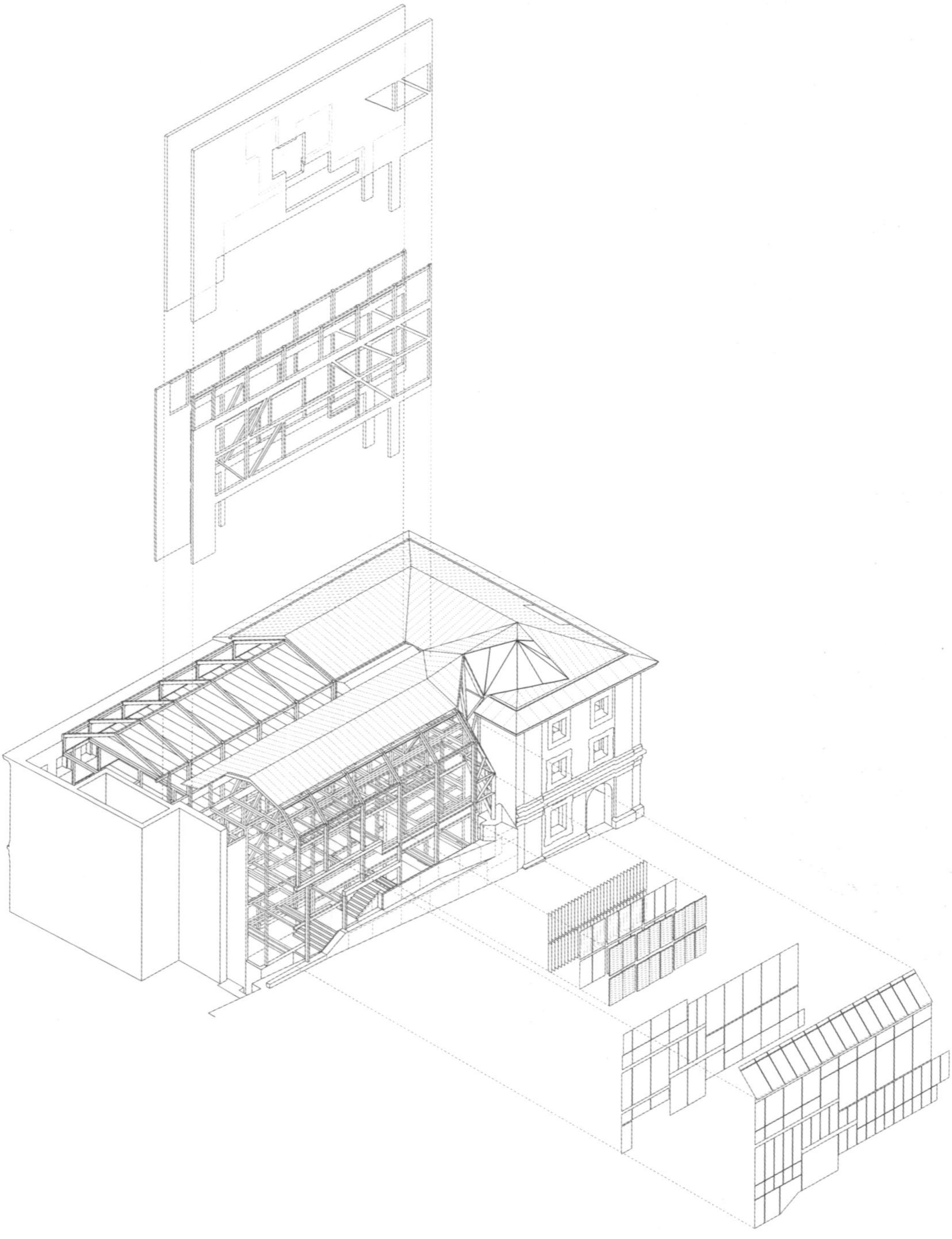

REAPPROPRIATION

PILGRIMS' MUSEUM
Manuel Gallego Jorreto

The former Bank of Spain in Santiago de Compostela was located in the Plaza de las Platerías and since its completion in 1949 it had the dubious honor of being the most controversial building in the city. The construction of the new pilgrims' museum by Manuel Gallego in the abandoned bank building succeeded in eliminating the negative energy that had always resided there. The need to conserve the stone facade didn't impede the reorganization of the building complex, nor did the phrase "contemporary architecture as a new reference on the urban scene" as stated in the specific urban planning guidelines for the historic city center. The new building is flexible and its visitor path is proposed as the continuation of the route of the Camino de Santiago, which culminates in a lookout from which to contemplate the cathedral.

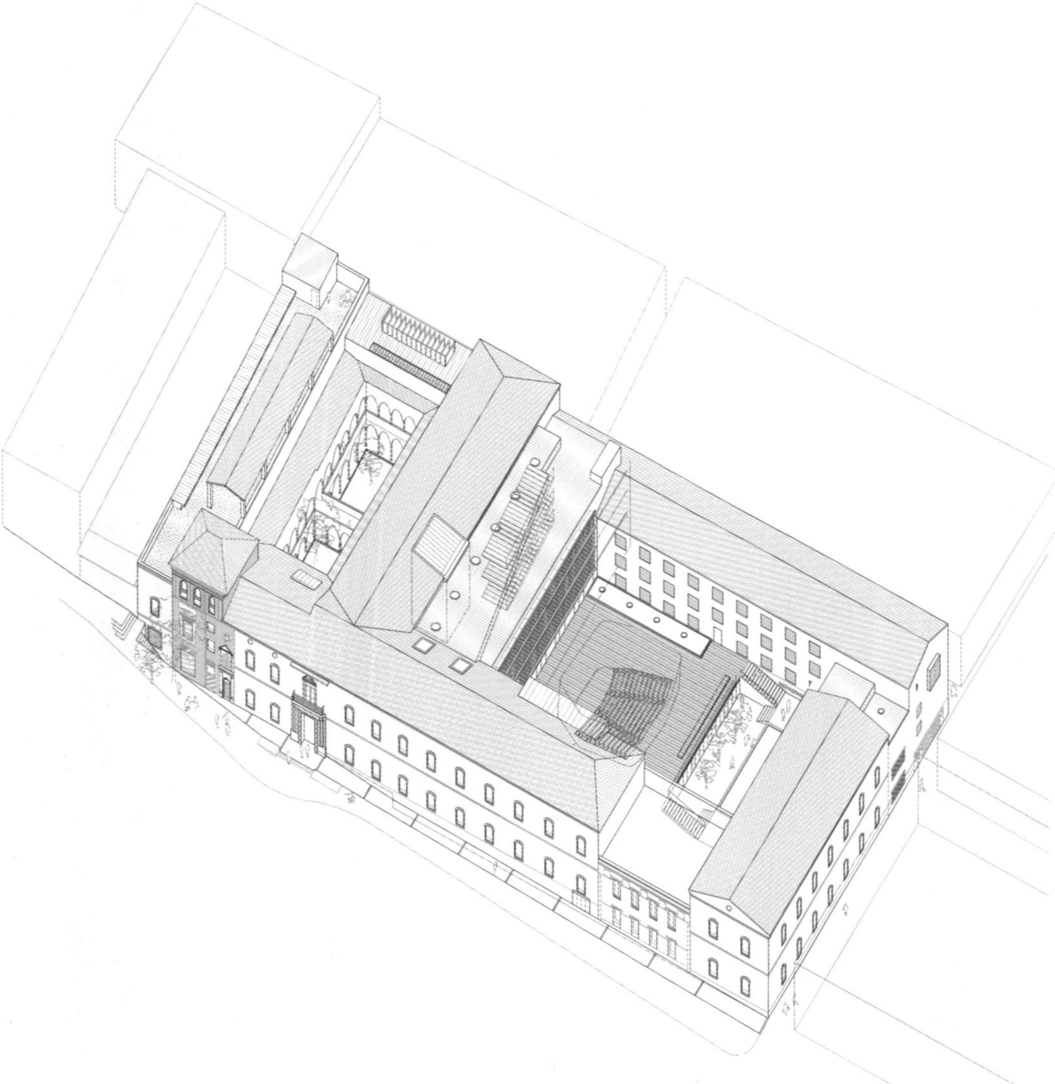

REAPPROPRIATION

GRANADA SCHOOL OF ARCHITECTURE
Víctor López Cotelo

This complex was formed through a protracted transformation process over more than five hundred years that started with the existence of a Nasrid house, continued in thesixteenth century with the construction of the "Admiral's house" and was gradually added onto until the twentieth century. Finally it was a monumental building, occupying an entire city block and overwhelming the small scale of its surroundings. The compound's structure was adequate to house Granada's new Architecture School; however an intervention was required to clarify the unity of the complex, not in a stylistic sense, but as an exercise in integration. In this heterogeneous composite there are elements that have specific architectural values together with others that have none. This intervention hopes that the tension generated between authentic elements from the past and new elements from the present will impregnate the rest in a way that helps the whole finally discover an architectural destiny. In this new phase the construction is the catalyzing agent of a new "whole," recognizing the materiality of each era and the light as the basic integrating principles of the historic process.

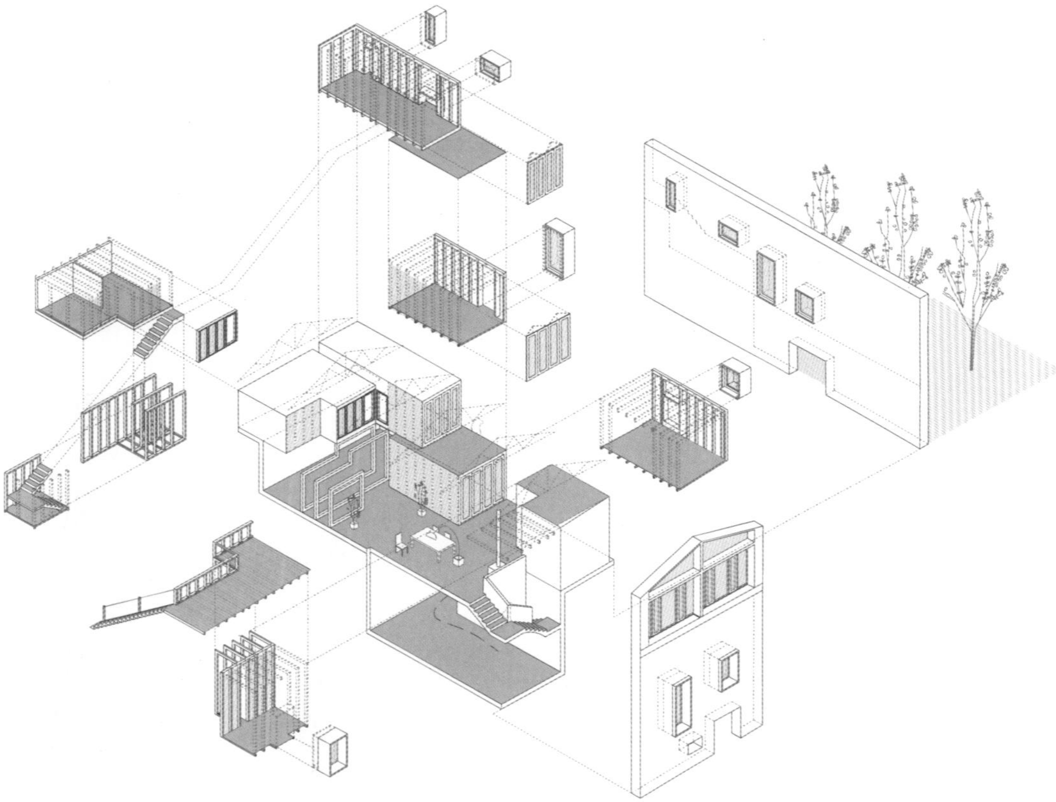

ADAPTABLE

LIDIA CINEMA
Núria Salvadó, David Tapias

How do you inhabit an abandoned cinema? How do you transform it into a comfortable home where you can relax without catching cold in the winter and still get a good dose of sunlight, while spending as little money as possible on construction and maintenance? This design features an open system of units that can be dismounted and modified within a "container" volume. A house within a house: a flexible and open group of wooden modules within the large space where the public sat watching movies. Variations and adaptations of a simple, lightweight and economical construction system. Each space can be heated or ventilated independently, and at the same time heat or cool the entire space. Each volume is intimately related to one of the windows and at the same time they are scattered throughout the building, forming a landscape of boxes within the space. A new module was built in 2011 and the configuration of the group of boxes was changed.

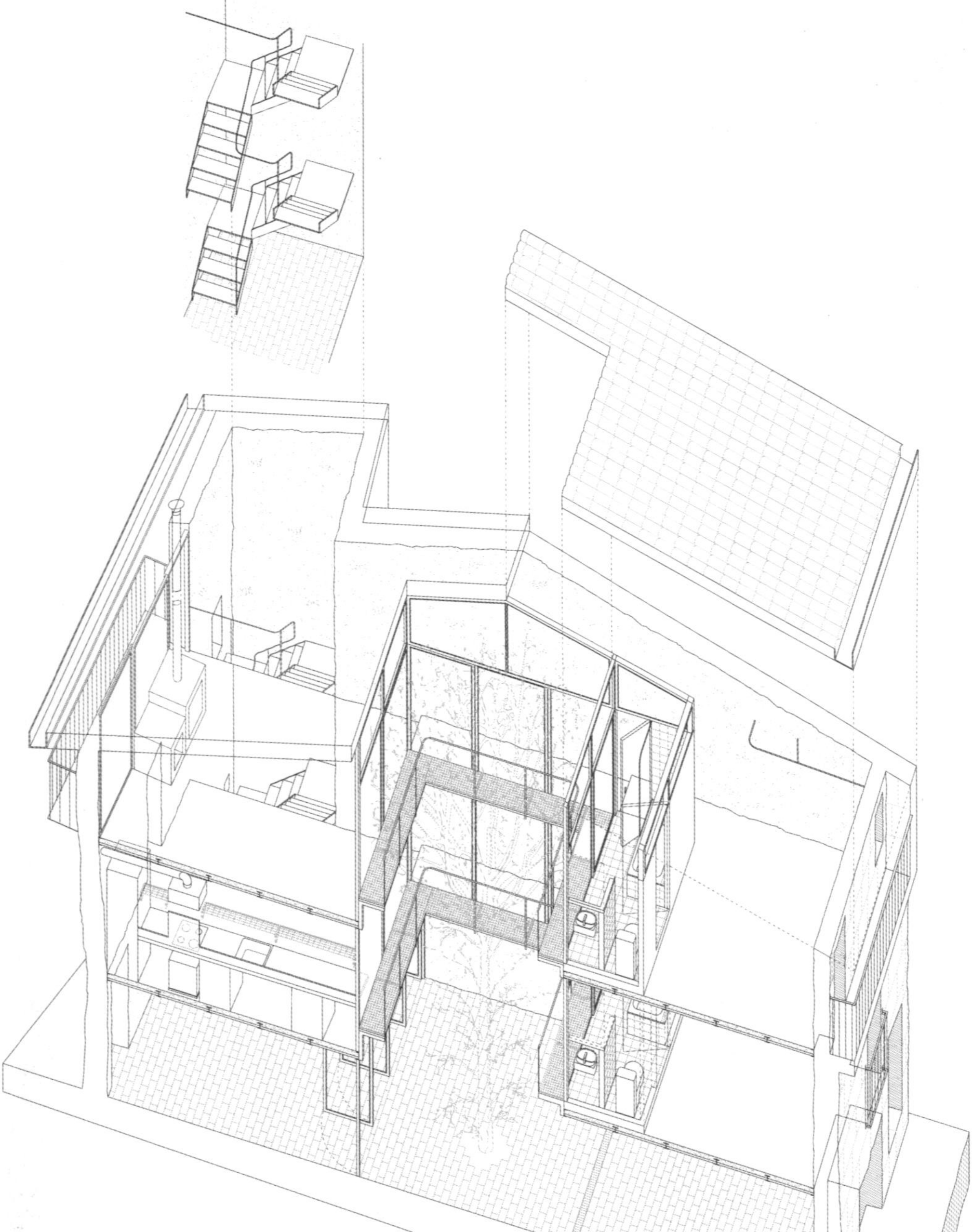

ADAPTABLE

LUZ HOUSE
ARQUITECTURA-G
Jonathan Arnabat, Jordi Ayala-Bril, Aitor Fuentes, Igor Urdampilleta

This townhouse has party walls, an elongated plan and a narrow span, and opens at the back onto a garden. Neglect and the passage of time had left the house in a state of ruin. Luz, the owner, wanted a light-filled house where she could enjoy the outdoors and the garden. The central part of the house had neither light nor ventilation, making it barely habitable. These constraints, compounded by a low budget, led to a simple design strategy, totally emptying and stripping the interior of the building, maintaining only the stone facades and the rammed earth party walls, and organizing a new interior around a courtyard.

There are times when a contemporary approach implies not using cutting-edge materials, but instead taking advantage of local know-how and the reliability of natural materials, adapting the architecture to its economic and geographic context. This is one of those occasions.

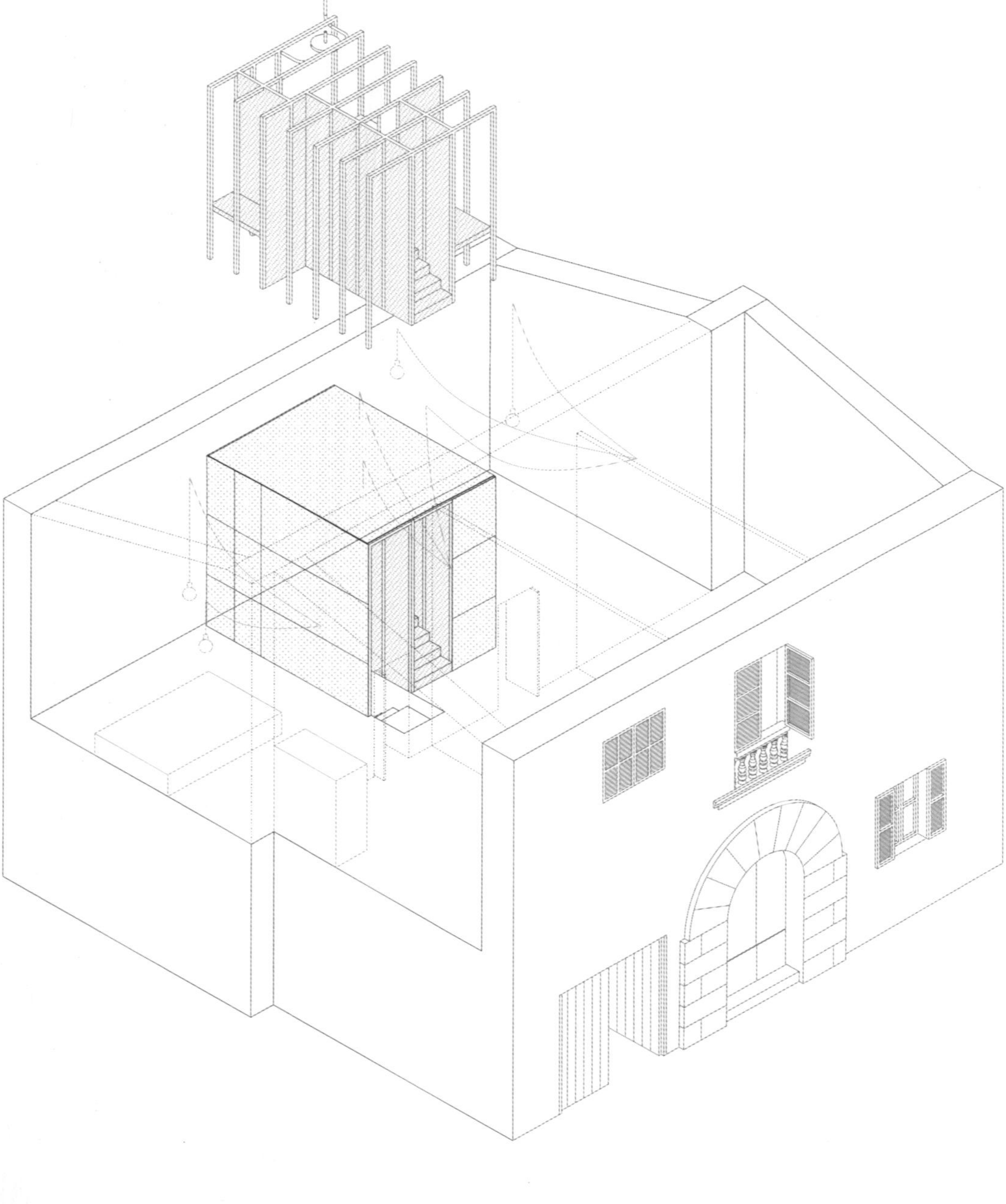

ADAPTABLE

NEW SPACE IN CASA NOVA
EXTUDIO
Toni Gilabert Amengual, Néstor Montenegro Mateos

The project for Sa Casa Nova in Lloret reconnects existing linear moments by inserting new moments. This intervention understands that agreements are always conflictive. A two-phase strategy is defined with a single tactical movement, and results in two luxuries: space and views. The construction of this new space in Sa Casa Nova is controversial: lightweight, prefabricated and completely reversible, compared to the values of the existing space: heavy, built-in-place and static. This project offers a sensitive interior space which gives order to the large volume of surrounding air, with a form that is bound to the popular imagination.

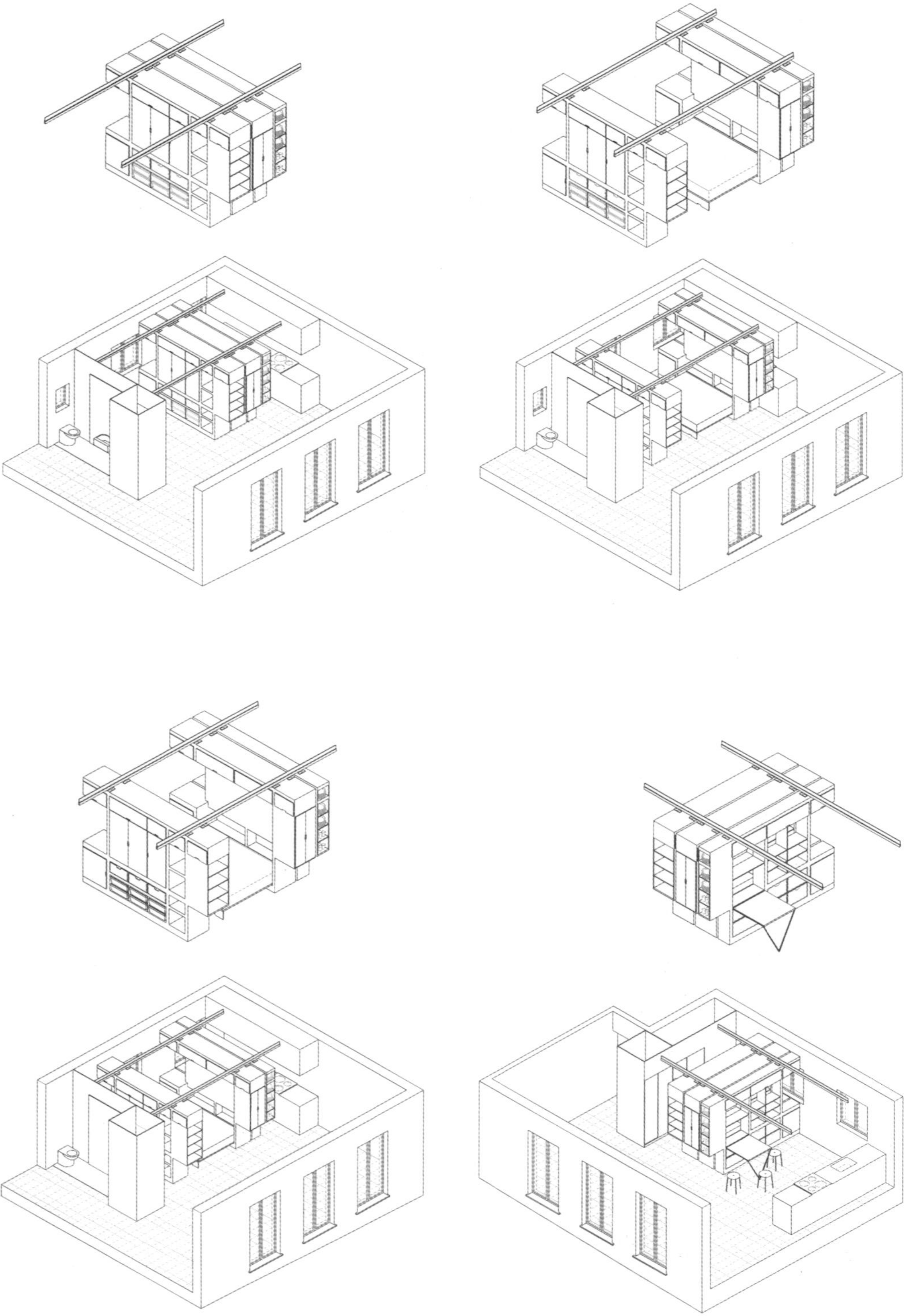

ADAPTABLE

ALL I OWN HOUSE
PKMN Architectures

All I Own House is a project that materializes the interior of a house through the personal belongings of the person or persons that occupy it. Through careful and totally custom design, and the combination of the cabinetry with a simple system of industrial linear rail guides, all of the house's service spaces are organized using three containers made from OSB wood panels that are suspended, mobile and transformable.

ADAPTABLE

SUSALOON
elii
Uriel Fogué, Eva Gil, Carlos Palacios

Susaloon is a minimal intervention in a domestic space to convert Susana's house into a flexible and transformable space. The project employs three simple strategies. The first, relocating certain domestic elements to optimize the layout and everyday use of the space. The second, opening certain partitions to enlarge some of the spaces, like the living room. The third, integrating a series of fold-down, retractable and sliding elements. The result is the main space of the house is configured like a black box theater: the stage can change its domestic scenery through simple operations that make the space many houses in one.

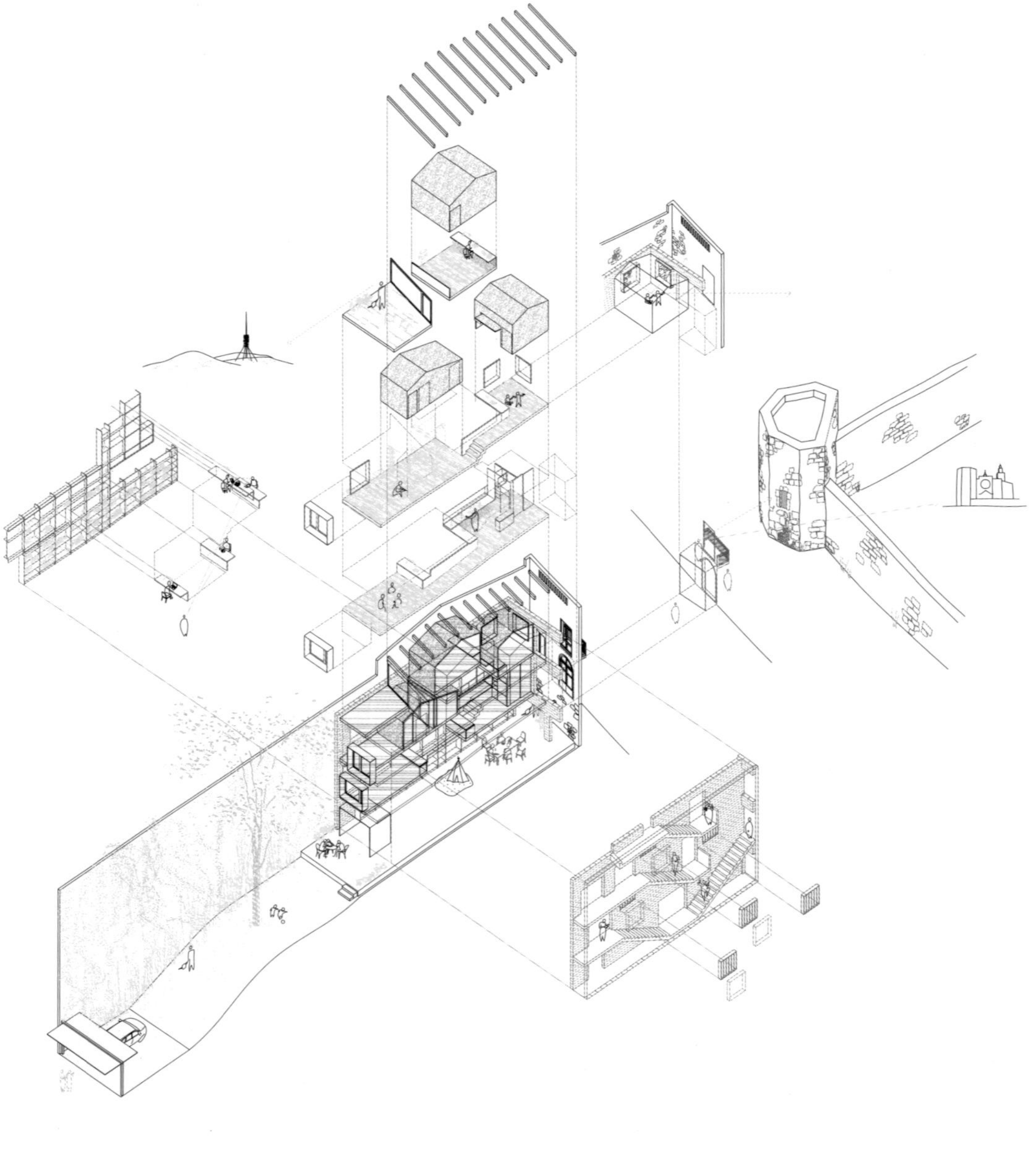

ADAPTABLE

HOUSE INSIDE A HOUSE
Josep Ferrando

The house is located on the old road that connects Valldoreix with Cerdanyola. It is a street with a suburban structure, characterized by long, narrow lots (around four meters wide); and is asymmetrical in nature where a strip of constructions faces the wall of a monastery. The constructions have been gradually adapted and substituted over time, and the house in question was the last of a row of similar two-story houses that shared a common facade and roof. Both these elements were protected by the city's architectural heritage register. The Monastery of Sant Cugat is higher than the level of the house and the street is parallel to the slope. There is almost a two-story difference in level between the upper and lower parts of the site, which means that the working volume includes not two, but three standard height floors, that are fundamentally designed in section. The existing house, defined by the facades facing the monastery, the roof and the party walls, is a volume in the rough that is converted into the landscape where the new construction is inserted.

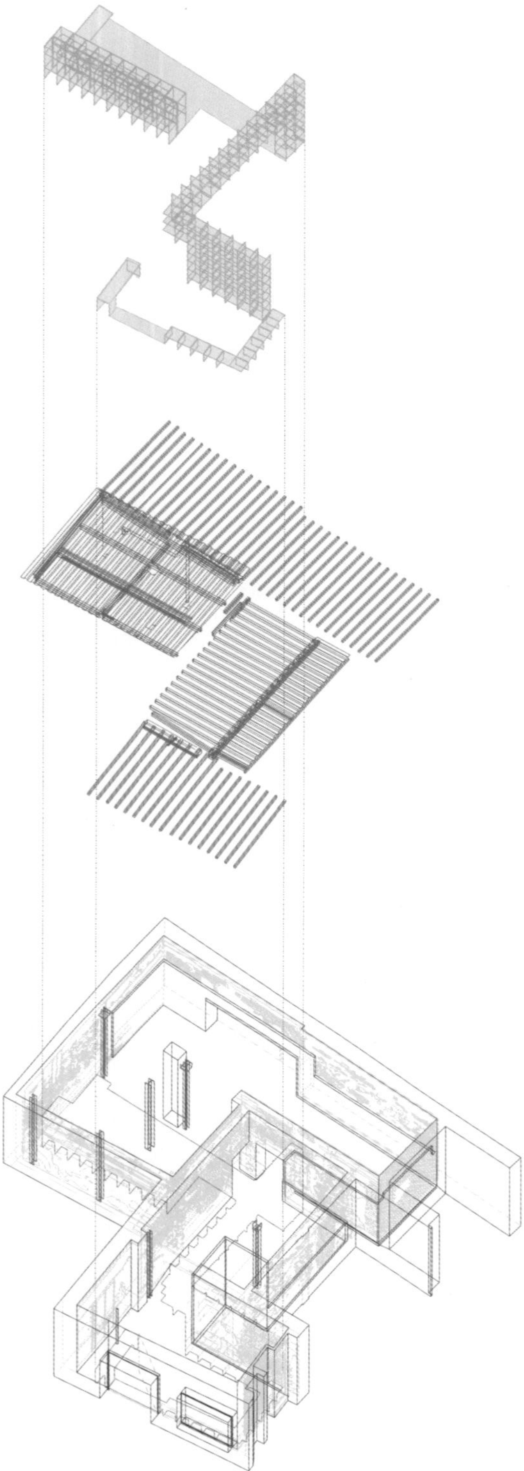

ADAPTABLE

SAN JERÓNIMO 17
CUAC Arquitectura
Javier Castellano Pulido, Tomás García Píriz

Ruin, recycled archaeology, infrastructure and memory converge in a proposal for the occupation of a space defined by the material traces of its successive alterations and repairs. Marked by the presence of a powerful brick masonry structure (the walls are from 60 to 80 centimeters wide) and wood floor structures from the end of the nineteenth century, the space is a palimpsest of successive interventions to be adhered to by the insertion of recycled elements. Above all, the desire emerges to make visible the continuous interventions made in this inherited space, revealing its different strata, mapping and modelling each brick, its wounds, dignifying its historic presence as part of the heritage of continuous overlapping elements that we incorporate, minimizing both the invested energy and its presence.

ULMA Trimax

THE CULTURAL FACTORY IN MATADERO
OSS, Office for Strategic Spaces
Ángel Borrego Cubero

The Cultural Factory is a reversible design project that advances, without negative impact, the aesthetic and technical qualities of the existing architecture of Matadero Madrid, a historic landmark of industrial architecture. The project is typical of crisis-stricken Europe, and particularly Spain, where architecture must chart a difficult course between the lack of economic resources and an urgent need for action.

Three volumes near the entrance organize the space, folding and compressing the circulation around them. This creates a gradient from compact to expansive, from busy to calm. The space requires minimal maintenance and, if the activity of the Factory were to cease, could be dismantled without any waste. The existing space would return completely to its pre-construction state. The materials used are predominantly polycarbonate and wood.

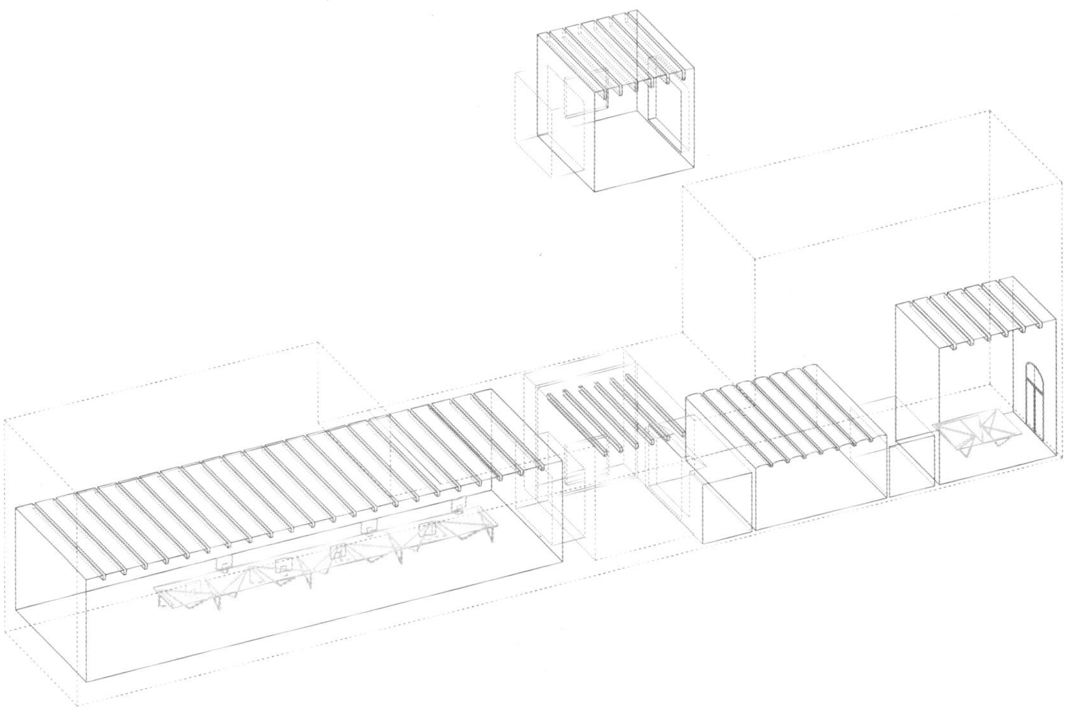

ADAPTABLE

RENOVATION AND ADAPTATION OF A HOME-STUDIO MAIO
Guillermo López Ibáñez, Anna Puigjaner Barberá

The new studio is located in a small pre-existing building that formerly housed a laundry, which consisted of a continuous space with a variable section some 40 meters long, and almost no natural light. To improve the lighting of the interior, the design proposal centers around opening up a central courtyard with windows, conceived of as yet another room. Special attention was paid to the depth of the three large openings in the courtyard, lining the jambs, lintels and sills with wood. This helps convert them into usable intermediate spaces that can be occupied to enjoy the open exterior room, as well as thresholds between the interior and exterior. The rest of the existing spaces are maintained, adding some small compartments to reinforce the subtle relationships between habitable areas.

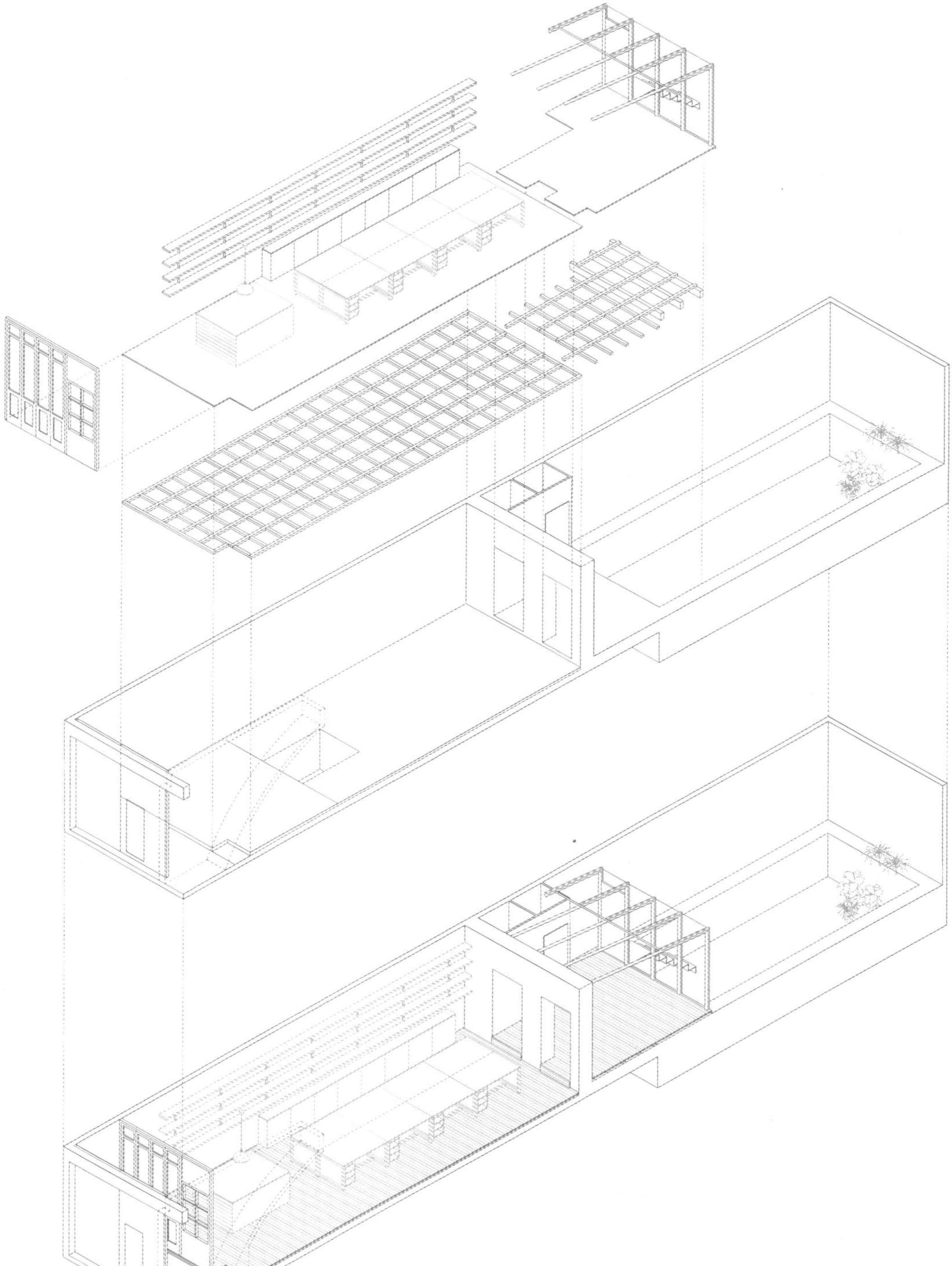

ADAPTABLE

STUDIO IN LACY STREET
Sauquet Architectes
Roger Sauquet, Guillem Bosch, Xavier Sauquet, Berta Fusté, Anna Bonet

The studio is located in a small former workshop, occupying the ground floor of a house. At the beginning of the last century it was a tannery, from the 1950s on it was used as a garage and for the past decade as a print shop. This project is the reappropriation of a space that was abandoned due to the financial crisis. It is a space in which the different uses have left architectural scars that the design doesn't try to hide. The largest scar that the intervention reveals is an open cistern located in the back courtyard. It is empty now. A meeting room had to be added onto the existing workshop space to accommodate the new architecture studio. This addition, in the form of a greenhouse, "floats" over the cistern and hides mechanical equipment and modelling materials underneath it. The greenhouse encloses a space that was previously outdoors without concealing the sediments of passing time revealed on the party walls.

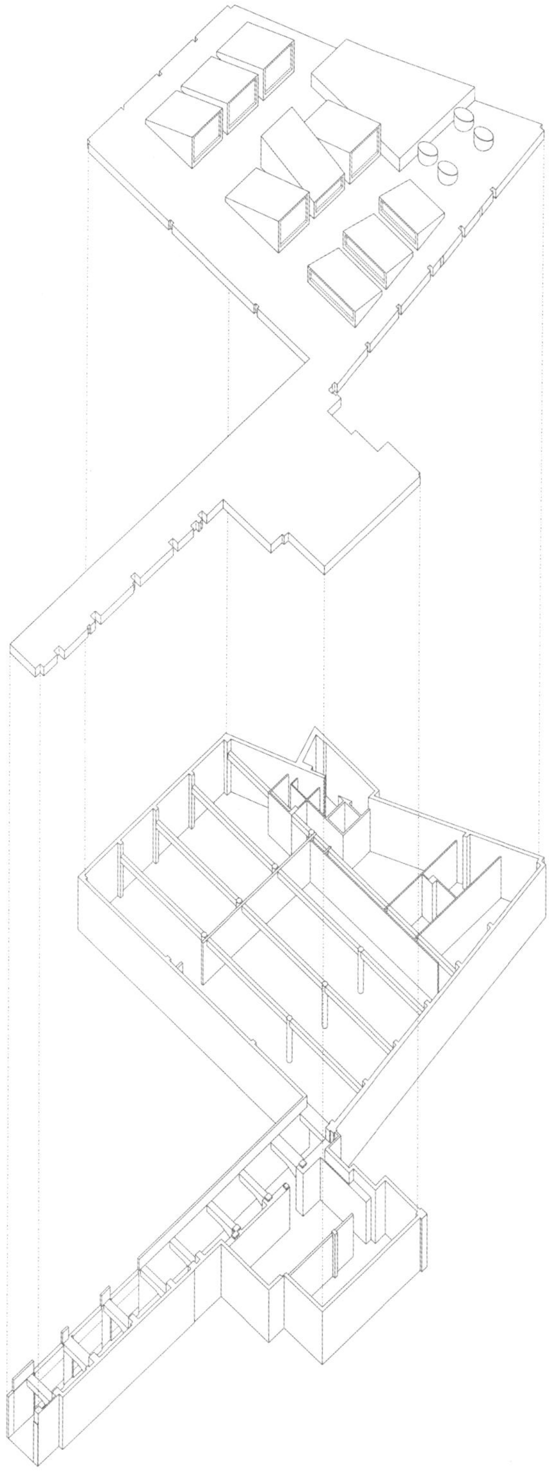

ADAPTABLE

CARRERAS-MÚGICA GALLERY OF CONTEMPORARY ART
estudio Herreros

A former warehouse occupies the interior of a city block in the *ensanche*, or urban expansion of Bilbao, with its access through a tunnel passing under the perimeter residential structures. The following program has been organized in this existing space: areas for storage and handling of artwork, administrative areas and meeting rooms, spaces for experimentation and specific projects and a large central space that is the focus of the project. The architecture adopts a limited number of materials—exposed concrete structures, continuous industrial paving, white walls levitating over recessed wall bases, and some furnishings—to construct the elemental ingredients of an exhibition space—floors, walls and ceilings—in which the artworks are responsible for determining the character of the space. The reinterpretation of the original system of skylights generates a series of periscope-like light-capturing devices, through which the landscape of the ensanche, in which the gallery is embedded, can be rediscovered. These volumes generate a new industrial landscape on the roof of the gallery, a gift to the city that threads through the past, the present and the future of this place.

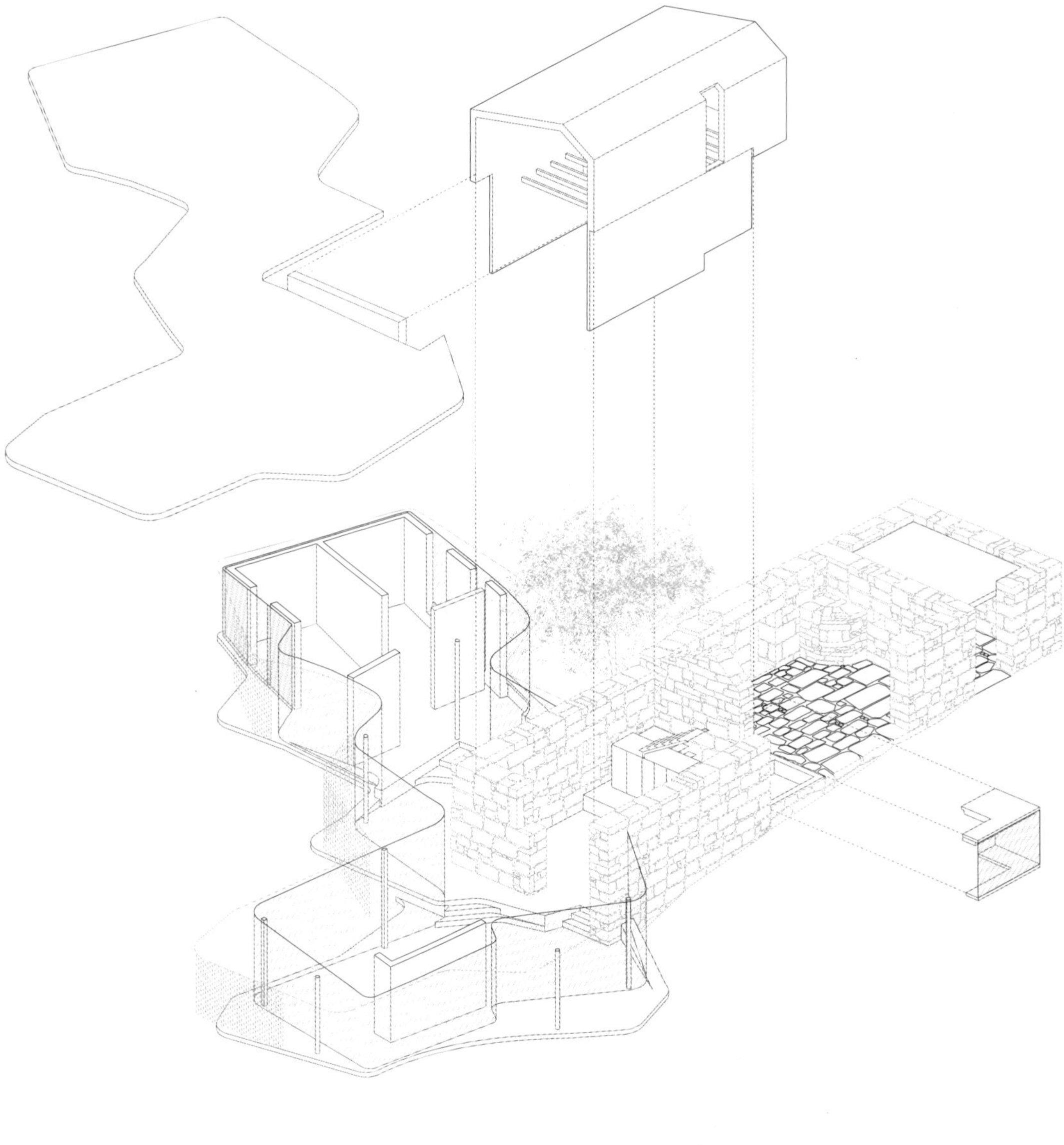

INFILL

SINGLE-FAMILY HOUSE IN TEBRA
Guadalupe Piñera Manso, Jesús Irisarri Castro

The prior character of the spaces in the ruins was more introverted and brings the most intimate moments to the domestic spaces, and the ones that contrast most with the exterior, like the open courtyards that were generated by the walls and the process of the ruin. A continuum of intermediate spaces of new construction joins their diverse states of conservation and the character of their position-orientation, bringing complementary spaces to the project. The generation of different filters for control, climate, light and privacy is explored, like a system of articulations connecting landscapes and moments. The remains of the existing building are treated like a consolidated ruin, with concrete walls and slabs that evoke the original volume, emphasizing the closed character of the former structure. The most private areas have a certain independence at their extremes, and between them they envelope a continuous space that adapts to the topography.

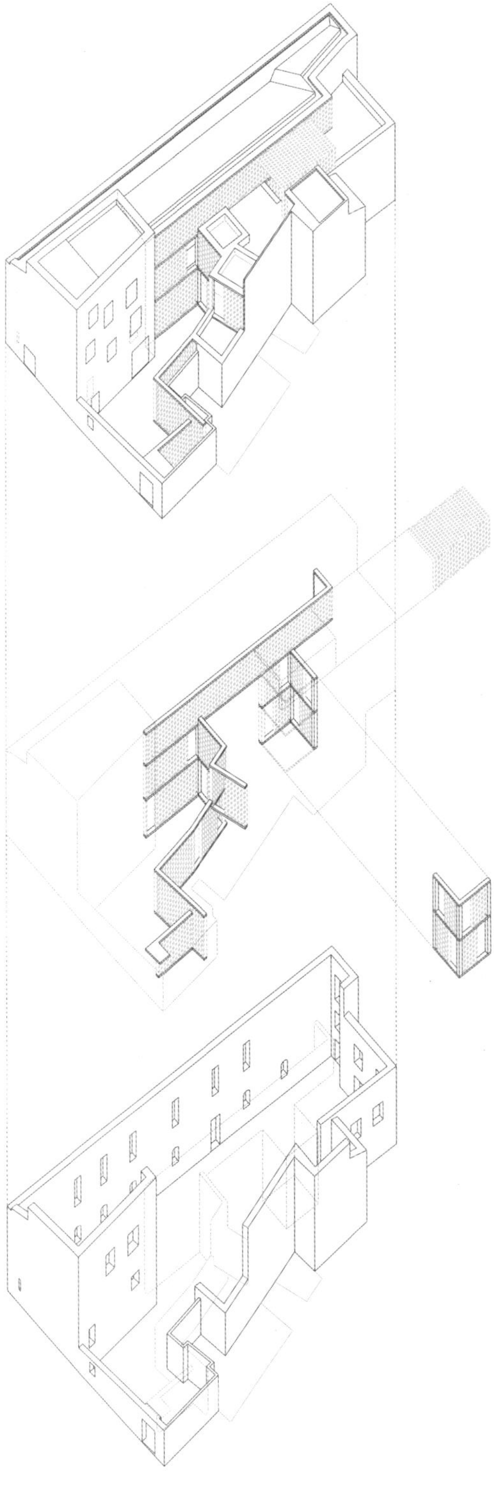

INFILL

ATRIO RELAIS CHÂTEAUX
Mansilla + Tuñón
Luis Moreno Mansilla, Emilio Tuñón Álvarez

Located in the medieval quarter of Cáceres, the compound onto which the new project was added consisted of two very different constructions, both quite dilapidated by years of disuse. The new building adapts to the existing structures like a hermit crab taking up residence inside an abandoned shell. The old structures are revitalized and rehabilitated by the new uses, and in turn, the contemporary architecture dwells harmoniously within its historic surroundings: a respectful and dignified coexistence. The resulting building accommodates two complementary activities: the new home of the Atrio restaurant and a small Relais-Châteaux hotel with fourteen guestrooms.

This new functional organism conforms to the irregularities it encounters along the perimeter of the existing buildings, revealing itself on the exterior only within the landscaped courtyard as a fabric of slender white concrete columns.

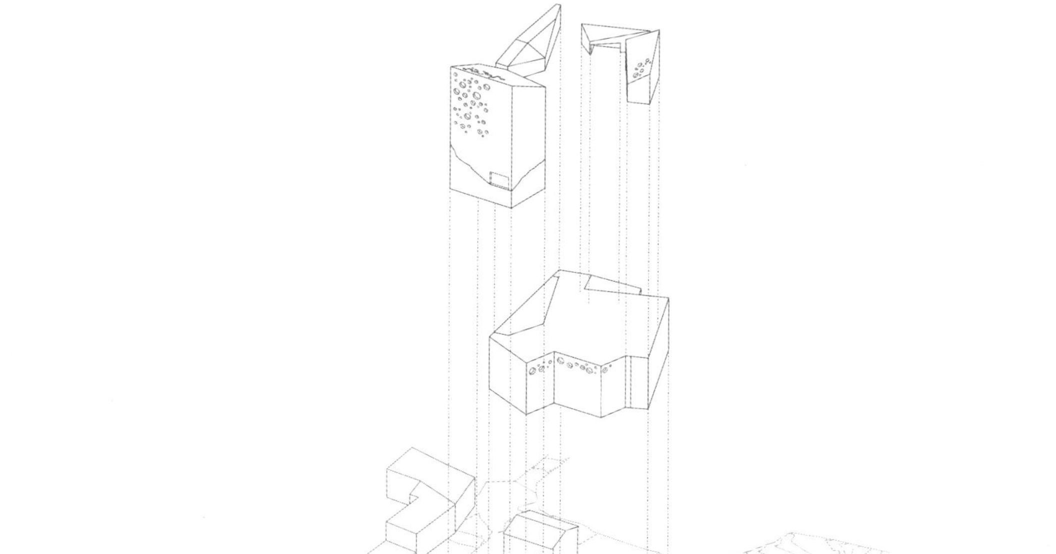

INFILL

DENOMINACIÓN DE ORIGEN RIBERA DEL DUERO HEADQUARTERS
Barozzi / Veiga
Fabrizio Barozzi, Alberto Veiga

The fundamental condition of this project is the edge, next to the historic rampart where the building is sited and at the limit of Roa de Duero, between the artificial and the natural, the urban and the rural landscape. The building program, intended to house the headquarters of the Consejo Regulador (Regulatory Board) of the Ribera del Duero wine region, includes offices, emblematic spaces and a small auditorium; uses that revolve around the idea of public space. The project is built in Roa with local stone masonry. It is conceived of as a solemn, massive element, reinforcing the idea of an anti-modern building, a building of unlimited durability, built with a material that mutates and changes with the passage of time. The relation between the building and the historical traces of the place reveal a reality that explains and revalues the specific context. A new reality, the fruit of a series of improbable and unexpected factors.

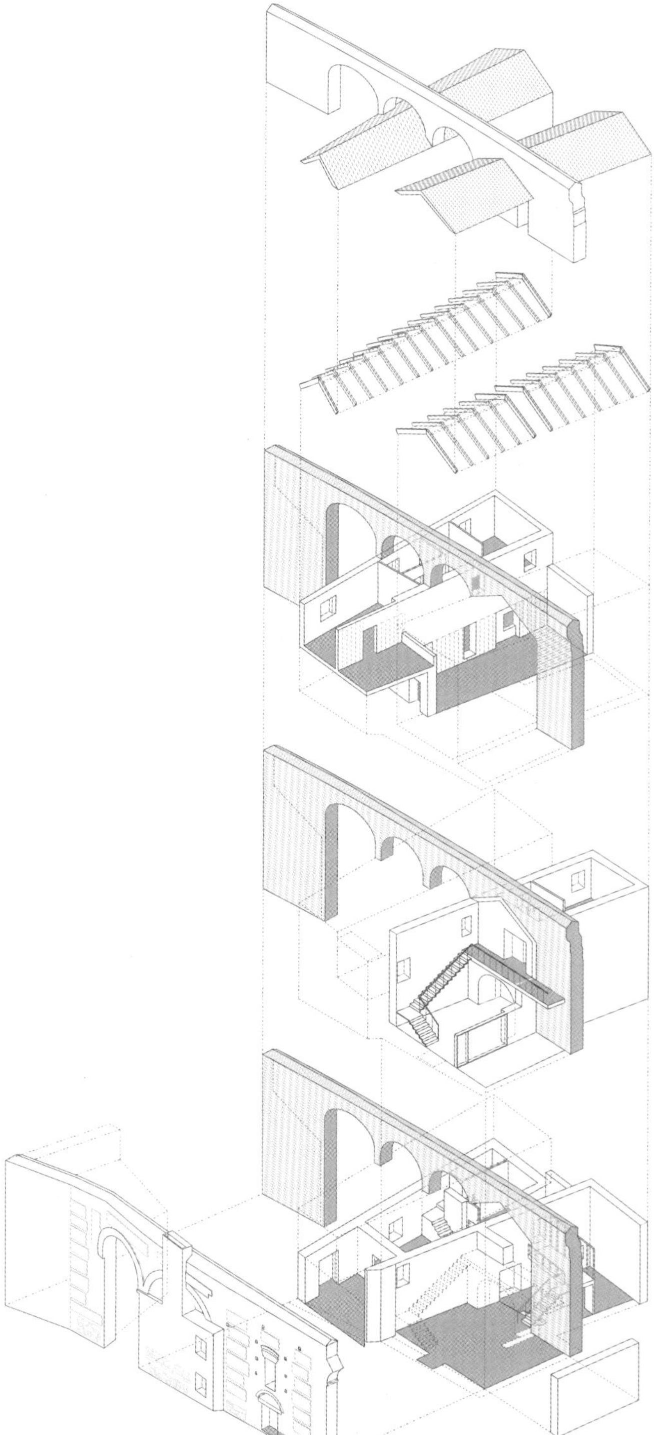

INFILL

TWO HOUSES IN OROPESA
Paredes Pedrosa Arquitectos
Ángela García de Paredes, Ignacio Pedrosa

Oropesa is known for its castle, built in 1402 as the residence for a noble family from Toledo, who undertook the construction of an unfinished aerial connection between the castle and the Nuestra Señora de la Asunción church. The structure is supported by arches and walls that cut across the city, and in which these houses are embedded. The houses were small, with many divisions, and in ruins. They had two shared courtyards behind one of the facades, with wide brick arches crossing them. The project opens a long, narrow courtyard/crack, which defines two asymmetrical houses on either side, built for two siblings. The roofs were dismantled and rebuilt a meter higher, reusing the clay roof tiles. The two structures are linked together by the two powerful brick arches, which are protected as historical monuments.

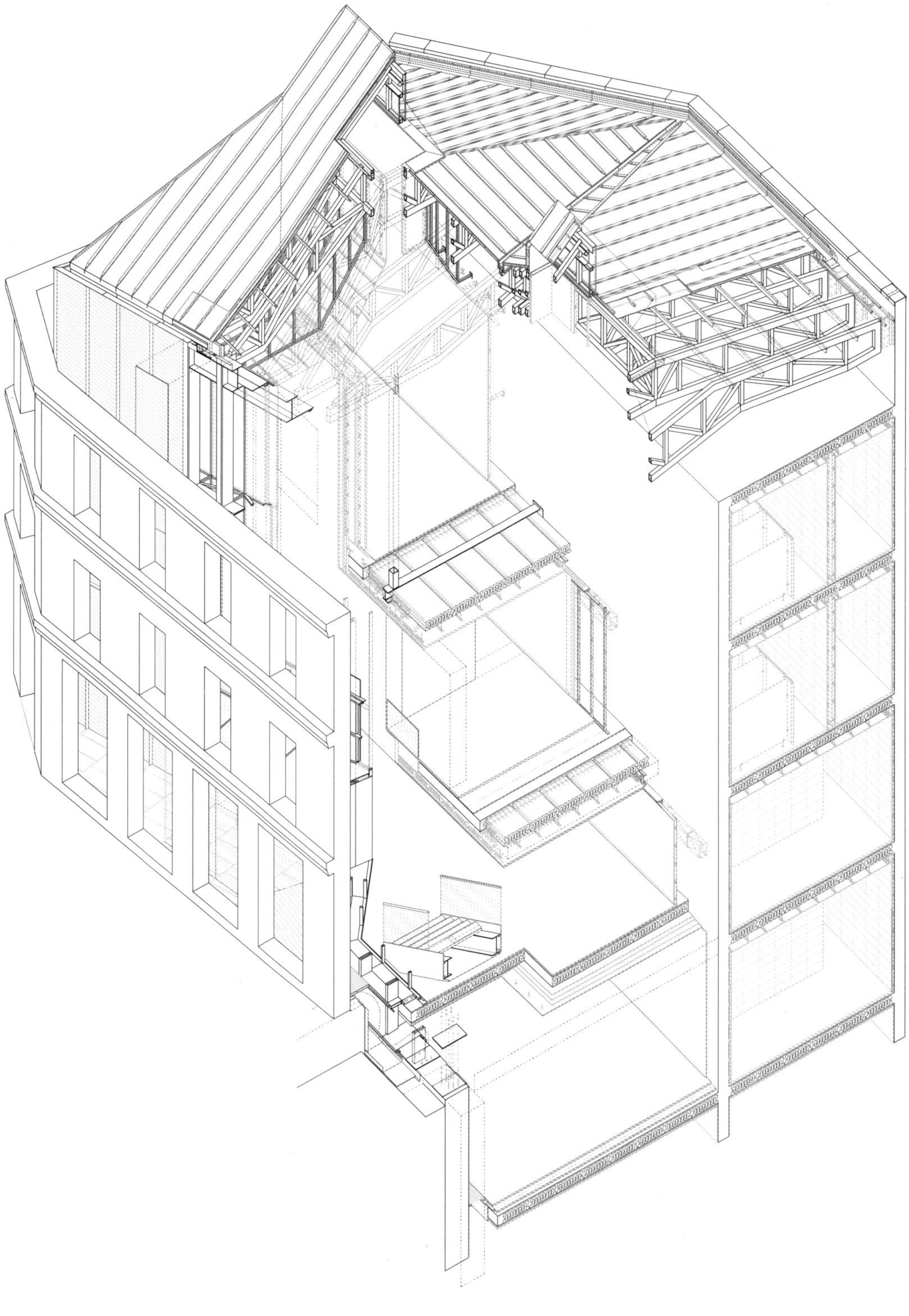

INFILL

FINE ARTS MUSEUM OF ASTURIAS
Francisco Mangado

The new addition to the Fine Arts Museum of Asturias is part of an urban complex which, through its successive enlargements, has been making room for what is now one of the best art collections in Spain. Before this addition the museum's most important architectural piece was the Palace of Velarde, a superb Renaissance palace, which was hidden on one side by an unfortunate new building from the 1970s, a construction that hopefully will be demolished when the second phase of the expansion project is built. The proposed addition, as is logical, is part of an analysis of the whole museum, including existing buildings as well as the two phases of the expansion. The project proposes a new building built behind the historic facade, which adapts to the structure of the existing urban fabric, generating a relationship of urban tension and great architectural intensity in the space between the two constructions.

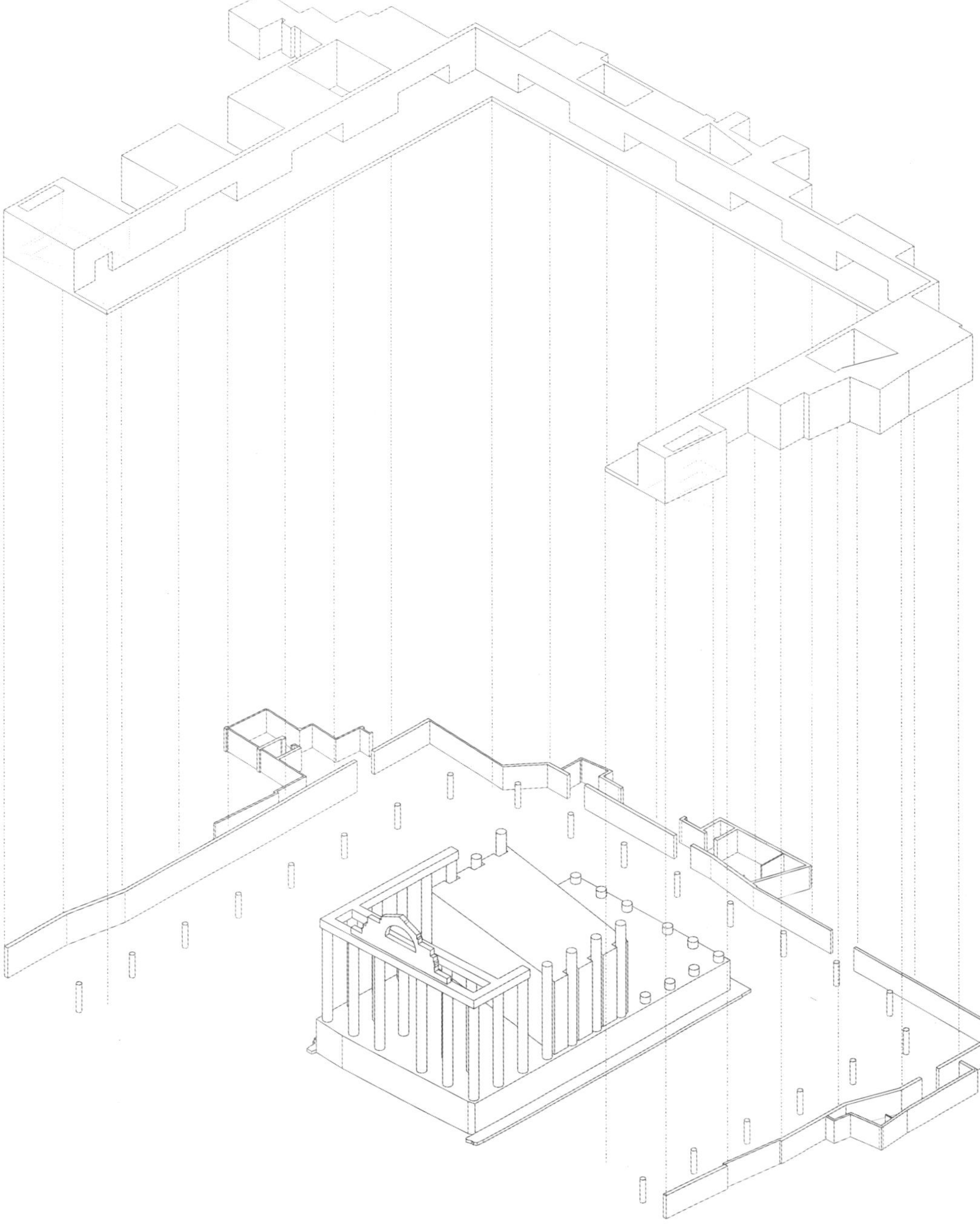

INFILL

BUILDING AND URBAN SPACE SURROUNDING THE TEMPLE OF DIANA
José María Sánchez García

This project reclaims and redefines the area surrounding the Temple of Diana in Merida, which was the ancient forum, or center, of the Roman city. Working together with the team of archaeologists a set of rules and guidelines for intervention were defined, which helped develop syntax for the project capable of absorbing the irregularities and modifications uncovered by the archaeological excavations.

To restore the outline of the Roman space, a perimeter structure was built along the edge of the site. This permits the recovery of the open plaza that existed in the Roman era, while respecting the archaeological elements that defined the ancient sacred space. The design takes the form of an "L" that stitches together the limit with the current city fabric and liberates a large area around the temple. Therefore, more than a building, the project is a structure that is capable of generating a new urban stratum, filled with program. At the same time, the structure casts a long shadow over the plaza.

NAKED

OE HOUSE
Fake Industries Architectural Agonism + Aixopluc
Cristina Goberna, Urtzi Grau, David Tapias

The OE house is a montage. The clients wanted a double house, which permitted them to move from one half to the other depending on their mood. The architects proposed using two well-known models of domestic space: the open plan of the Case Study Houses for hedonistic pleasures in the warm summer months, covered by the existentialist interiors of Le Corbusier's Maisons [the LC project is a pair of houses] Jaoul for the windy months in the Sierra de la Mussara. This was accomplished literally. The departure points for the design were a typological investigation of local rural constructions and the invention of a seasonal membrane that could be reconfigured depending on changes in the weather. Learning form neighboring constructions, the resulting building is a cross between an agricultural storehouse and a *mas*, or a Catalan farmhouse. The house transcends its two schizophrenic uses, creating multiple environments depending on the weather and the mood of its inhabitants. The OE, who lived across the street, spent every evening on the construction site.

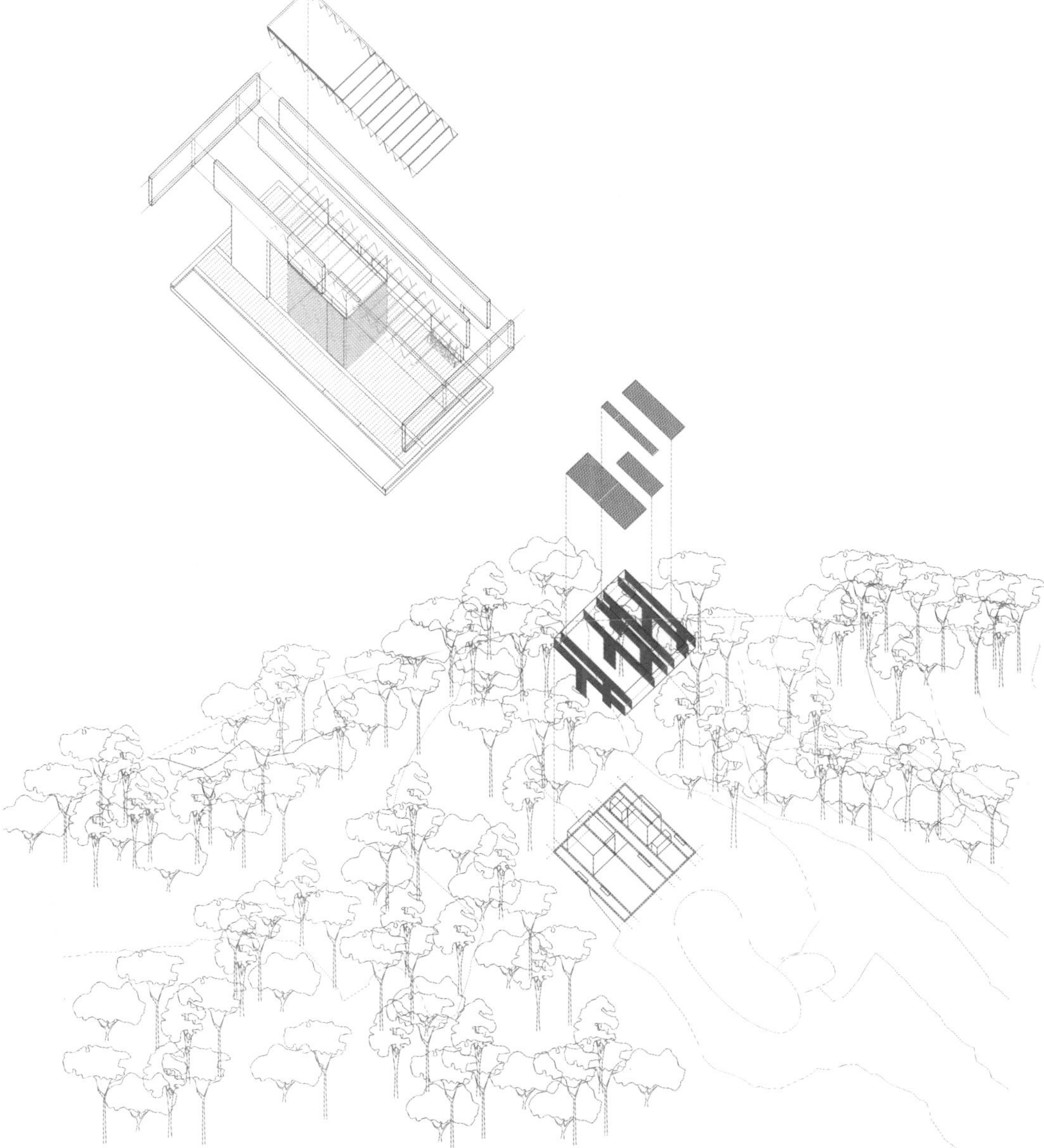

NAKED

SAN LUCAS PAVILION
FRPO Rodríguez & Oriol Arquitectos
Pablo Oriol, Fernando Rodríguez

The final configuration of the pavilion responds largely to the quick response exercised during the project. A design system was generated that on the one hand would be sufficiently flexible to assume the inevitable changes that occur during construction and, on the other hand, would have a strong and unequivocal character, ensuring that the personality of the building would not suffer due to changing circumstances in the future. The pavilion delimits a square area in plan measuring eleven by eleven meters, at the border between a dense copse of pines and a carefully groomed lawn, on the same site as a former pavilion from the 1950s, which was demolished in 2011. The geometric order of this "field" is heir to previous projects designed by this studio. The pavilion is organized into six strips, which are parallel to the axis that leads from the pines toward the lawn. This layout is reflected in the slab that supports the floor, which is perforated at points to permit plantings. Small white brick boxes, independent of the structure and reminiscent of the former building, house the more specific program functions.

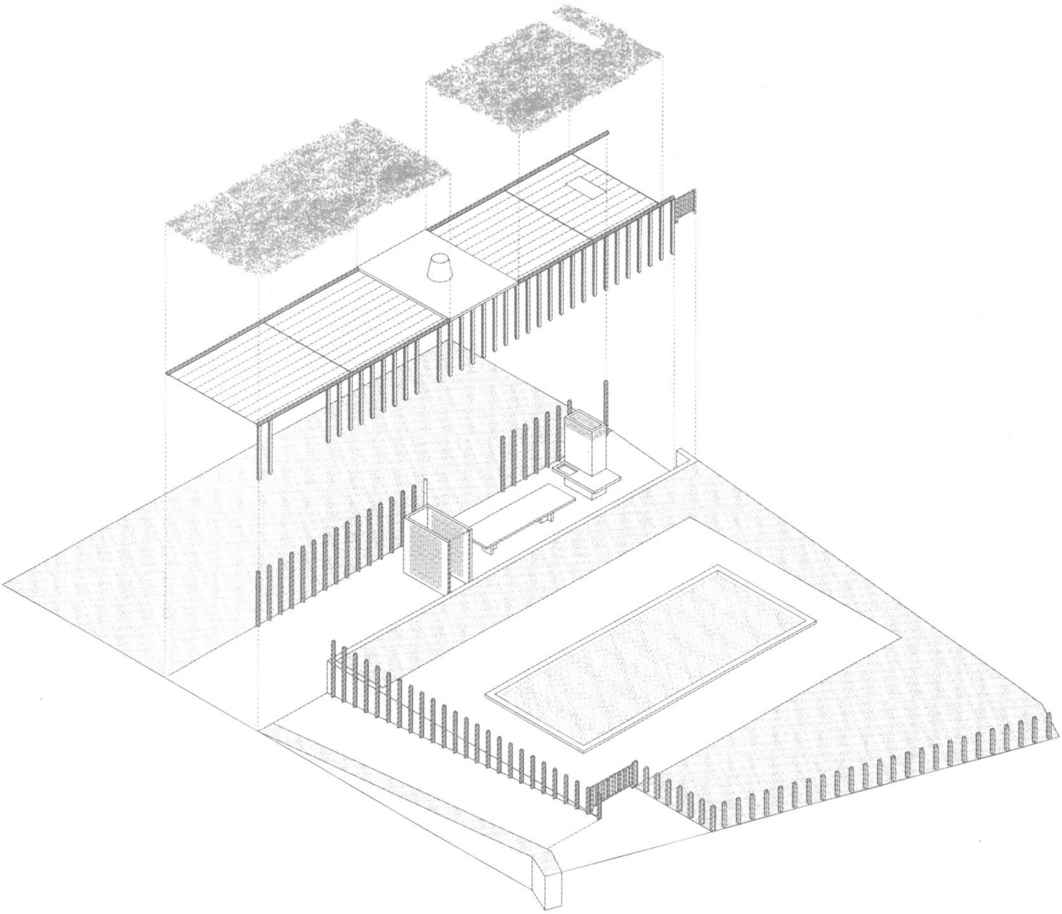

NAKED

SWIMMING POOL IN MACEDA

trespes.arquitectos

Alberte Pérez Rodríguez, Carlos Mosquera del Palacio, Enrique Iglesias Lima

The site is irregular, with a break at its midpoint, which slopes down toward the house. This change of level is used as a way to relate and separate the two parts of the program. The swimming pool is placed on the upper platform and the annexes are located on the lower platform. Since the design requirements included two distinct zones, the double portico andchange of level good climatic characteristics for both uses. In this aspect the existing trees and the new arbor are especially important, as they provide shelter from the wind and shade the dining and preparation areas.

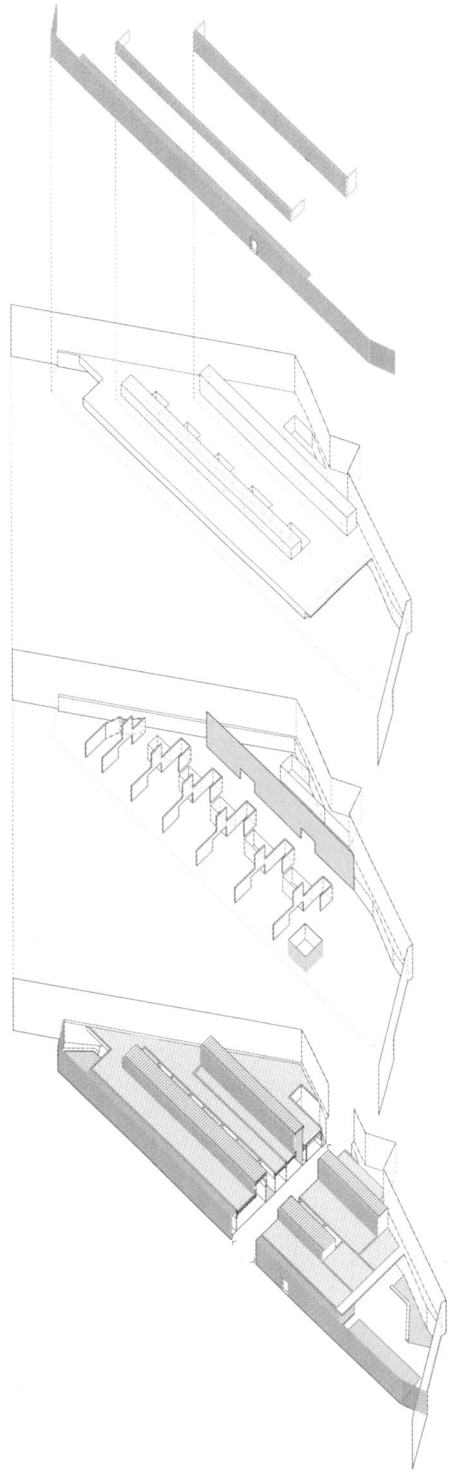

SCHOOL IN LA MILAGROSA
Pereda Pérez Arquitectos
Carlos Pereda Iglesias, Óscar Pérez Silanes

The main influence in this project is the site without which it is impossible to understand the design. It is located at the edge of a peripheral neighborhood in Pamplona. Given the extreme conditions of the surroundings and the program characteristics, two primary design goals were determined: the logic of where to locate the building program elements and the need to capture daylight, which took precedence over a other more complex or exuberant approach. With this strategy the project reappropriates the place, preventing the rough aesthetic of the surroundings from undermining the new building. Its condition as a base for the adjacent buildings unaffectedly assumes the presence of the unfinished rear facades of the housing blocks. As a result, the surrounding buildings are inextricably incorporated into the landscape of the new building.

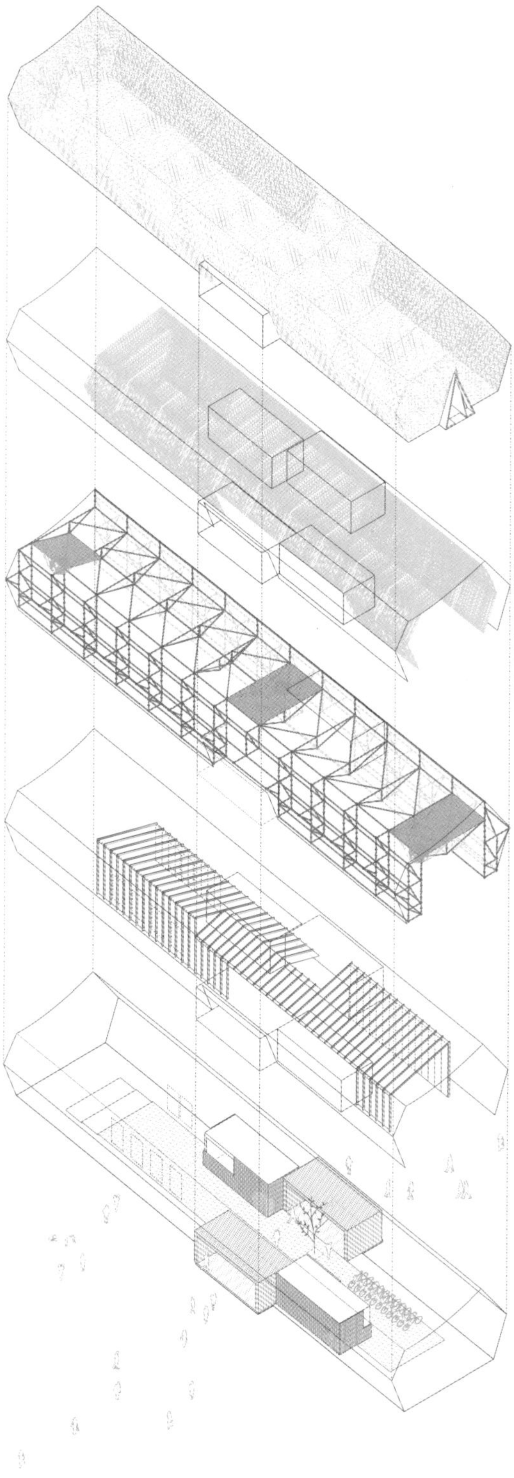

NAKED

GLÒRIES INFORMATION POINT

peris+toral.arquitectes

Marta Peris Eugenio, José Manuel Toral, Izaskun González

The temporary building forms part of the provisional public space installed in the Plaza de las Glorias of Barcelona. The program includes an information area, an exhibition space explaining the project for transforming the plaza and a bike rental service. Given the large scale of the adjacent buildings, this project proposes a linear element with a building envelope that blurs its outline to minimize its presence. The intention is that the building doesn't compete, but rather melts into its surroundings and that it is permeable to transit, views and air. Three envelopes with differentiated functions are combined to form a certain depth, which is visible especially at night when an artificial light source is located at floor level between the polycarbonate layer and the shade netting. Both layers take advantage of the diffusion qualities of the material, and in addition to producing two radiant surfaces, the interstitial space is also illuminated. Through light, the void acquires presence, adding the successive envelopes together to form a whole: a halo of light. At nightfall, the light gravitates like a line that underlines the building. At night, the light ascends to occupy the interstitial space and complete the halo. The building, permeable to passersby, views and air, more than occupying a space, densifies a void.

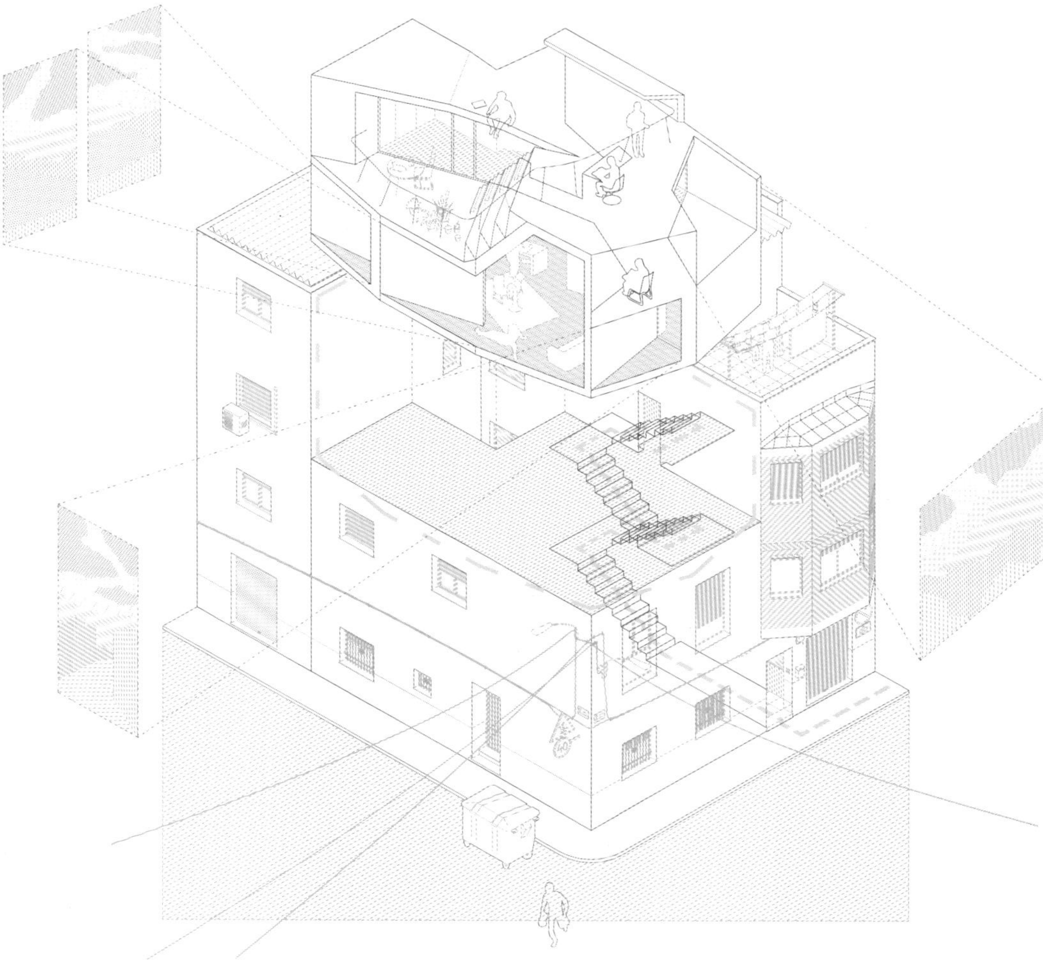

PERCHING

LUDE HOUSE
Grupo Aranea
Francisco Leiva Ivorra, Martín López Robles

Lude wanted a house in the historic center of the village of Cehegín, built on top of a building housing the apartments of his mother and his sister. The Lude house proposes a particular way to relate to its immediate surroundings. Immersed in a dense urban fabric, it avoids opening windows directly on the facade, like the neighboring buildings, but instead focuses views down the narrow streets to the nearby mountains of the Sierra de Burete (to the south) and the Cabecico San Agustín (to the east). Although apparently alien to the buildings around it, the Lude house doesn't renounce the massive and introverted character of the local traditional architecture. The result is a complex, light-filled interior, which Lude will fill with music, and which still contains many secrets.

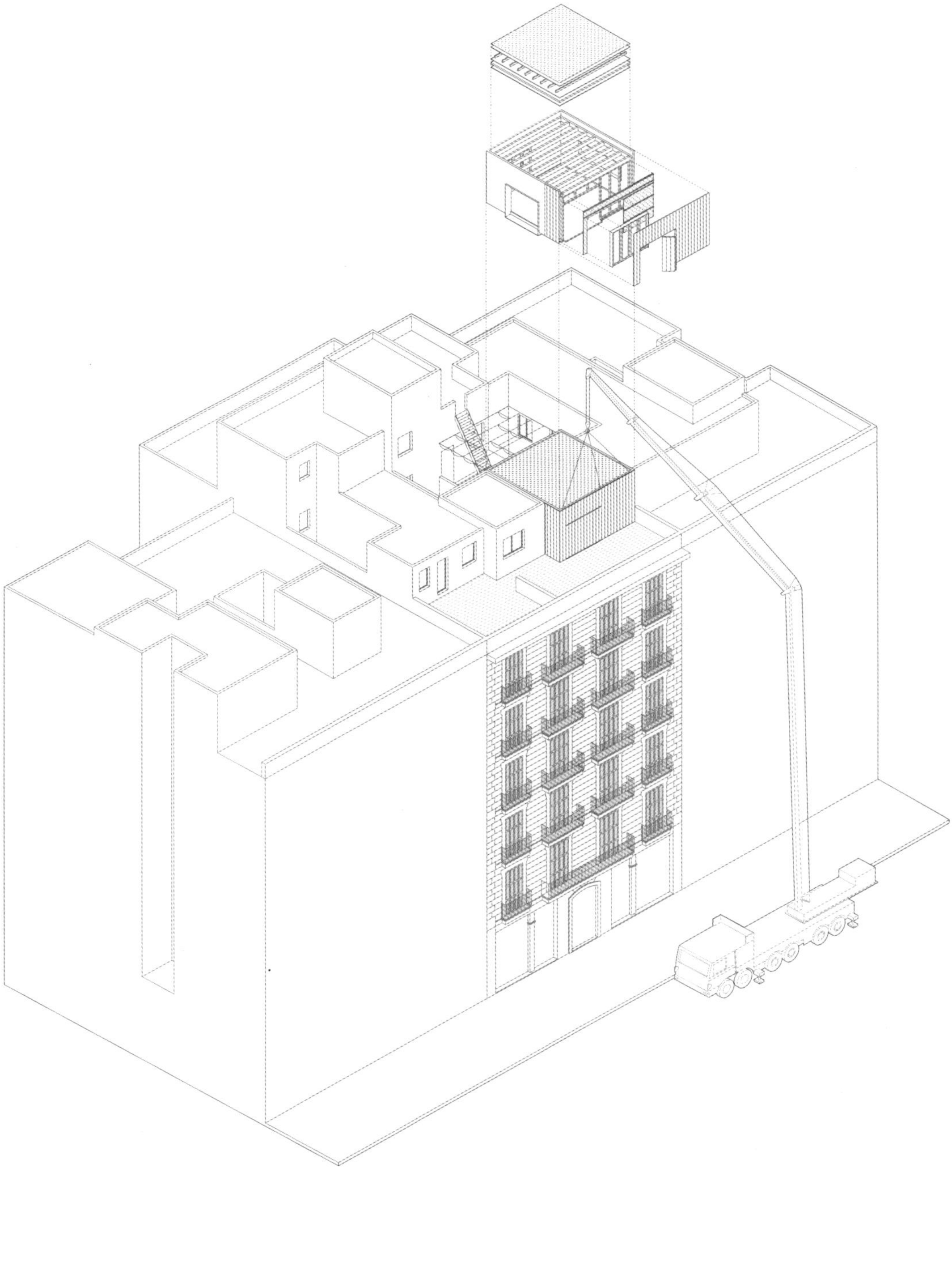

PERCHING

PAVILION FOR AN EXISTING HOUSE
Flexo Arquitectura
Aixa del Rey García, Tomeu Ramis Frontera, Barbara Vich Arrom

This proposal reflects on the need to reactivate residual spaces found on the roof terraces of a large part of the city of Barcelona. Available low-impact mechanisms take advantage of the opportunities offered by existing geometries and materials (load-bearing party walls, changes of level, orientation, etc. offering versatile and flexible spaces that don't jeopardize future uses. With this in mind, the pavilion was designed with a lightweight wood-frame structure that took advantage of the existing conditions of the terrace to define a versatile space with an independent entrance from the apartment to which it belongs. The pavilion includes all the services necessary for it to house different uses over time (related or unrelated to the existing apartment), bedroom, studio, workshop, playroom, living room or kitchen. The space is designed to permit its use indefinitely, until the renovation of the original apartment is completed.

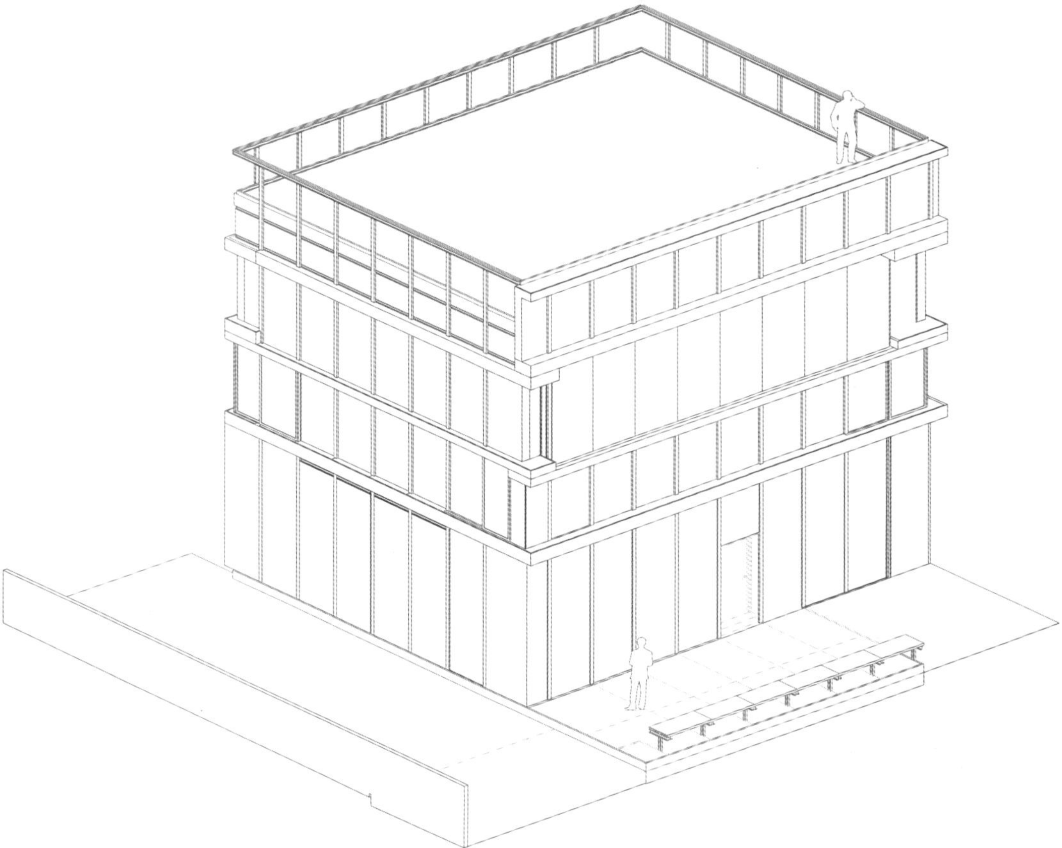

PERCHING

CYCLOPEAN HOUSE
Ensamble Studio
Antón García-Abril, Debora Mesa

The Cyclopean House is a house without a site. It is a kit of prefabricated domestic parts designed to occupy different locations. Each part has a purpose: structure, building envelope, mechanical services, finishes and cabinetwork, within the large prefabricated element. Dimensions of the pieces are adjusted to fit into a shipping container or a standard truck, permitting easy transport from their place of fabrication—in Madrid, Spain—to the place where they will be installed. This architectural assembly defines a large two-story room, an empty space in which the structure and infrastructures are concentrated at the perimeter, while the rest of the floor plan is free to be used for different functions or divided up and transformed over time depending on the lives of its inhabitants. Each prefabricated element is specialized in a different action—cooking, washing, storage, eating, sleeping, working or looking—and together they provide a space for all basic domestic activities and create a dense container that embraces the space to provide thermal comfort, privacy, cross-ventilation, natural light and diagonal views.

JLG LIFT
BlueLine Rental
MULTIBOARD
450AJ
USDOT 398741

PICK
CRANE SERVICE
PICKCRANE.com

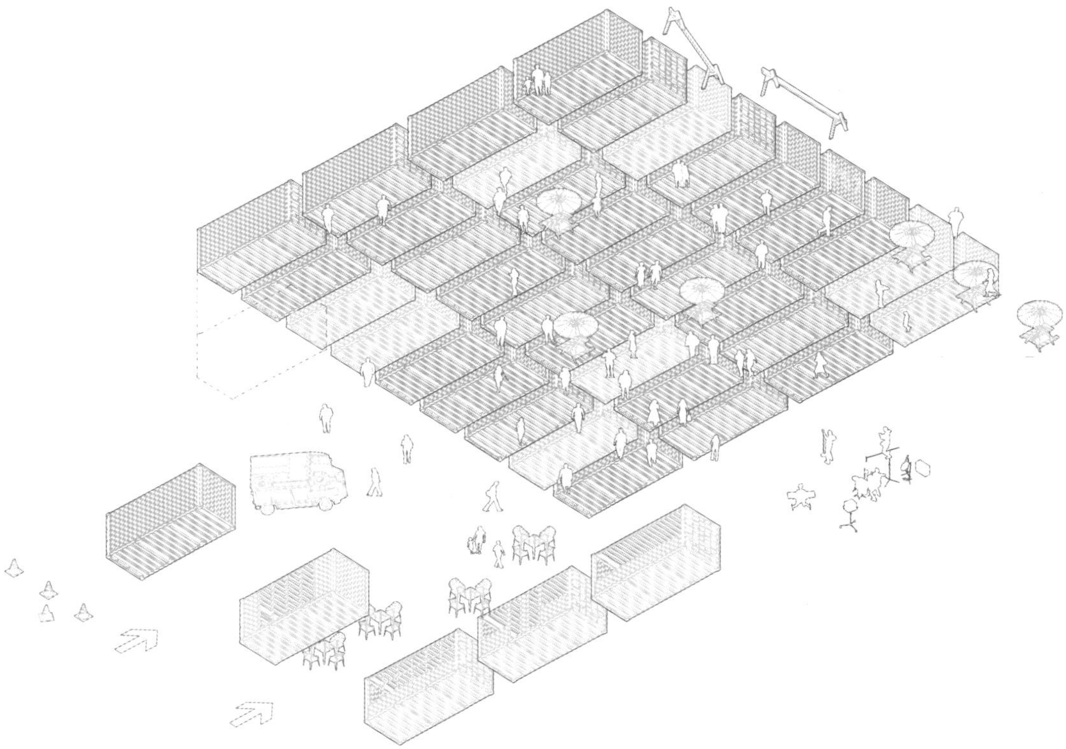

PERCHING

PIER 57 INTERIM PROJECT
Jose María de Churtichaga + Cayetana de la Quadra-Salcedo

At Aviation Pier on Pier 57, the future New York Superpier, there is an intervention with shipping containers from Spain hung from the ceiling like a magic carpet. The containers have motors so they can be raised and lowered. The different ways they can be transformed allow hundreds of different types of events to be held here. A magic carpet of floating shipping containers forms a colorful ceiling, a grid of possible scenarios, a space that defies gravity with a single-layer backdrop that resolves everything.

STOP

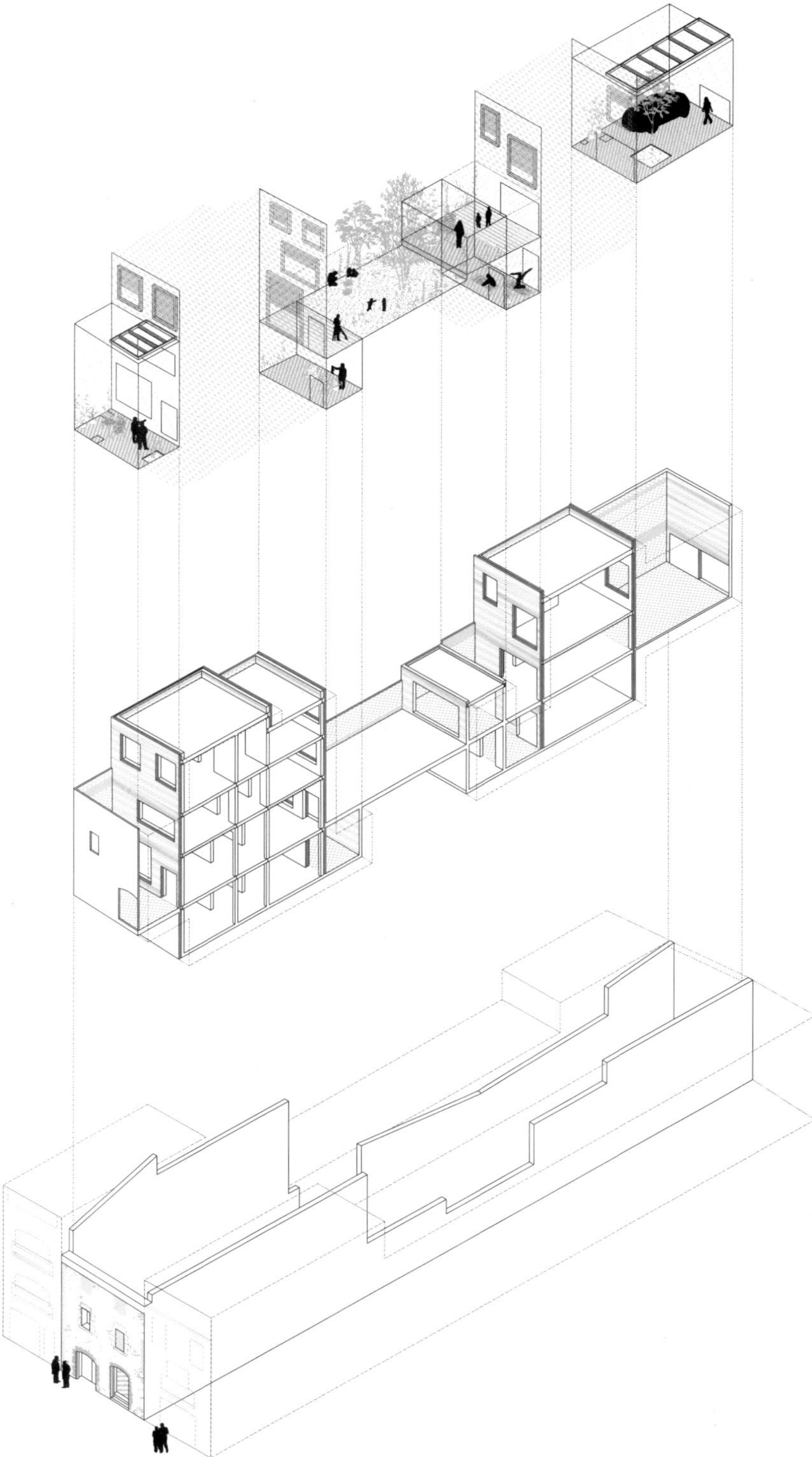

REASSIGNMENTS

HOUSE 1014
HARQUITECTES
David Lorente, Josep Ricart, Xavier Ros, Roger Tudó

The site is six-and-a-half meters wide and very long, between two party walls, with access from two streets in the historic center of Granollers. The existing construction was in a state of ruin; only the main street facade was preserved, as it was fairly sound and had certain historic value. The clients wanted to clearly differentiate two zones in the house: a domestic area for family life and a second area that could function independently, serving both as a more isolated and calm space as well as to receive guests or sporadically organize large communal meals. The sequence of spaces tries to create a certain ambiguity between interior and exterior, however, the exterior spaces are intentionally differentiated by more intensive vegetation and the use of unclad clay brick. The brick, with its more material and natural presence, creates a less domestic atmosphere and helps construct landscapes in this site without views. The organization of the materials and spaces tries to prioritize optimal passive environmental performance, starting with the improved climate of the intermediate courtyards that reduces energy demand in the directly related spaces.

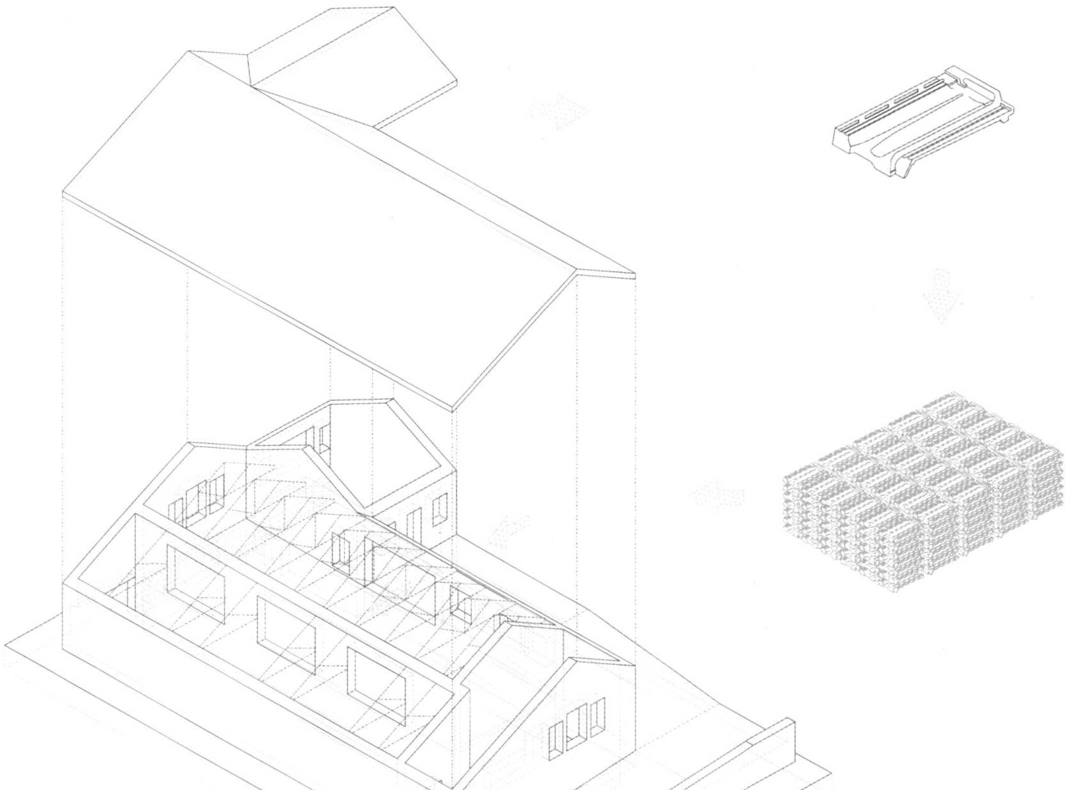

REASSIGNMENTS

MATADERO MADRID—BUILDING 8B
Arturo Franco

In Building 8B, a small building within a former slaughterhouse complex in Madrid, the clay roof tiles have been removed from a roof that needed to be replaced and stacked up inside of the space to solve a problem. Building 8B is programmed to be an administrative space, with a small work space, a storage area and a multipurpose space for talks or presentations. It is a small building, but spatially very interesting. This intervention aims to respect a valid spatial configuration, with no adulteration. It is a test. This project retraces some paths that were taken, trying to find meeting points. The inert industrial elements are understood differently, decontextualized and installed with the unpredictability of manual labor. The tiles are used in another way. This project tries to understand architecture as an intellectual, cultural and ethical experience.

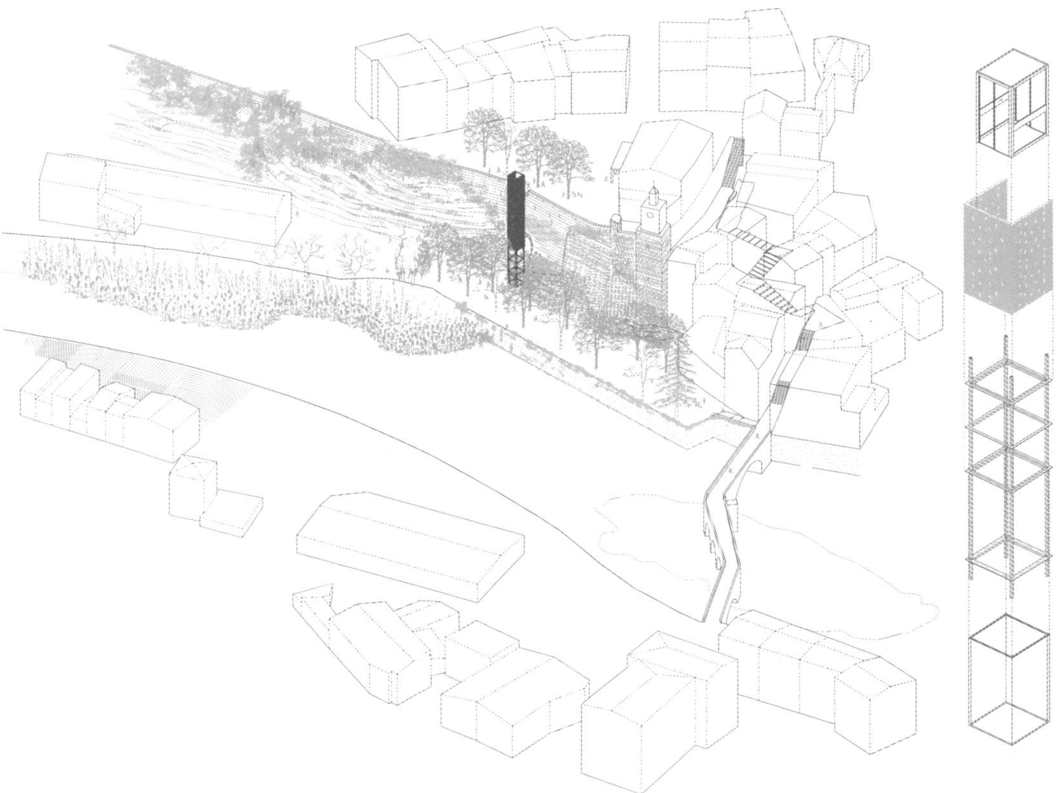

NEW ACCESS TO THE HISTORIC CENTER OF GIRONELLA
Carles Enrich Arquitectura + Urbanisme

Gironella is a town that has grown in the past few decades divided by the Llobregat River. The historic center is on the top a hill some 20 metrer from the right bank of the river, while the modern part of the town is located on the other bank. This project proposes the insertion of an elevator to improve accessibility to the old town and promote the urban connection between the two parts of the town, encouraging the use of the historic center and preventing the risk of social exclusion. The selection and placement of materials was determined by a set of criteria related to industrial buildings, economic concerns (low cost, ease of installation and zero maintenance), climatic considerations (sun protection for the elevator cab, ventilation of the shaft) and the possibility of creating an entry for indirect light.

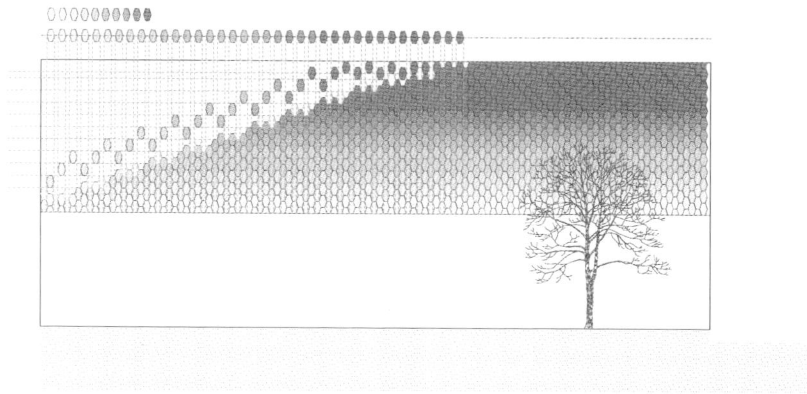

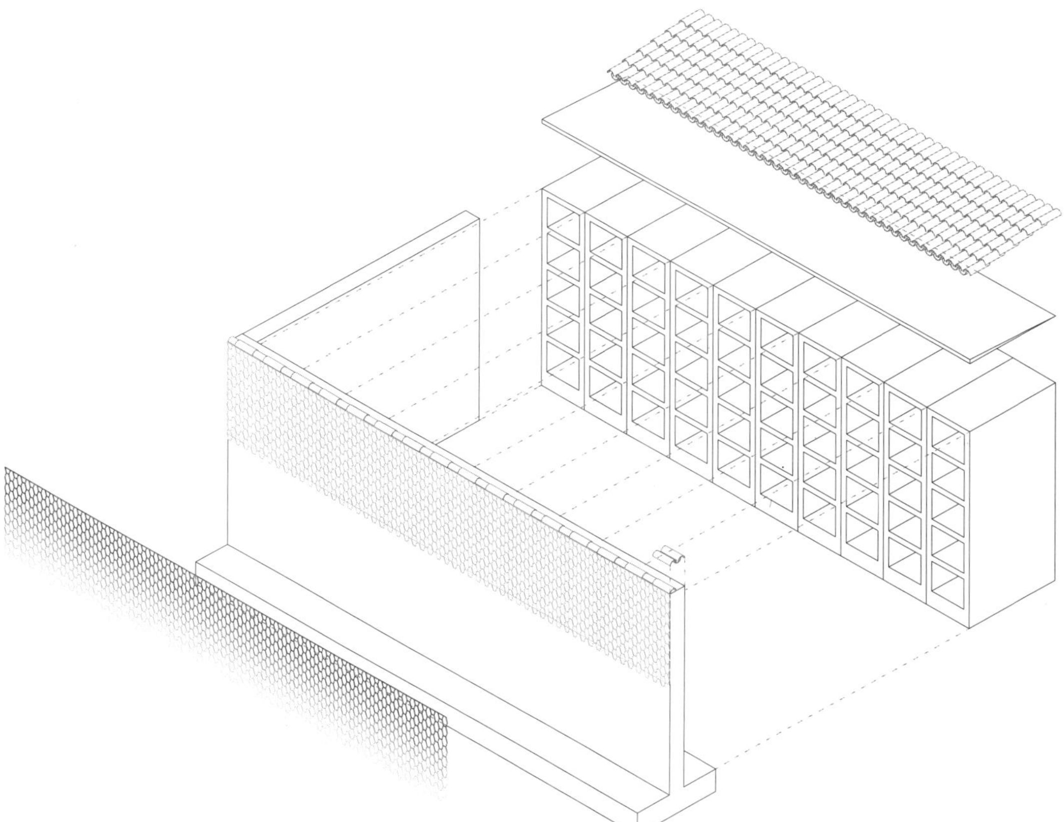

GRAO CEMETERY
Inés García Clariana

The cemetery is sited as the end to many unfinished processes in the city of Valencia, the end of the Avenida de Francia, the end of the interventions in the former riverbed and abutting with another urban sector (that of Arts and Sciences). In this undefined space a simple intervention is made, both providing a finish for a constructed element, as well as giving it an identity and unity with the simple operation of installing a ceramic cladding in different tones of green.

JORDI AND AFRICA'S HOUSE
TEd'A arquitectes
Jaume Mayol, Irene Pérez

The house occupies a corner site and is ordered in two directions. The house doesn't have a dominant direction. The house looks in all directions. In order for the structural walls to dominate the space, the mechanical systems are located along the perimeter, creating a thick facade, freeing up the center of the plan and permitting visual and program connections between the spaces. The materialization of these walls is a fundamental part of the project. There was an existing structure on the site built with bearing walls of *marés*, a local sandstone. Common sense led to reusing these elements. The strategy was implemented. The stone gives the facade its texture and character; a texture that with the passing years will absorb a patina added by time. The old pieces of stone, due to their limited number, were combined with new pieces. The new ones came from the same quarry and were used at points where it was necessary to build more precise edges: window frames, roof copings, etc.

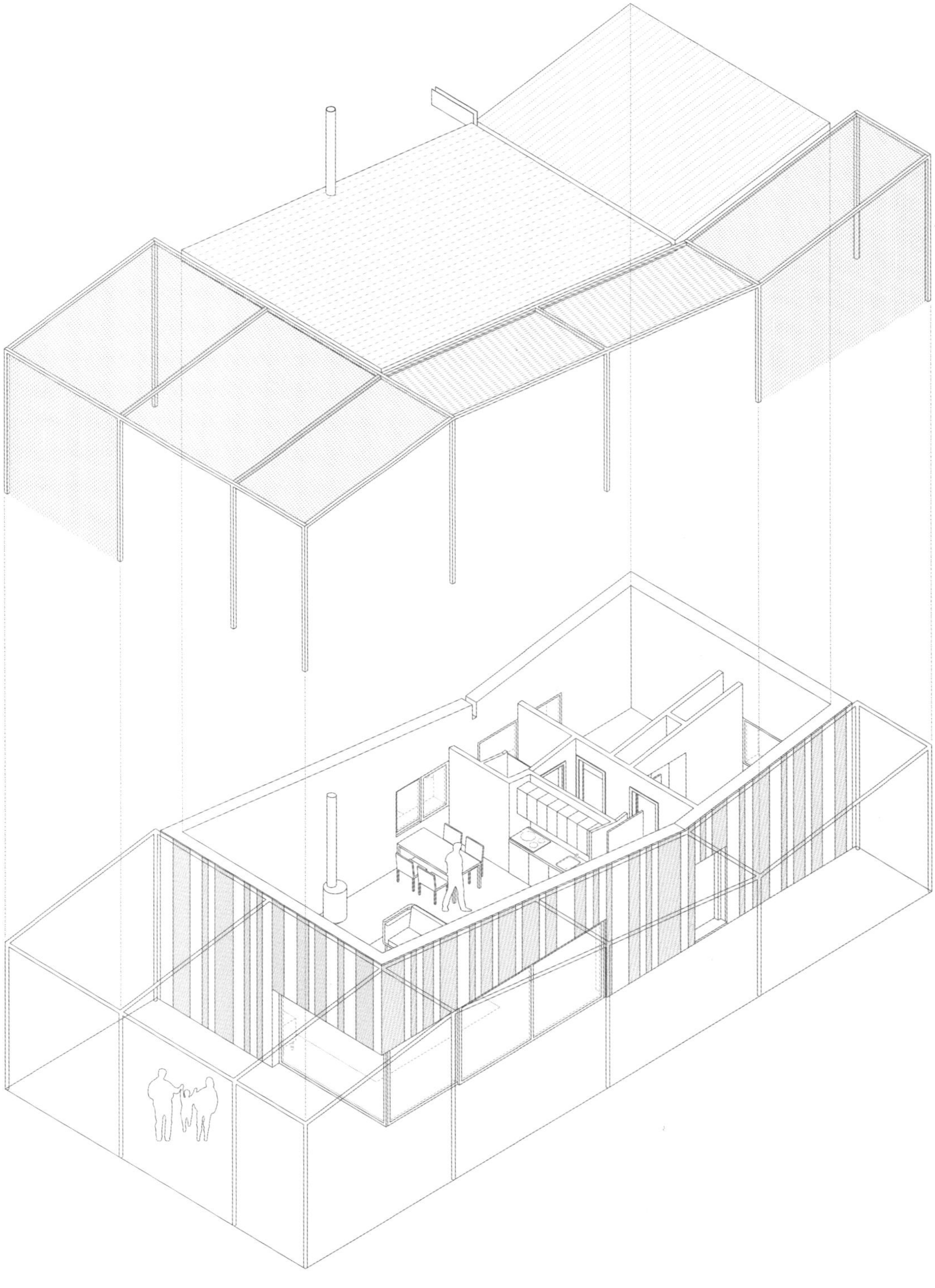

REASSIGNMENTS

HOUSE IN GAÜSES
Anna & Eugeni Bach

This main constraint of this project was the economic aspect; the design needed to be viable with a minimal budget (70.000 €). This factor limited structural possibilities, and finishes. This led to a clear premise: the architects would have to work with local craftsmen and fabricators (if possible from the same town), and use the technical solutions that they were accustomed to, traditional solutions adopted in the typical local construction techniques. This led us work with load-bearing walls, one-way slabs, aluminum windows with reasonable dimensions and conventional finishes like painted stucco. The diaphanous space contains the living room, dining room and kitchen. This space is designed to maximize its area, so that the heart of the house and the space where the majority of daily functions take place is as pleasant as possible. The bedrooms, on the other hand, are basic spaces, with the minimum space required for sleeping and a small desk.

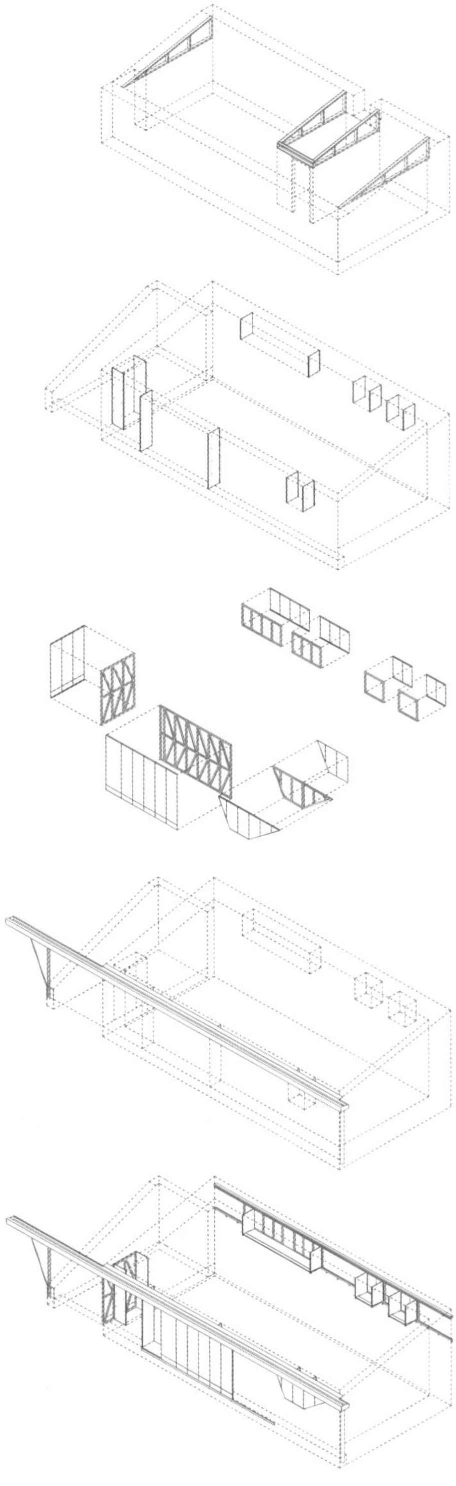

REASSIGNMENTS

HABITAT STOREHOUSE

Ferran Grau Valldosera, Nicola Regusci, Xavier Bustos Serrat

The habitat-storehouse is located in a rural area dedicated to livestock, vegetable gardens and fruit trees. The topography of the site defines the project's position and basic geometry. The shed roof follows the slope of the ground, which naturalizes its integration into the surrounding site. The construction is placed between a pine forest to the north and existing terraces with olive, almond, fig and apricot trees to the south. The example of the nearby rabbit farm defines the habitat's architectural language. The program consists of a multipurpose space: living/kitchen/bedroom/storeroom, a bathroom and a small bedroom. On the exterior there is a small outdoor storage space (west) and a paved area facing south.

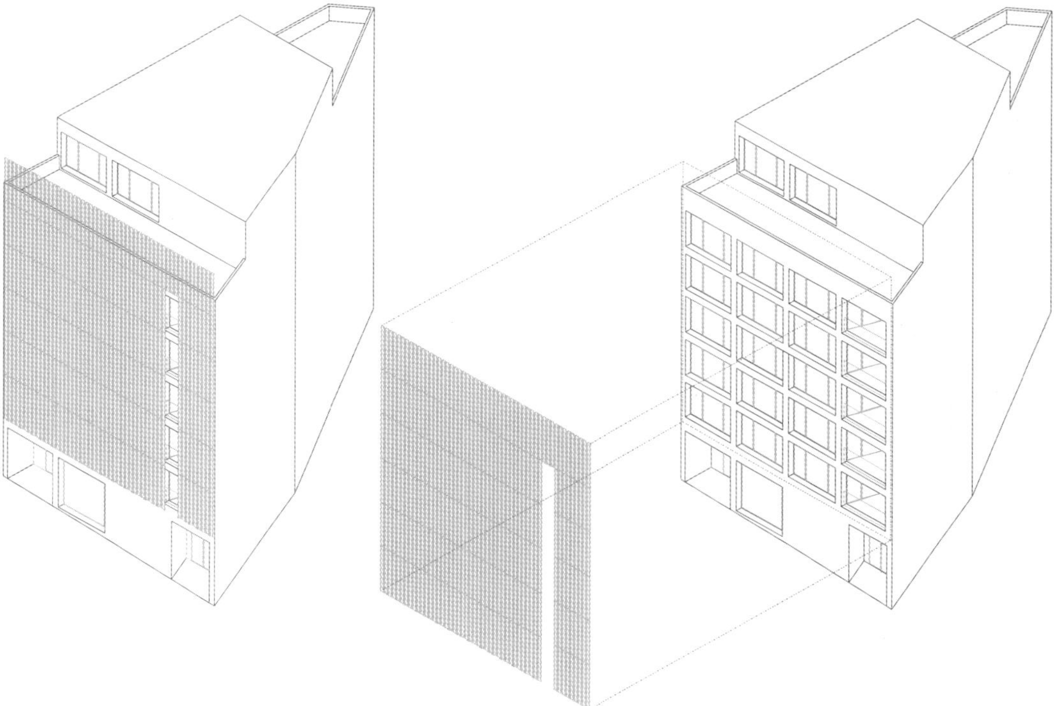

AUZO FACTORY IRAZÁBAL-MATIKO
Suárez Santas Arquitectos
Asier Santas Torres, Luis Suárez Mansilla

Bilbao has a continuous ring of districts that surround the more touristic and mediatic city center, many with evident necessities for architectural intervention. Matiko is one of them. In this district the city has provided an industrial building to be converted into an entrepreneurship center, based on a model that uses the recovery of old buildings to revitalize the place where they are located. The most significant aspect of the project was the idea to design a facade that made the whole operation visible, with minimal cost and maximum expressivity. The proposal is a uniform skin with a large scale that covers the exterior structure to create a taut plane. The material chosen for this facade is commonly used for mechanical installations, but here it is conferred with an aesthetic virtue: galvanized steel raceway pans. Behind this surface the old fascia panels and windows will be replaced with new ones that infill between the structural bays, increasing the amount of day lighting. The budget for the facade material (one kilometer of pans) is around 10,000 € (28.40€ per square meter), which can be considered strikingly low taking into account the impact of the image achieved by this operation.

BAR
EDER

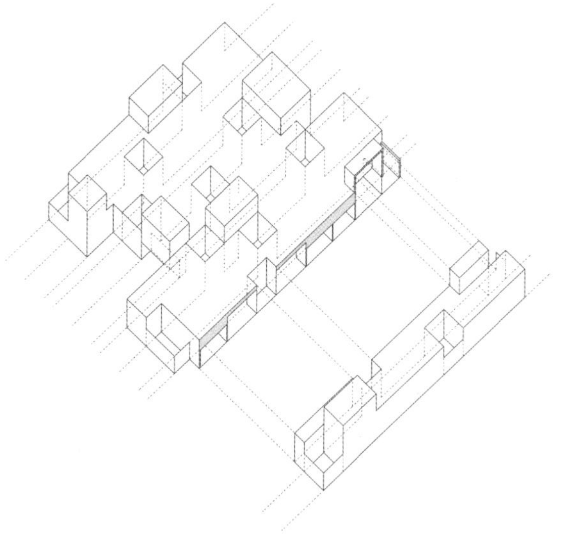

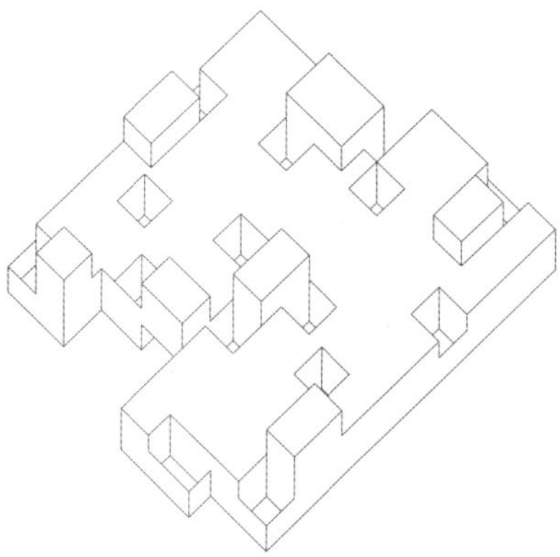

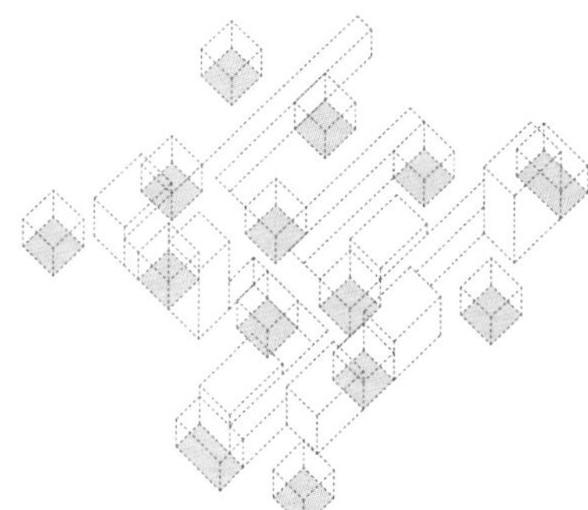

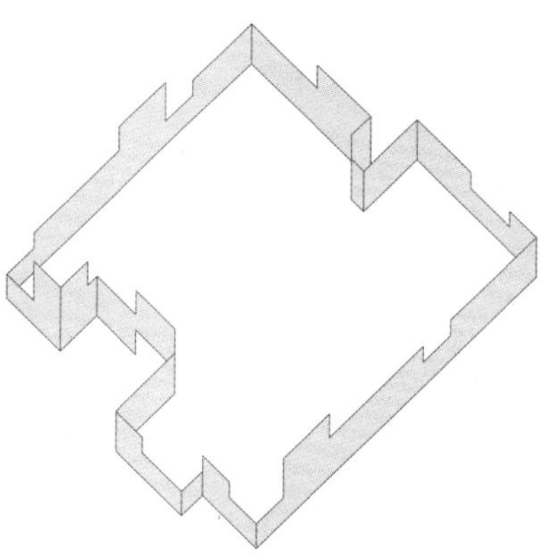

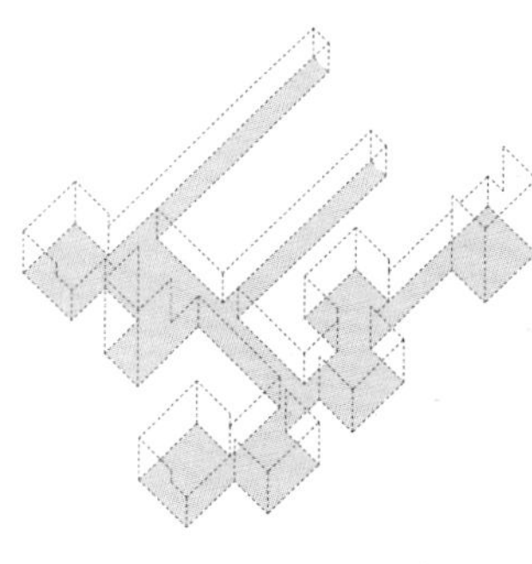

3X1 / 3 MUNICIPAL HEALTH CENTERS IN MADRID

Entresitio

María Hurtado de Mendoza Wahrolén, César Jiménez de Tejada Benavides, José María Hurtado de Mendoza Wahrolén

The inception of these three buildings goes back to an unusual competition held for the construction of two identical buildings (same client, same program and same budget) in two different sites in Madrid (Usera and San Blas), whose common characteristic consisted in their lack of urban significance. This proposal was the only building whose formal and functional autonomy were sufficient for it to "exist" independent of its location. A second competition for the Villaverde site served as an occasion to verify that the spatial model and the plan solution were newly viable, although in this case in a more sensitive urban setting, due to the street alignments and the proximity of the building to pedestrians. The program for the health center is laid out entirely on the ground floor. The different program areas are ordered on a loosely-formed, irregular orthogonal grid, with thirteen courtyards staggered among the public and private areas, following three parallel (non)-corridors. A relationship of opposites is established between the exterior facade and the interior space, a synthesis between the intellectual and the experiential, the classic and the picturesque.

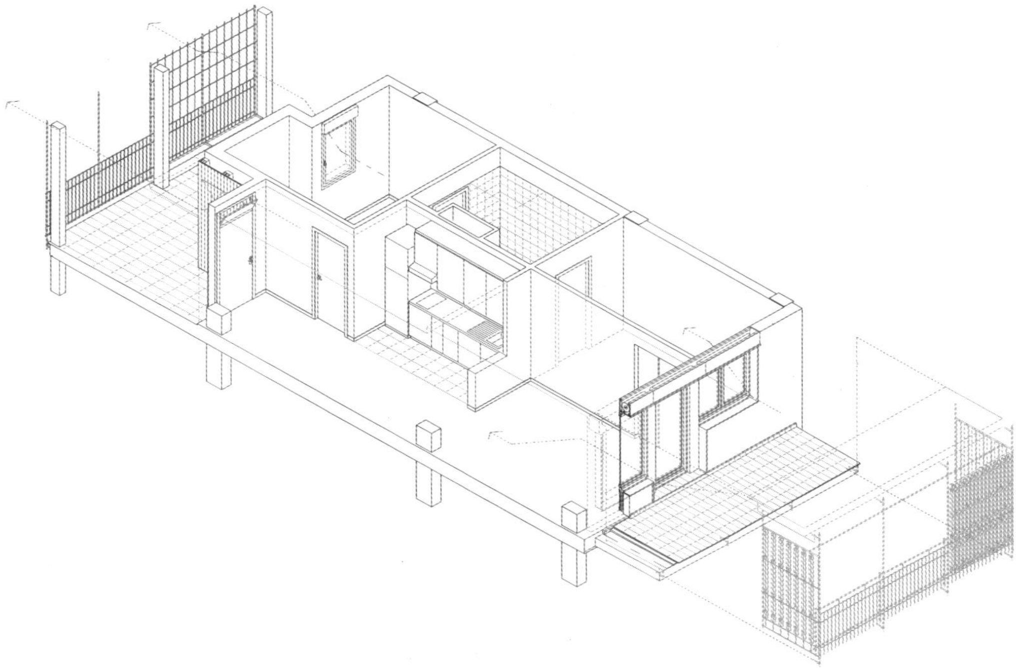

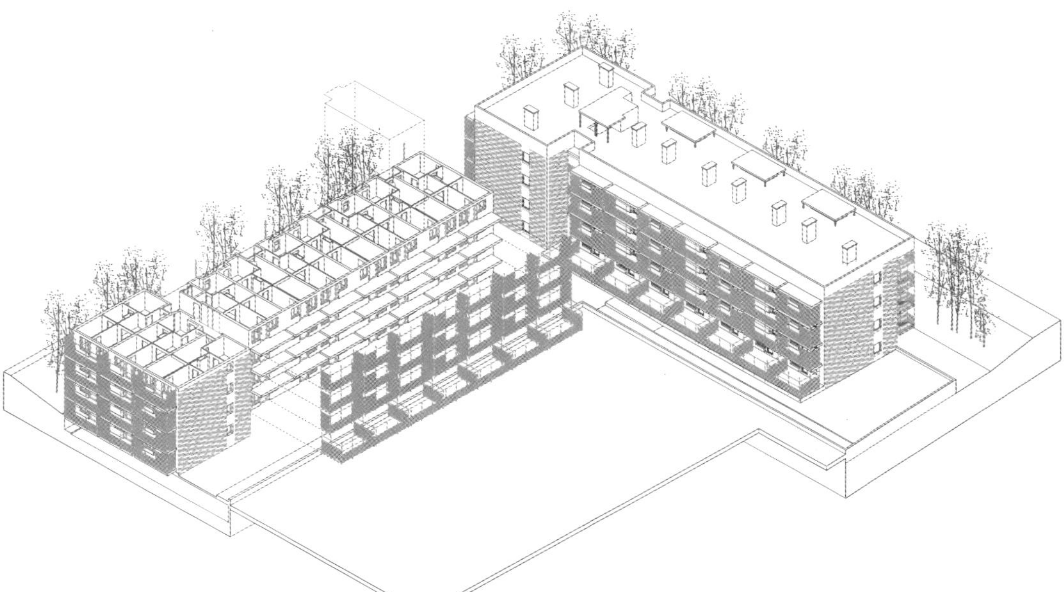

80 HOUSES IN SALOU
Toni Gironés

Set out as a new urban pattern overlaid onto the existing agricultural layout, the new place originated with large lots containing free-standing buildings, arranged orthogonally.

The project proposes a fabric with various scales of intervention, with a program for social housing that develops its relationship properties, constructing an architecture understood as a support and closely related to the users' reality. At the same time, the entry areas and the community spaces are designed as places for relaxation in the intermediate areas between the apartments and the exterior space.

The apartments have two opposite orientations and have a transversal sequence of spaces: breezeway, apartment and terrace, which lends them versatility and the capacity for adaptation linked to use and climatic circumstances. The proposal is built with simple, low-cost and low-maintenance materials, but carefully detailed and built.

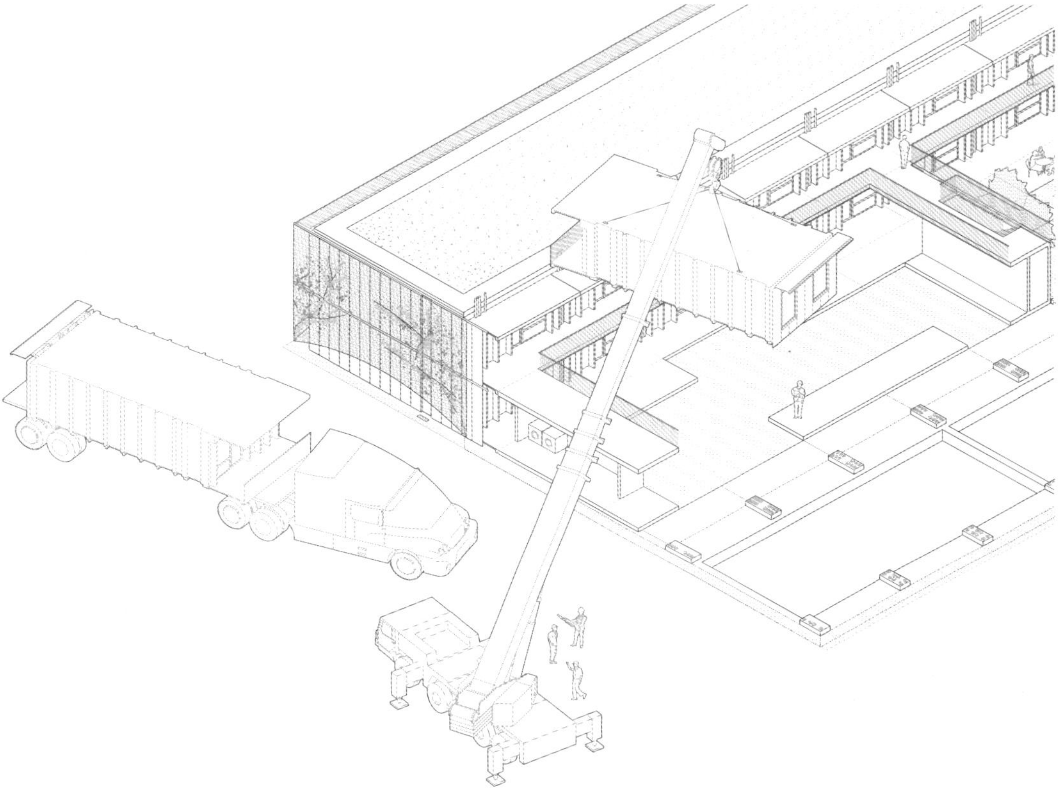

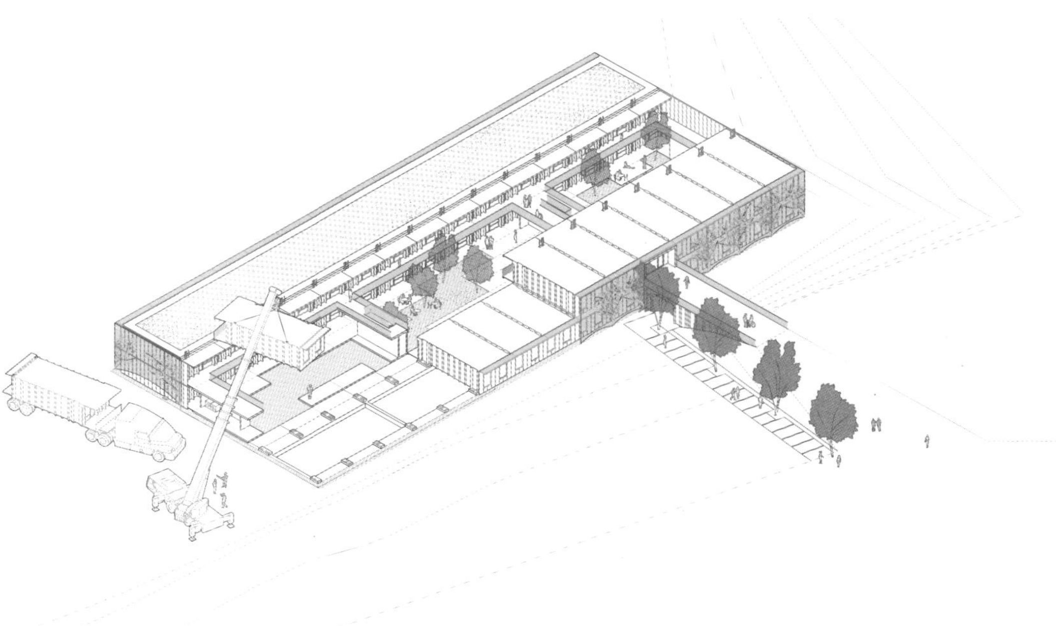

57 HOUSING UNITS ON THE ETSAV CAMPUS
DATAAE + HARQUITECTES

Conceived of as empty spaces, free of interior compartments, the university housing units on the campus in Sant Cugat are formed by a series of precast reinforced concrete drawers, stacked up two high and aligned in two parallel blocks, with a large central atrium. The residential program for architecture students provides the possibility of intensifying the coexistence between users, both individually, due to the interior flexibility of the housing, and collectively, thanks to the potential use of the atrium as a space for social events. The central atrium will be covered in the future to create an intermediate, bioclimatic space, which will permit a major improvement in the energy efficiency of the building at the same time it economizes on the building envelope.

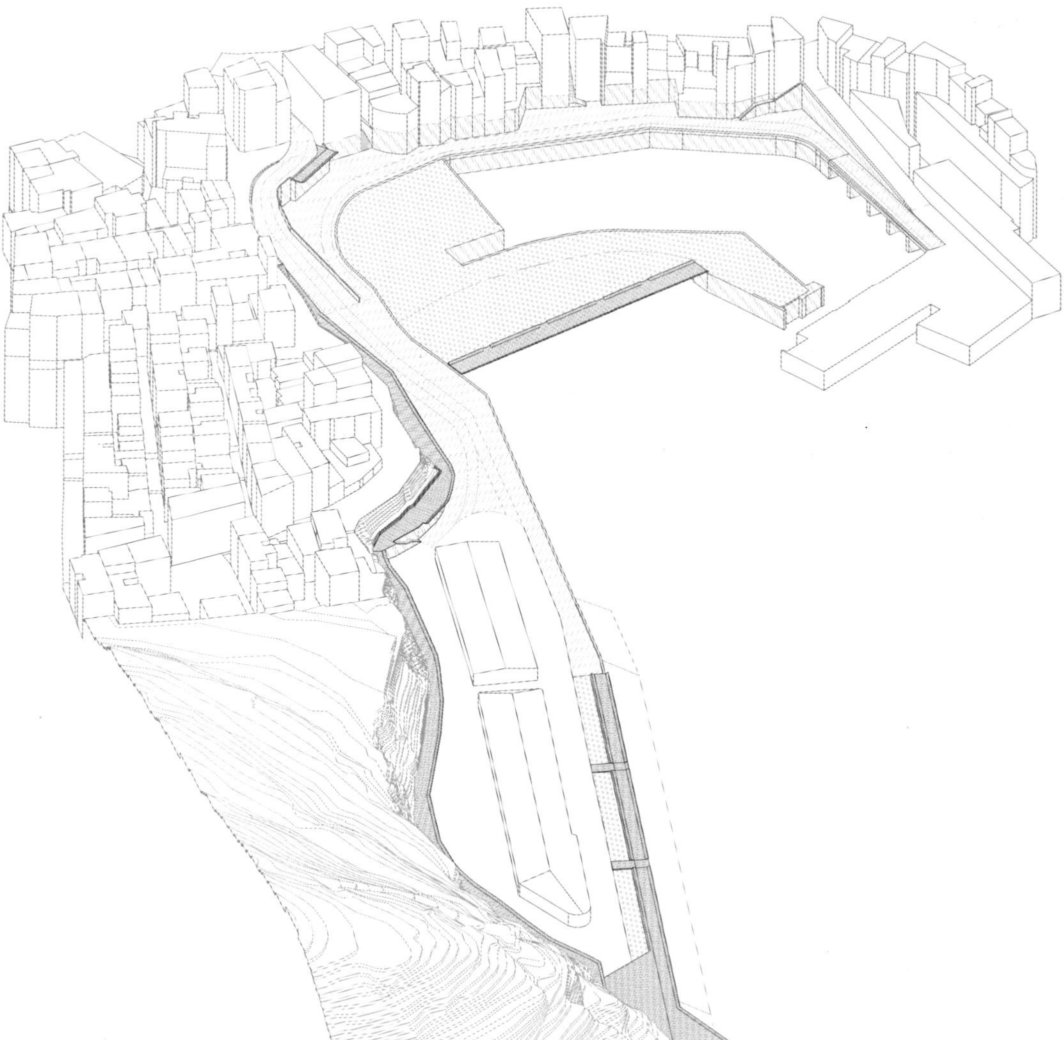

PAVEMENTS

RENOVATION OF MALPICA HARBOR
CREUSeCARRASCO
Juan Creus Andrade, Covadonga Carrasco López

Guidelines to walk without a floor, on top of a wall, a freeboard or rip-rap. Starting with a single base element: precast concrete with a standard width of 122 centimeters and variable lengths. A system for the creation of public space was postulated using a limitless sequence, which could admit complex situations of position and use. The construction, whose extent and form is established according to necessity, can be extended, modified and even transported to another location. In fact, the system was invented for the opposite hillside from the one that where it finally built. This is a project in which the architect and engineer focus their investigation on how to open and expand the space of a port from which public use has been gradually disappearing, while preserving activity and work flows. The project discovers an intermediate level on which it is extended, creating a new, unexpected ground level. This new space, constructed using cantilevers and ramps of variable widths and shapes, connects the different levels between the elevated streets of the town and the water level, providing a new way to pass through and perceive this enclave defined by the force of a highly constructed natural landscape that maintains the identity of the towns of A Costa da Morte.

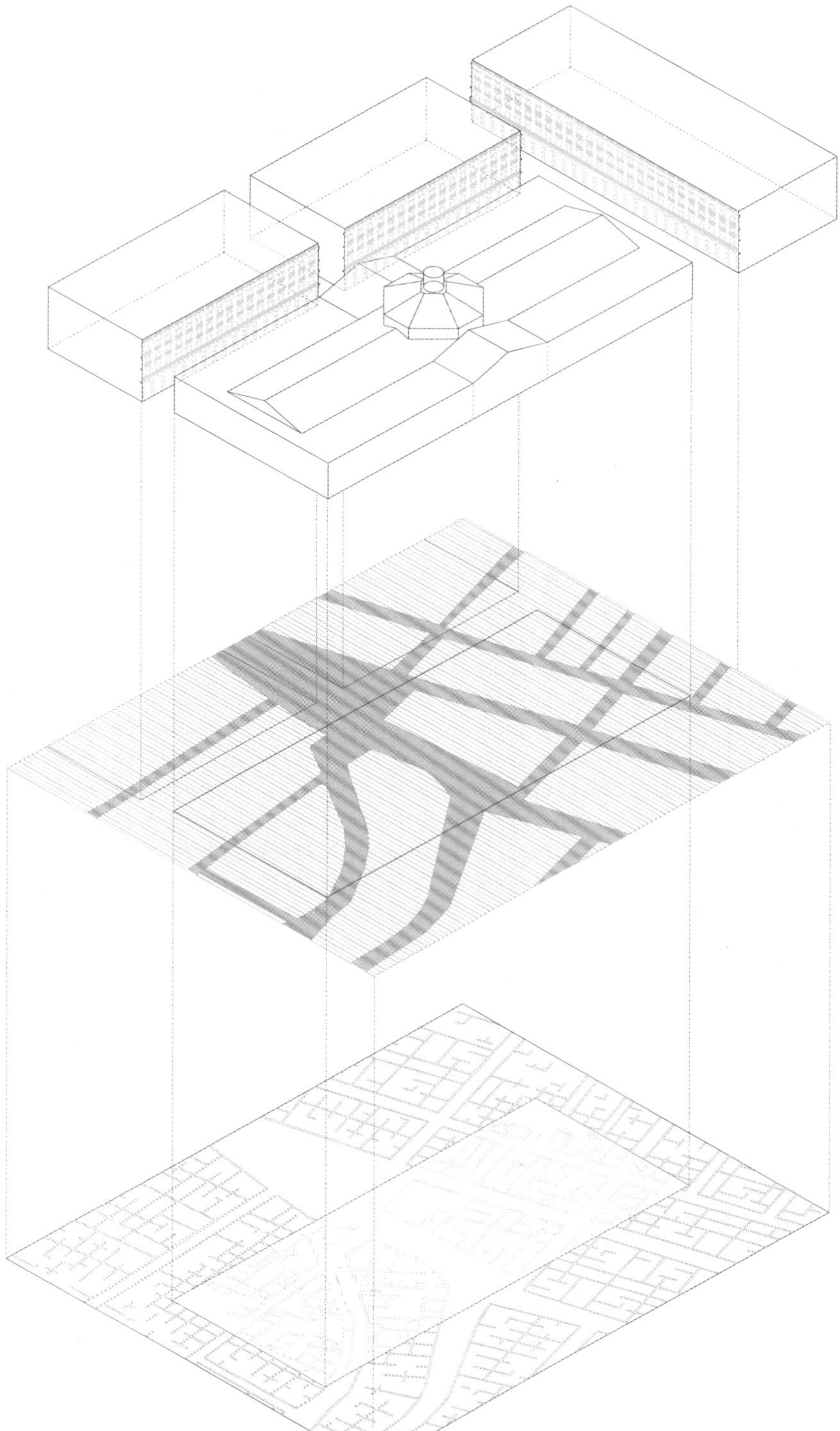

PAVEMENTS

ENVIRONS OF THE BORN MARKET
Vora Arquitectura
Pere Buil, Toni Riba

The market building, which contains a huge piece of the medieval city that was destroyed in 1714, has reopened its doors as a historic-cultural facility. A reopening that, at an urban level, offers an enormous new covered public space, almost like a porch, framed by a unified architectural backdrop, the Fontser porches. The paving is an element of connection with the history and memory of the place. The final result permits a reading on two levels. On one level, the reading of distant memory: the definition of the layout of the medieval streets through subtle changes in the cobblestones and the reproduction of the location of built elements uncovered during the excavations. On the other level, the materiality is linked to the more recent memory of the place. Its use as a market within the continuity of the unified character of Fontser's nineteenth-century operation. The continuous granite cobblestone paving identifies the intervention and makes a sensory connection with the collective imagination. A large number of the cobblestones were removed from the existing streets and reused in the same area.

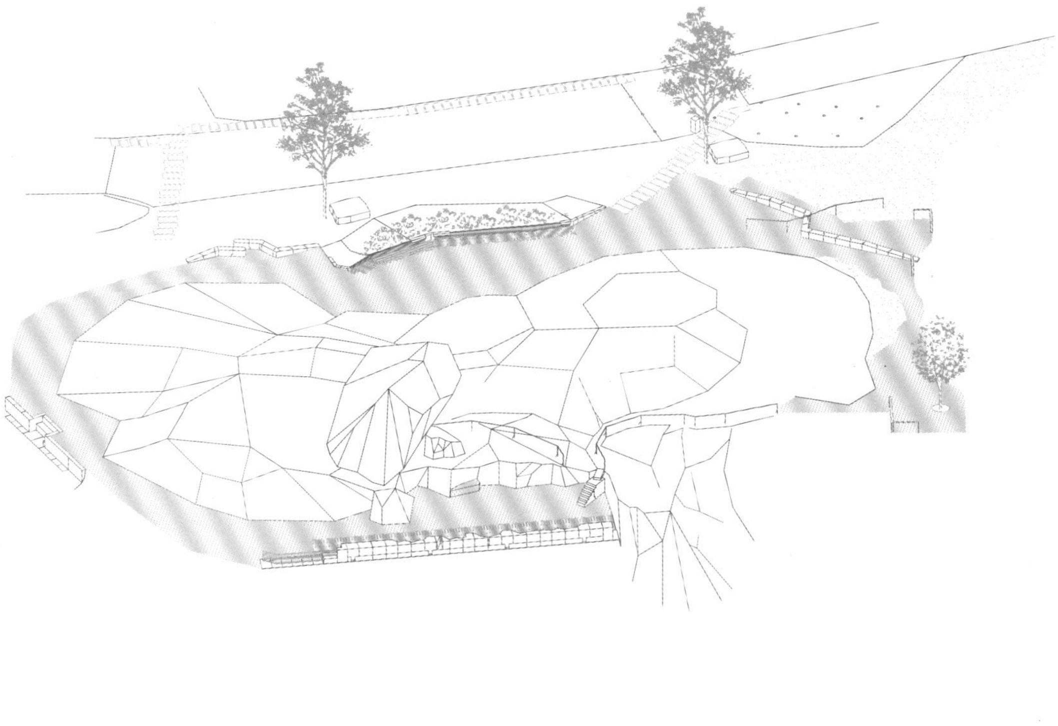

PAVEMENTS

PEDRA DA RÁ OVERLOOK
Carlos Seoane

This intervention originated as a proposal to improve the space associated with a geological formation known as the "Pedra da Rá"—frog rock. First, an existing lookout built in the 1980s in the form of a concrete stair that led to the top of the rock formation was demolished. In addition, excavation and earth movements were undertaken to reveal the rock formation in its original state, highlighting its exceptional geological and formal characteristics. Once the aggressive elements were eliminated, a space was constructed around the stone outcropping that serves as the origin point of a multitude of paths leading to other nature areas, including the Playa do Vilar, the Corrubedo dunes and theCastro da Cidá, a recently excavated Celtic fort. The project is a collection of different possibilities for manipulating granite to form paving, limits, benches, stairs, etc., all of which contributes to the delicate relationship of the great rock to its surroundings.

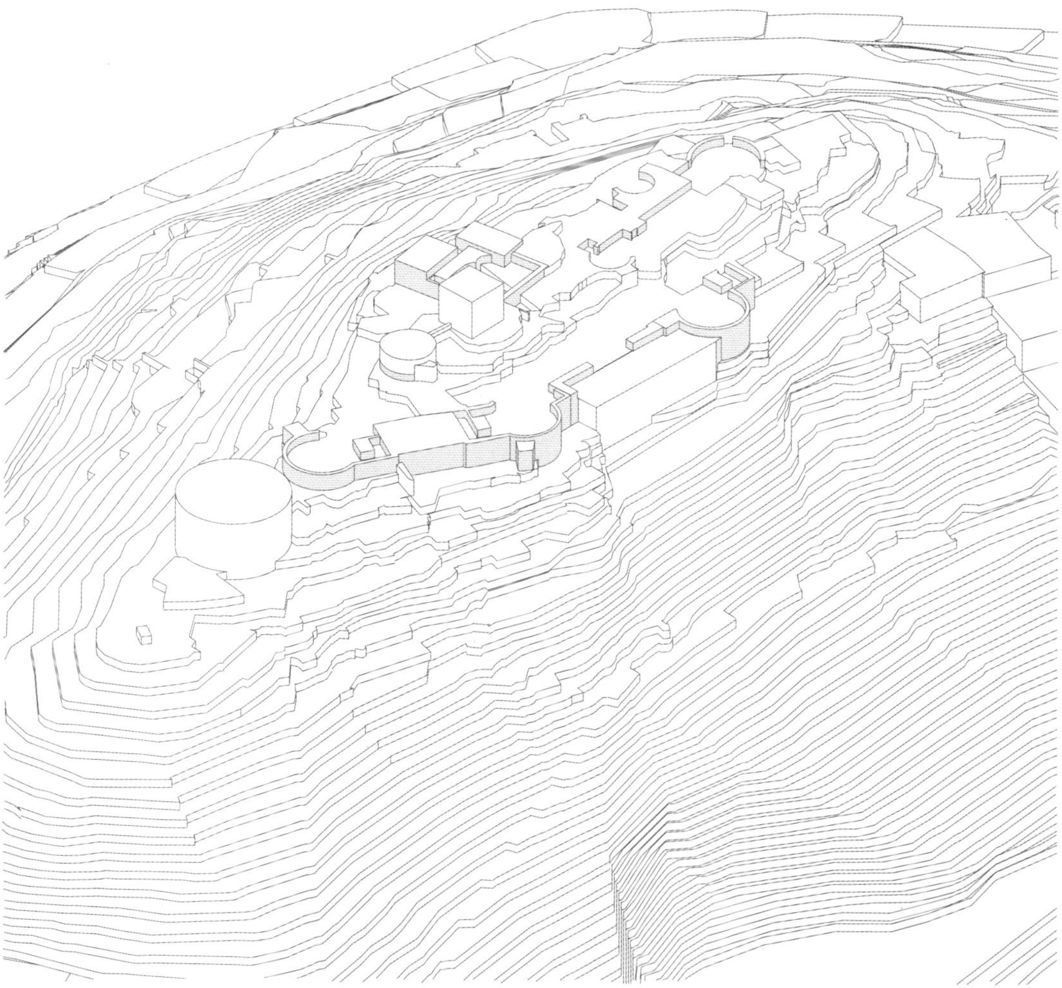

PAVEMENTS

TURÓ DE LA ROVIRA
Jansana, de la Villa, de Paauw Arquitectes S.L.P.
AAUP Jordi Romero Associats S.L.P.

Iberian village; agricultural settlement; anti-aircraft defence bunkers for Barcelona (1937-38), to defend the city from the attacks of the fascist air force; from 1940 to 1990 the "Los Cañones" shantytown; communication tower; abandoned space; 360 degree lookout point over the city of Barcelona; and, finally, open-air museum. The Turó de la Rovira is all of these things. The restoration highlights the scars left by everything that has existed on the site; it permits the appreciation of the different uses that a space can have depending on the era. We could say that there is an appropriation of the space depending on the interests of society at any particular moment. The new use of the space, superimposed now on top of the previous ones, is an imperceptible frame that makes visible everything that has gone before. The Turó de la Rovira has changed from being a space in movement, everyday, to a space for contemplating history, an open-air museum and, for the city, a lookout point.

PROJECT INFORMATION

SANTA MARÍA DE LOS REYES CONVENT
MGM, Morales de Giles Arquitectos
C/ Santiago 33, Seville
1,680 m^2
2015

Technical architect: Francisco Duarte
Construction supervision: Francisco Alcoba
Health and safety supervision: Francisco Sanchez
Landscape: Juan José Guerrero Álvarez, REDIAM
Structure: Paco Duarte y Asociados
Mechanical systems: INSUR JG

RE-HABITAR
Escuela Técnica Superior de Arquitectura de Toledo
Callejón de Menores 12, Toledo
710 m^2
2015

Client: Toledo School of Architecture, UCLM
Technical architect: Vicente Gómez Padilla

RESTORATION OF THE OLD CHURCH OF CORBERA D'EBRE
Ferran Vizoso, Núria Bordas, Jordi Garriga, David Garcia
Poble Vell, Corbera d'Ebre
Terra Alta, Tarragona
1,050 m^2
1999–2011

Project team: Mónica Company, Giovanni Bautista, Xosé Domínguez
Technical architects: Teresa Arnal, Ernest Valls

INTERMEDIATE HOUSE
Carmen Moreno Álvarez
Carrera del Darro 11, Granada
2009–2017

Architecture students: Pablo Fernández Carpintero, Juan Moreno Romero, María Zurita Elizalde, Carmen Álvarez Vílchez
Mechanical engineering: Ábaco Ingenieros

SAN ISIDRO SUGAR FACTORY
Juan Domingo Santos
Granada
1901–2016

Special thanks to the students and professors of the architecture schools of Granada, Seville, Munich, Rome, Madrid, Valencia, Coimbra, and Barcelona, the International School of Catalonia, the European School of Madrid, and to the directors of the Andalusia Museum of Contemporary Art, the Board of Trustees of the Alhambra and Generalife, the Commission of Industrial Heritage of Andalusia, the Architectural Association, the Office of Architecture and Urban Planning, and to the citizens of Granada and of the world.
Axonometric drawing: Pablo Fernández Carpintero, Paloma Ramírez Sanjuán

CONTEMPORARY ART SPACE IN MADRE DE DIOS CONVENT
Sol 89
María González García, Junjo López de la Cruz
San José 4, Seville
830 m^2
2012–2013

Project team: Andrés Pino
Mechanical systems: Alejandro Cabanas

ESPACIO BARBERÍ
RCR Arquitectes
Rafael Aranda, Carme Pigem, Ramon Vilalta
Fontanella 26, Olot, Girona
2004–2006

REI MARTÍ WATER RESERVOIR
ARCHIKUBIK
Marc Chamalank, Miquel Lacasta,
Carmen Santana + Enllaç arquitectònic Arc-Roig
Bellesguard 14, Barcelona
966 m²
2014–2015

Construction supervision: ARCHIKUBIK
Jero Steinger, project architect
Building process management: Francesco Belart, technical architect
Structure: Eskubi Turró Arquitectes
Acoustic design: David Casadevall

OLIVA ARTÉS
BAAS
Jordi Badia
Espronceda 144, Barcelona
1,450 m²
2014–2015

Project team: Jero Gutiérrez, Eva Damià, Viki Llinares, Cristina Anglés, Andreu Egido

COLLAGE HOUSE
bosch.capdeferro arquitectures
Elisabet Capdeferro Pla, Ramon Bosch Pagès
Calle de la Força, 19
Ballesteries 30–32, Girona
1,515 m²
2003–2010

Project team:
Josep Grau, construction manager
Joan Anglada Ruiz, project architect
Blázquez Guanter, structural consultants

CASA DEL CONDESTABLE
Tabuenca&Leache
Fernando Tabuenca, Jesús Leache
Calle Mayor 2, Pamplona, Navarra
6,820 m²
2005–2008

Project team:
Belén Beguiristain Lahuerta, architect
Arturo Pérez Espinosa, technical architect
José Luis Sola, technical architect
Structural design: Susana Iturralde, Raúl Escrivá, Mikel Landa
Engineering: GE & Asociados
Archaeology: Gabinete Trama
Restoration: Sagarte, S.L.
Historical research: Asunción Orbe
Axonometric drawing: bcsarchitects.wix.com

CASAL BALAGUER CULTURAL CENTER
Flores & Prats + Duch-Pizá
Ricardo Flores, Eva Prats, Sé Duch, Xisco Pizá
Unión 3, Palma de Mallorca
3,675 m^2
1996–2014

Fabrizio Barozzi, project leader
Project team: Caterina Anastasia, Ankur Jain, Els van Meerbeek, Cristian Zanoni, Carlos Bedoya, Guido Fiszson, Ellen Halupczok, Julia Taubinguer, Paula Ávila, Nicolás Chara, Eugenia Troncoso, Israel Hernando, Hernán Barbalace, Benedikte Mikkelsen, Mar Garrido, Celia Carroll, Jorge Casajús, Juan Membrive, Oriol Valls, Tanja Dietsch, Sergi Madrid, Sergio Muiños, Lucas Wilson, Anna Reidy, Maria Amat Busquets, Fabrizia Cortellini, Veronica Baroni, Elvire Thouvenot, Carlotta Bonura, Francesca Tassi-Carboni, Tomás Kenny
Technical architect: Anastasio de la Peña

PILGRIMS' MUSEUM
Manuel Gallego Jorreto
Plaza de las Platerías, Santiago de Compostela
3,500 m^2
2008–2012

Architects: Eduardo Cruz, Julio Grande, Alejandro Álvarez
Architecture student: Cándido Couceriro
Drafter: Lourdes Mosquera
Structural design: Javier Estévez Cimadevila
Mechanical systems: Quicler-López
Axonometric drawing: M. Gallego-Tectónica

GRANADA SCHOOL OF ARCHITECTURE
Víctor López Cotelo
Campo del Príncipe, Granada
13,785 m^2
1998–2015

Project management: Pedro Morales Falmouth (phase 1), Juan Uribarri Sánchez-Marco (phase 2)
Assistant architects, construction: Flora López-Cotelo, Isabel Mira Pueo, Rafael Medina Iglesias, Elena Lucio Bello, Francisco García Toribio
Assistant architects, design: Juan Manuel Vargas Funes, Jesús de la Fuente Moreno, Francisco García Toribio, Álvaro Guerrero Aragoneses, Flora López-Cotelo, Rafael Medina Iglesias, Isabel Mira Pueo, Pedro Morales Falmouth, Jesús Placencia Porrero, Ana Torres Solana, Juan Uribarri Sánchez-Marco, Frank Furrer, César Leal
Restoration: Kika Martín, Irene Orueta
Structural design: José María Fernández, Ingeniero de Caminos Proyectos de Ingeniería y Arquitectura S.L.
Mechanical systems: J.G. Ingenieros
Axonometric drawing: Echeocai

LIDIA CINEMA
Núria Salvadó, David Tapias
L'acarredor 16, Riudecols
20 m^2
2003–2011

Mechanical systems: Josep Ma Delmuns
Technical architect: Vicens López

LUZ HOUSE
ARQUITECTURA-G
Jonathan Arnabat, Jordi Ayala-Bril, Aitor Fuentes, Igor Urdampilleta
Cilleros, Extremadura
136 m^2
2011–2013

Structure: Toni Casas

NEW SPACE IN CASA NOVA
EXTUDIO
Toni Gelabert Amengual, Néstor Montenegro Mateos
Camí de Sa Casa Nova, Lloret de Vistalegre (Mallorca), Baleares
36 m^3
2014–2015

Coordinating architect: Pepe Herrero
Project team: Cristian Cabaña, Juan Rol

ALL I OWN HOUSE
PKMN Architectures
Madrid
2014

Structural engineering: Mecanismo S.L.
Mechanical systems: Alberto Espinosa

SUSALOON
elii
Uriel Fogué, Eva Gil, Carlos Palacios
Madrid
23 m^2
2014

Project team: Pedro Pablo García, Alicia García, Claire Laborde

HOUSE INSIDE A HOUSE
Josep Ferrando
C. de la Torre 8, Sant Cugat, Barcelona
225 m^2
2011–2014

Project team: Marta Arias, Carol Castilla, Jordi Pérez, Félix Platero, Goun Park, TaeGweon Kim, Adrià Orriols, Clara Vidal, Borja Rodríguez
Technical architect: Toledo-Villarreal
Structural engineering: Josep Nello

SAN JERÓNIMO 17
CUAC Arquitectura
Javier Castellano Pulido, Tomás García Píriz
Calle San Jerónimo 17, Granada
146 m^2
2015

Project team:
Álvaro Castellano Pulido, architect
Fernando Álvarez de Cienfuegos, graphic designer
Technical architect: Miguel Ángel Jiménez Dengra

THE CULTURAL FACTORY IN MATADERO
OSS, Office for Strategic Spaces
Ángel Borrego Cubero
Paseo de la Chopera 14, Matadero, Madrid
484 m2
2013–2014

RENOVATION AND ADAPTATION OF A HOME-STUDIO
MAIO
Guillermo López Ibáñez, Anna Puigjaner Barberá
Bruniquer 23, Barcelona
197 m^2
2012

Studio team: Anna Puigjaner Barberá, Guillermo López Ibáñez, Alfredo Lérida, Maria Charneco

STUDIO IN LACY STREET
Sauquet Architectes
Roger Sauquet, Guillem Bosch, Xavier Sauquet, Berta Fusté, Anna Bonet
Lacy 38, Sabadell, Barcelona
2014

CARRERAS-MÚGICA GALLERY OF CONTEMPORARY ART
estudio Herreros
Heros 2, Bilbao, Vizcaya
900 m^2
2013–2014

Local architect: E2 Arquitectura, Germán Hurtado
Project architect: José Baldo
Project team: Carmen Antón, María Franco, Abraham Piñate, Víctor Lacima, Leonardo Tamargo
Structural design: Eduardo Barrón
Lighting design: Antón Amann

SINGLE-FAMILY HOUSE IN TEBRA
Guadalupe Piñera Manso, Jesús Irisarri Castro
O Casal, San Salvador de Tebra
Tomiño, Pontevedra
290 m^2
2006–2011

Project team: Martín Rivas, Francisco Fariña
Technical architect: Manuel Tabeada Acevedo
Structural design: Ibinco S.L., Exinor S.L.

ATRIO RELAIS CHÂTEAUX
Mansilla + Tuñón
Luis Moreno Mansilla, Emilio Tuñón Álvarez
Plaza de San Mateo, Cáceres
3,000 m^2
2005–2013

Project team: Carlos Martínez de Albornoz, Andrés Regueiro, Marceline Ruckstuhl, Carlos Brage, David Orkand, Arabella Masson, Elke Gmyrek, Ignacio Peydro, Teresa Cruz, Anna Partenheimer, Joao Leitao, Bárbara Silva, Carlos Cerezo
Technical architect: Fernando Benito Fernández Cabello

DENOMINACIÓN DE ORIGEN RIBERA DEL DUERO HEADQUARTERS
Barozzi / Veiga
Fabrizio Barozzi, Alberto Veiga
Hospital 6, Roa, Burgos
4,146 m²
2006–2008

Project team: Agnieszka Samsel, Paulo Lopes, Tanja Oppowa, Antonio Pinto, Antonis Vourexakis
Structural design: BoMA S.L.
Mechanical engineering: Grupo JG S.A.

TWO HOUSES IN OROPESA
Paredes Pedrosa Arquitectos
Ángela García de Paredes, Ignacio Pedrosa
Iglesia 1 + 3, Oropesa, Toledo
316 m²
2011–2015

Project team: Álvaro Rábano, Clemens Eichner, Roberto Lebrero, Blanca Leal
Construction supervision: Inés Cobisa
Structural design: Alfonso G. Gaite, GoGAITE S.L.
Mechanical engineering: Nieves Plaza

FINE ARTS MUSEUM OF ASTURIAS
Francisco Mangado
Santa Ana 1–3, Oviedo, Asturias
10,702 m²
2006–2014

Project team: Idoia Alonso, Luís Alves, Ricardo Ventura, Sergio Rio Tinto, Abraham Piñate, Hugo Pereira, André Guerreiro, Diogo Lacerda, Justo López García
Technical architects: Luis Pahissa, Fernando Pahissa, Alberto López Diez, Ángel Garcia Garcia
Structural and mechanical engineering: IDoM
Lighting design: ALS Lighting

BUILDING AND URBAN SPACE SURROUNDING THE TEMPLE OF DIANA
José María Sánchez García
Romero Leal / Santa Catalina, Mérida, Extremadura
2,159 m²
2005–2011

Project team: Enrique García-Margallo Solo de Zaldivar, Rafael Fernández Caparros, Daniel González Guerrero, Maribel Torres Gómez, Laura Rojo Valdivielso, Mariló Sánchez García, Marta Cabezón López, Mafalda Ambrósio, Francisco Sánchez García, José García-Margallo, Carmen Leticia Huerta, Julia Ternström
Technical architects: Ángel García Blázquez. Fernando Benito Fernández Cabello
Structural design: CDE Ingenieros, GoGAITE S.L.
Mechanical engineering: Aro Consultores

OE HOUSE
Fake Industries Architectural Agonism + Aixopluc
Cristina Goberna, Urtzi Grau, David Tapias
Camí de Sant Antoni 26, Alforja, Tarragona
330 m²
2010–2015

Project team:
Ricard Pau, architecture
Jordi Royo, technical architect
Josep Maria Delmuns, engineer

SAN LUCAS PAVILION
FRPO Rodríguez & Oriol Arquitectos
Pablo Oriol, Fernando Rodríguez
Madrid
110 m²
2013–2014

Project team: Inés Olavarrieta, María Domínguez, Carmen Sanz
Structural design: Pablo Urbano

SWIMMING POOL IN MACEDA
trespes.arquitectos
Alberte Pérez Rodríguez, Carlos Mosquera del Palacio, Enrique Iglesias Lima
2014–2015

Project team: Alejandra Elvira García Macías, Ylenia López Giménez
Structural design: Francisco Carballo

SCHOOL IN LA MILAGROSA
Pereda Pérez Arquitectos
Carlos Pereda Iglesias, Óscar Pérez Silanes
Plaza Alfredo Floristán, Pamplona
1630 m^2
2009–2012

Project team: Teresa Gridilla Saavedra, Sara Andorinho
Structural design: Fernando Sarría
Technical architect: Marc Buxó, GLSL

GLÒRIES INFORMATION POINT
peris+toral.arquitectes
Marta Peris Eugenio, José Manuel Toral, Izaskun González
Plaça de les Glòries, Barcelona
300 m^2
2014

Project team: Ana Espinosa, Leticia Soriano
Technical architect: ICC S.L.
Structural design: Manel Fernández
Mechanical engineering: Jaume Pastor

LUDE HOUSE
Grupo Aranea
Francisco Leiva Ivorra, Martín López Robles
Cehegín, Murcia
128 m^2
2007–2011

Technical architect: Antonio Martínez Sánchez
Ábaco Aparejadores

PAVILION FOR AN EXISTING HOUSE
Flexo Arquitectura
Aixa del Rey García, Tomeu Ramis Frontera, Barbara Vich Arrom
Barcelona
28 m^2
2013–2014

CYCLOPEAN HOUSE
Ensamble Studio
Antón García-Abril, Debora Mesa
240 m^2
2014–2016

Project team: Javier Cuesta, Ricardo Sanz, Borja Soriano, Walter Cuccuru, Massimo Loia, Juanjo Fernández, Valentina Giacomini, Marietta Spyrou, Federica Zunino, Marian Stanislav, Chung-Wen Wu, Yannis Karababas
Structural engineering: Jesús Huerga

PIER 57 INTERIM PROJECT
Jose María de Churtichaga + Cayetana de la Quadra-Salcedo
New York City
2013

Project team: Mauro Doncel, Natanael López

HOUSE 1014
HARQUITECTES
David Lorente, Josep Ricart, Xavier Ros, Roger Tudó
Granollers, Barcelona
673 m²
2010–2014

Project team: Blai Cabrero Bosch, Montse Fornés Guàrdia
Technical architect: Carla Piñol Moreno, Ramon Anton
Interior design: Fátima Vilaseca
Structural engineering: DSM Arquitectes
Systems engineering: Igetech / Àbac Enginyers
Landscape: Anna Esteve

MATADERO MADRID, BUILDING 8B
Arturo Franco
Paseo de la Chopera 14, Matadero, Madrid
1.000 m²
2009

Project team:
Diego Castellanos, interior architect
Yolanda Ferrero, architect
Jose H. Largo Díaz, technical architect

NEW ACCESS TO THE HISTORIC CENTER OF GIRONELLA
Carles Enrich Arquitectura + Urbanisme
Gironella
2013–2015

Project team: Adriana Campmany, Àngel Rosales, Ada Sánchez
Structural design: MA+SAad

GRAO CEMETERY
Inés García Clariana
El Grao, Valencia
2012

Project team: Shunichiro Higashi, Enrico Cavallo, Mónica Ibáñez

JORDI AND AFRICA'S HOUSE
TEd'A arquitectes
Jaume Mayol, Irene Péreza
Montuïri, Mallorca
311 m²
2010–2015

Project team: Toni Ramis, Tomeu Mateu, Margherita Lurani
Technical architect: Guillem Mas
Structural engineering: Raimon Farré
Security and health: Bernat Parera

HOUSE IN GAÜSES
Anna & Eugeni Bach
Afores, Gaüses, Vilopriu
90 m²
2007

Technical architect: Alfons Brugué

HABITAT STOREHOUSE
Ferran Grau Valldosera, Nicola Regusci, Xavier Bustos Serrat
Tarragona
20 m²
2008–2010

Project team:
Isabella Pintani, architect
Raimon Grau, engineer
Javier Monte, structural design
Albert Faus, technical architect

AUZO FACTORY IRAZÁBAL-MATIKO
Suárez Santas Arquitectos
Asier Santas Torres, Luis Suárez Mansilla
Matiko, Bilbao
2014

Technical architect: Julián Echevarría

3X1 / 3 MUNICIPAL HEALTH CENTERS IN MADRID
Entresitio
María Hurtado de Mendoza Wahrolén, César Jiménez de Tejada Benavides,
José María Hurtado de Mendoza Wahrolén
San Blas + Usera + Villaverde, Madrid
1,920 m^2
2005–2007

Project team: Jorge Martínez, Laura Frutos, Vincent Rodriguez, Fabrice Quemeneur, Filipe Minderico, Clara Rodríguez, Marco Plazzogna, Álvar Ruiz Villanueva, María Urigoitia Villanueva
Structure and mechanical systems: Geasyt AT, Juan Carlos Corona Ruiz, David Gil Crespo

80 HOUSES IN SALOU
Toni Gironés
Sector 5 Emprius-Sud
Salou, Tarragona
8,670 m^2
2007–2009

Technical architect: Brufau, Cusó S.L.P.
Structural engineers: Xavier Saura (Orpa S.A.)

57 HOUSING UNITS ON THE ETSAV CAMPUS
DATAAE + HARQUITECTES
Carrer de Pere Serra, San Cugat del Vallès
3,670 m^2
2009–2010

Project team (DATAAE): Claudi Aguiló Aran, Albert Domingo Ollé (Data AE)
Project team (HARQUITECTES) David Lorente Ibáñez, Josep Ricart Ulldemolins, Xavier Ros Majó, Roger Tudó Galí

RENOVATION OF MALPICA HARBOR
CREUSeCARRASCO
Juan Creus Andrade, Covadonga Carrasco López
Port of Malpica, A Coruña
13,710 m^2
2006–2009

Project team: Francisco Rosell, Estefanía Vázquez, Roi Feijoo, Belén Salgado, Alexandre Antunes, Bárbara Mesquita, Laura Coladas
Structure: Thema

ENVIRONS OF THE BORN MARKET
Vora Arquitectura
Pere Buil, Toni Riba
Born Market, Barcelona
14,000 m^2
2009–2013

Project team: Adrià Guardiet, Miquel Camps, Jordi Riba, Eva Cotman, Ondrej Fabian
Mechanical engineering, specifications, and quantity surveying: PCG Arquitectura e Ingeniería

PEDRA DA RÁ OVERLOOK
Carlos Seoane
Riveira, A Coruña
3,300 m^2
2013–2016

Project team: María Montero, Eduardo Castrillón, Oscar Fuertes, Adrián Río, Raquel Ferreiro
Technical architect: Luis Romero
Engineering: Marcial de la Fuente

TURÓ DE LA ROVIRA
Jansana, de la Villa, de Paauw Arquitectes S.L.P.
AAUP Jordi Romero Associats S.L.P.
Turó de la Rovira, Barcelona
2009–2014

Technical architect: MOR Arquitectura Técnica, Modest Mor
AAUP architect: Guillem Gascón
Archaeology: Jordi Ramos
SGS, LIMONIUM S.L.
Eduardo Soler
History Museum of Barcelona, Democratic Memorial

PHOTOGRAPHIC CREDITS

By order of appearance of the photographers, grouped by works.

Jesús Granada: Santa María de los Reyes Convent, Lude House.

Ángel Baltanás: Re-Habitar.

José Hevia: Restoration of the Old Church of Corbera d'Ebre, Collage House, Lidia Cinema, Luz House, Renovation And Adaptation of a Home-Studio, Studio in Lacy Street, Building and Urban Space Surrounding the Temple Of Diana, OE House, Glòries Information Point.

Carmen Moreno Álvarez: Intermediate House.

Juan Domingo Santos: San Isidro Sugar Factory.

Fernando Alda: Contemporary Art Space in Madre de Dios Convent, San Jerónimo 17.

Sophie Mayer: Espacio Barberí.

Adrià Goula: Rei Martí Water Deposit, Casal Balaguer Cultural Center, House Inside a House, Carreras-Múgica Gallery of Contemporary Art, House 1014, New Acces to the Historic Center of Gironella, 57 Housing Units on the ETSAV Campus, Environs of the Born Market.

Marcela Grassi: Oliva Artés.

Luis Prieto: Casa del Condestable.

Manuel González Vicente: Pilgrim's Museum.

Luís Casals: Granada School of Architecture.

Coke Bastrina: New Space in Casa Nova.

Javier de Paz: All I Own House.

Miguel de Guzmán: Susaloon, San Lucas Pavilion.

Simona Rota: The Cultural Factory in Matadero Madrid.

Santos-Diez: Single-Family House in Tebra.

Luís Asín: Atrio Relais Châteaux, Two Houses in Oropesa.

Pedro Pegenaute: Fine Arts Museum of Asturias, School in La Milagrosa.

trespes.arquitectos: Swimming Pool in Maceda.

Ensamble Studio: Cyclopean House.

Churtichaga: Pier 57 Interim Project.

Carlos Fernández: Matadero Madrid–Building 8B.

Mariela Apollonio: Grao Cemetery.

Ted'A arquitectes: Jordi and Africa's House.

Jordi Bernadó: House in Gaüses.

Rafael Vargas: Habitat Storehouse.

Roland Halbe: 3X1 / 3 Municipal Health Centers in Madrid.

Xoan Piñón: Renovation of Malpica Harbor.

Héctor Santos: Pedra da Rá Overlook.

Lourdes Jansana: Turó de la Rovira.

UN
FIN
ISHED

Housing Development Neumünsterallee, Zurich, Switzerland 121
2003–07

The building turns a corner at the intersection of Neumünsterallee and Signau-strasse, creating a sunny garden area between its two wings that faces southeast. In addition, portions cut out of the overall volume form small courtyards on three sides, resulting in a meandering shape that links outside and inside spaces. One of the cutouts faces the morning sun and the garden, another the noonday sun and the avenue of plane trees, and the third the evening sun and the gardens of the villas opposite. Bridge-like balconies frame the courtyards, emphasizing the main volume of the building and, at the same time, offering views into its depths. Thanks to these "balcony bridges," the courtyards, which measure approximately 7.5 by 8.5 meters, receive daylight not only from above but from the side as well.

The apartments angle around the courtyards, thereby substantially enlarging the sense of space therein. The three main stories accommodate two 5.5-room units facing the East and West Courts and two 4.5-room units facing the South Court; the top floor holds one 4-room unit facing the East Court, one 2.5-room unit facing the West Court, and a 7-room unit facing the South Court.

The courtyards allow optimal use to be made of the building's considerable depth, because they ensure that the living spaces as well as the kitchens and the large bathrooms can all be supplied with natural daylight. The heart of each flat is a spacious hallway. Laterally illuminated from the courtyard, it is a link between the private bedrooms and the living room. Its use is not defined, but it can function, for example, as a dining room or study, or provide space for children to play. The living room opens onto the lateral terrace and the outside and has direct access to the kitchen, which also faces the courtyard.

The ground floor is lowered slightly below street level so that a half flight of stairs and a ramp lead down to the large lobby of the building, which is illuminated from the central courtyard and provides access to the two circulation cores. There are also studios that can be accessed directly from the lobby and rented as office space or for recreational activities.

The load-bearing structure of the building consists of concrete walls and slabs. Wood/metal windows, 20-centimeter-thick thermal insulation, and plaster skim on rear-ventilated cladding slabs form the shell of the building, which meets the Minergie® (energy-saving) standard.

In collaboration with the artist Adrian Schiess, the walls in the courtyards were coated with silvery paint to "guide the light," while the outside façades are painted a darker gray. The lobby is rendered in a luminous copper color, and the spectrum of iridescent "light-suffused" shades continues inside the flats,where the doors of the built-in wardrobes have been given a high-gloss, mother-of-pearl finish.

A pool of water in the central courtyard reflects the light from the sky and forms the focal point of the entrance area. The other courtyards are planted with tall, delicately leafed ash trees. The slightly staggered levels of the garden each have their own vegetation. Ground-covering evergreen shrubs and grouped bushes form together with the preserved garden wall and wrought-iron fence the traditional front garden area. The area to the southeast, designated both for adults and for children at play, consists of a grassy lawn with groups of trees.

Color concept

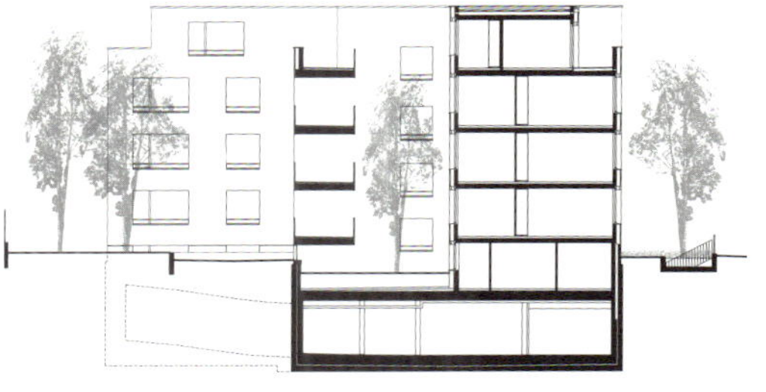

Section through light courtyard and terraces

Housing Development Neumünsterallee, Zurich, Switzerland

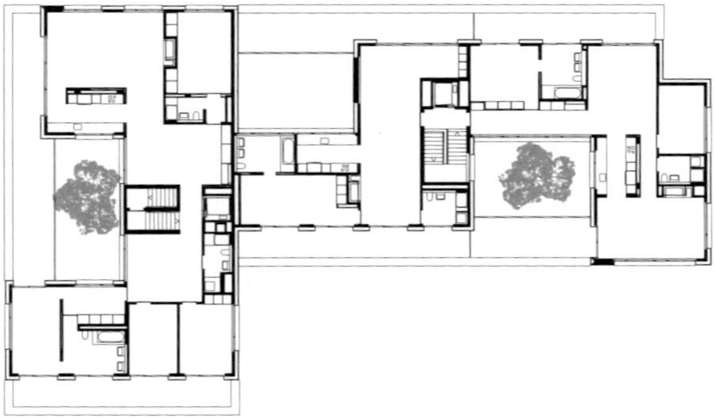

4th floor

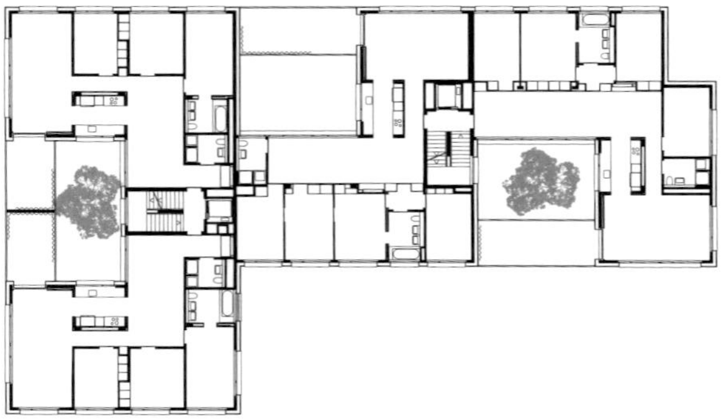

2nd and 3rd floors

Ground floor

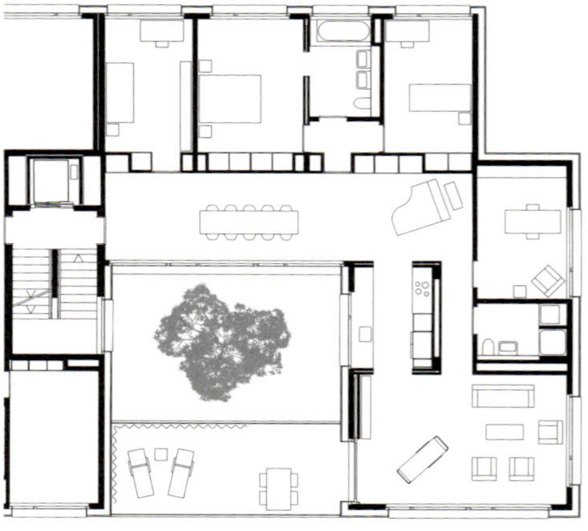

Northeast apartment, 1st–3rd floors

Northwest apartment, 1st–3rd floors

Housing Development Brunnenhof, Zurich, Switzerland 135
2003–07

The former, noise-exposed three-story apartment buildings owned by the Foundation for Large Families in Zurich have been replaced by two slightly angled, elongated volumes of different heights. The larger, six-story building follows Hofwiesenstrasse but is oriented toward the park, which it shields from the street and hence from traffic noise. The smaller, four- to five-story building on Brunnenhofstrasse is in a certain sense within the park, surrounded by green on both sides with its height corresponding to that of the neighboring buildings. Both buildings are conceived as "stacks" of horizontal slabs which cantilever to varying degrees and form generous balconies on the park side.

For the noise-affected building on Hofwiesenstrasse, access to the apartments is via longitudinally arranged staircases and spacious entryways that adjoin the eat-in kitchens. All bedrooms face the quiet park side and are connected by a projecting balcony. The living rooms extend through the apartment, facing both east and west and giving onto the park-side balconies.

Within the smaller Brunnenhofstrasse building, the living rooms are positioned along the façade and look onto the park to the south and southeast via adjoining balcony areas. In the four-story north- and south-facing part of the building, the eat-in kitchens are connected to the living rooms on the south side, while in the angled part of the building the kitchens enjoy the evening sun.

A circuit-like layout grants all apartment types spaciousness, freedom of movement for both children and adults, and enhanced flexibility of use. The latter is further augmented in the ground floor apartments by means of extra rooms between them that can be used by either apartment. The entrance lobbies on the ground floor are connecting rooms that link to the park and provide space for strollers, scooters, and toys. The naturally lit laundry and drying rooms are located in the basement, adjacent to the stairs.

A kindergarten and nursery are housed at the end of both buildings where the pathway to the park is situated. A multi-purpose common room takes the most prominent position at the corner between street and pathway. A continuous hedge along the street creates a green zone that provides the necessary privacy for the slightly elevated ground floor apartments. The park-facing apartments are elevated by half a story to allow the inclusion of a garden and play area between the park and the building. The hedges that run alongside the building approaches establish the border between these zones and the park.

The façades are formed by the balconies and the concrete bands that wrap horizontally around the building. Between them, floor-to-ceiling windows alternate with colored glass panels, joining together with sliding glass shades to create an interplay of reflecting and matt, opaque and translucent or transparent surfaces. The color concept was developed together with the artist Adrian Schiess. Facing the street, the glazing is dark blue and violet, while toward the park the tonality flows over large areas from blue tones to orange to yellow. The impression of the fluid, changing play of colors is enhanced by the varying positions of the sliding elements—ultimately the residents modify and create new color compositions every day, even every hour.

Color studies

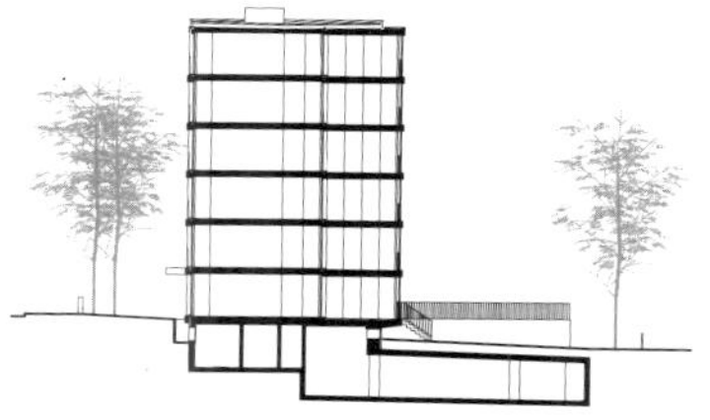

Section through building on Hofwiesenstrasse H3

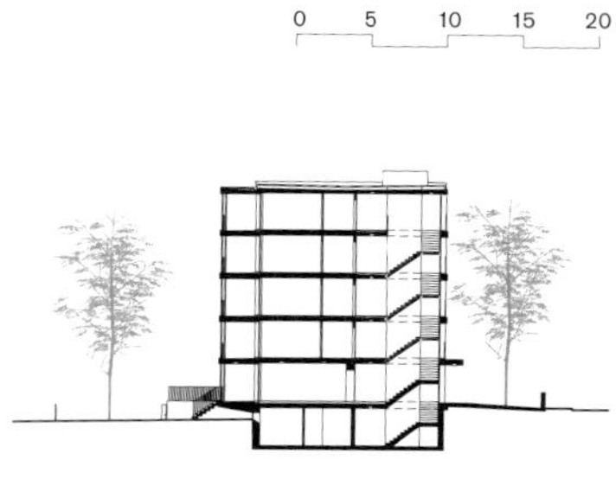

Section through building on Brunnenhofstrasse B7

Typical floor plan with surroundings

6.5-room apartment, building on Hofwiesenstrasse H4

Typical floor plans

0 1 2 3 4 5

6.5-room apartment, building on Brunnenhofstrasse B6

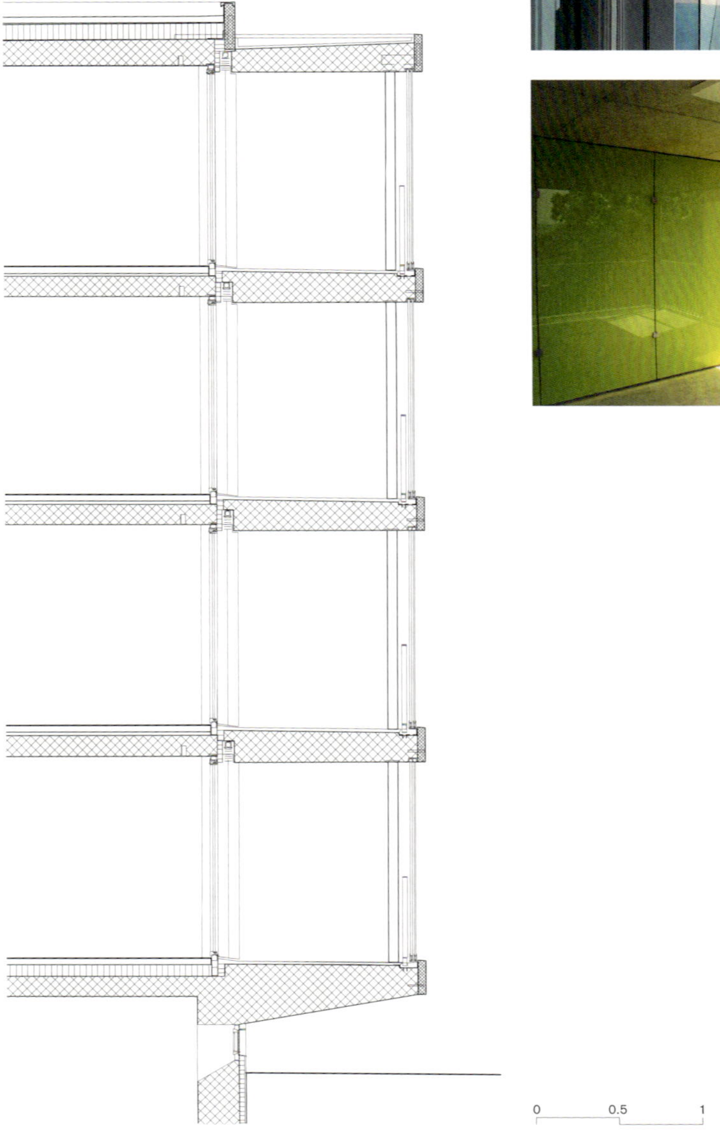

Construction detail

Three Single-Family Row Houses, Rüschlikon, Switzerland 115

2002–05

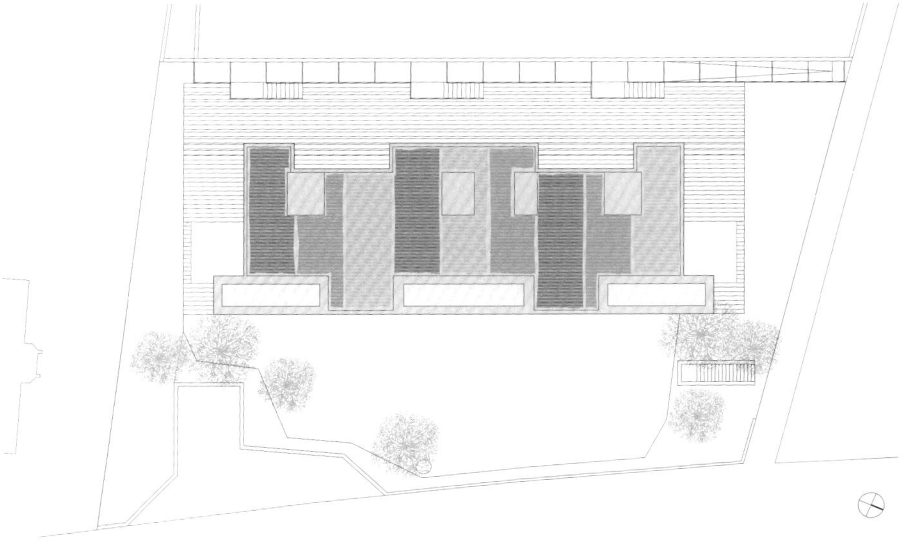

The building, comprising three residential units, is a longitudinal, flat volume set in the middle of the property parallel to the lake, the street, and the retaining wall at the rear of the plot. Two stories of balconies running the entire length of the lakeside façade include cantilevered indoor rooms that extend beyond the length of the building on both sides.

The enclosed slope-side entrance area is defined by the building and the steel trellis fence overgrown with hanging plants, and is accessed via a raised path and staircase along the painted retaining wall. Projecting volumes mark and protect the three entrances, which access the units on the middle floor.

The building consists of three floors, with a ground floor built into the slope and a parking garage underneath. The living and dining areas are situated on the top floor of the building to take maximum advantage of the lake view. On the floor below, in addition to the entrance, there are two large rooms of different sizes, which can be used as studies, guest rooms, or bedrooms. There are two more rooms on the ground floor, on garden level.

The loads are borne on the outer walls and the firewalls, allowing residents to individualize the floor plan of each unit. The balcony layer is formed by an open concrete structure, and the façades are clad in rear-ventilated panels seamlessly covered with fine-grained plaster. Metallic silver paint is combined with anodized aluminum window frames, the silvery reflections of the glass parapets, and aluminized fabric blinds to generate a unified "light-charged" effect. The pink of the retaining wall along the access path both contrasts and complements the overall metallic and silver coloring of the building.

Lawns, trees, and bushes form private garden areas protected from the street. Elongated bands of concrete alternate with gravel on the ground of the rear entrance courtyard and the outdoor seating areas. The roof, planted with undulating rows of thyme in various shades of pink, optically extends the gardens of the neighboring buildings above it.

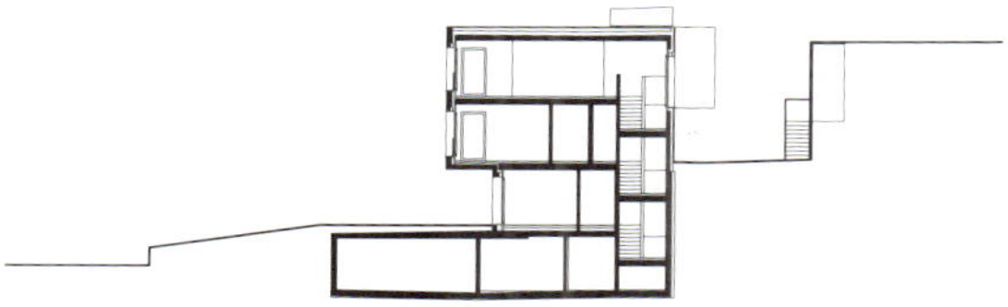

Section A–A

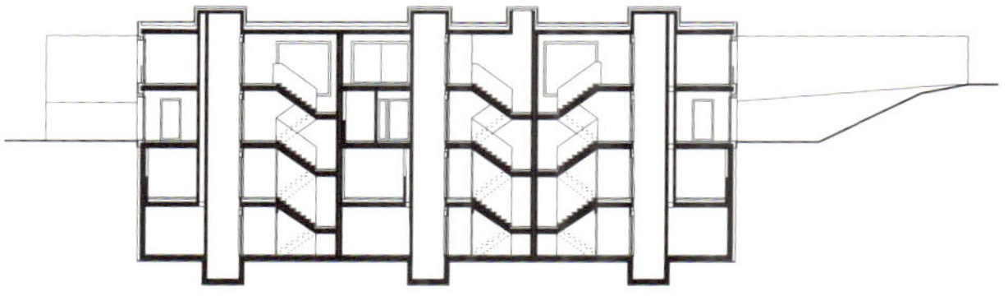

Section B–B

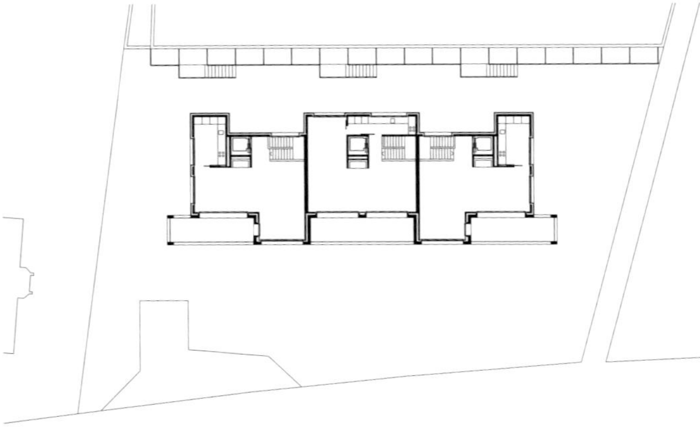

Upper floor

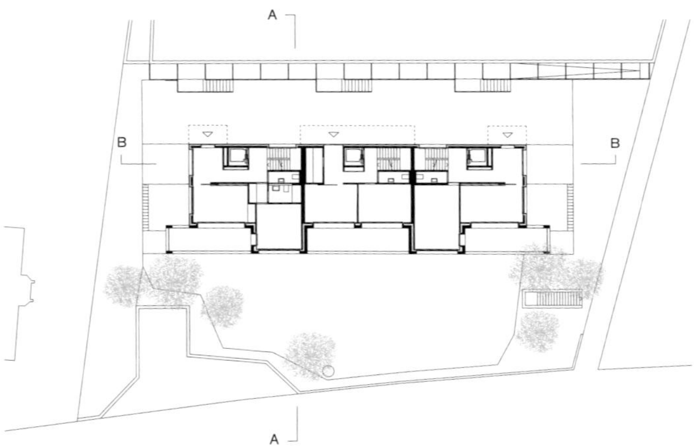

Ground floor

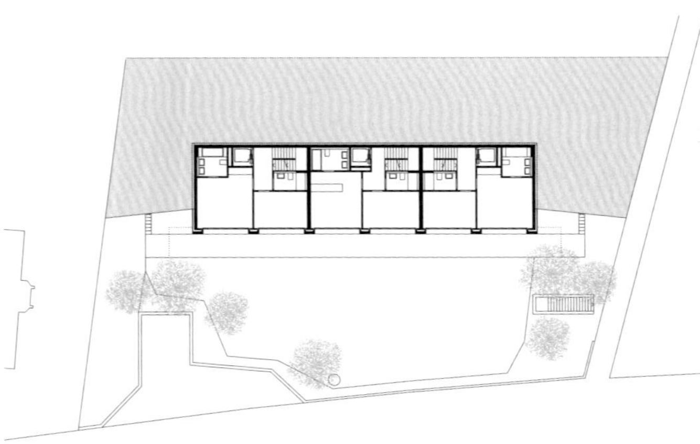

Lower ground floor

Grebler-Weg

Housing Complex Diggelmannstrasse, Zurich, Switzerland 139
2003–07

The small-scale and heterogeneous structure to be found in Zurich's Albisrieden residential district was the reason for dividing up the projected volume into several units. The multiple occupancy buildings with their polygonal volumes and varied footprints are grouped together on one plot. The materials used provide a common link, with the overall color scheme defining the buildings as a group, but also differentiating them and establishing a correlation with the surrounding built environment.

Access to both buildings in the north is gained directly from the street at basement level. A path leads to the building behind, to the south. It forms part of a star-like figure made of large slabs set in a continuous stretch of lawn. Deciduous trees accentuate the open space and provide shady areas for relaxation.

The apartments have between 2 and 4 bedrooms and varied, polygonal floor plans. Generously-sized balconies facing different directions lead off the living areas. The amount of direct sunlight and the degree of privacy required on the balconies can be "adjusted" using curtains. The kitchens can be left open to the living-dining areas or closed with sliding doors.

The façades are articulated by alternating bands of windows and sill-height walls, which link the projecting balconies and recessed roof terraces to form one entity. The rear-ventilated cladding of colored, enameled glass sheets alternates with translucent glazed panels of the same color around the balconies and terraces.

The color scheme was devised in close cooperation with the artist Adrian Schiess. The two colors selected for the smaller buildings closer to the road are a yellowish-green up to sill height and a purple shade for the wall areas between the windows. A combination of pink and beige was chosen for the larger building in the garden to the south. The overlapping reflections across the colored glazed panels interweave not only the "color layers" of the buildings, but also the neighboring structures, trees, and the color of the sky to form part of the optical impression created.

Color studies

Building 2

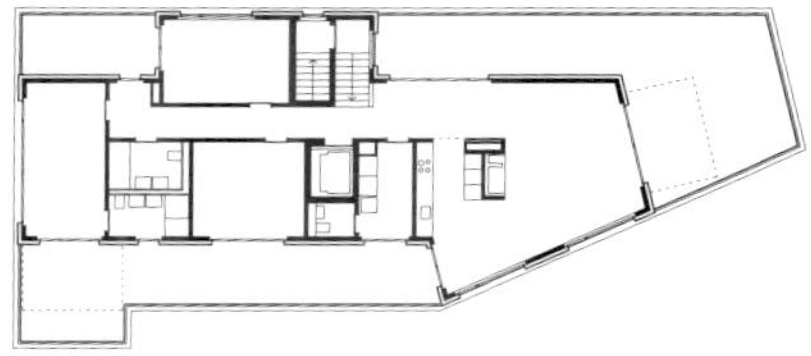

Building 1

Building 3

Top floor

Ground floor

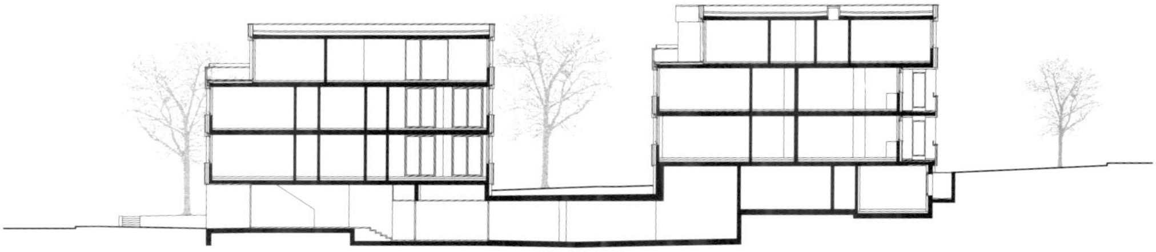

Building 2 Building 3

Section

0 1 2 5 10

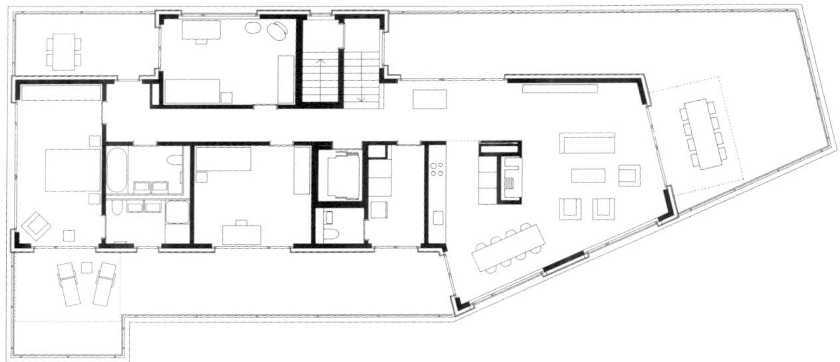

Top floor

0 1 2 3 4 5

Building 1

Ground floor and upper floor (part)

Building 2

Housing Development, Färberei-Areal, Thalwil, Switzerland

House 1, 1998/2005–08 043
Houses 2 and 3, 1998/2008–12 215
House 5, 1998/2005–08 176

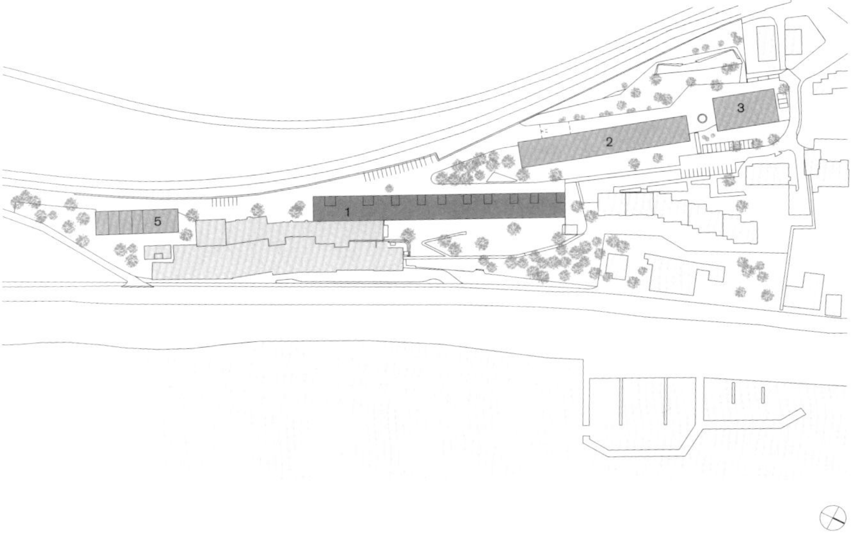

Four new buildings were planned for the site of the former "Färberei," or textile-dyeing factory, to be constructed in successive stages in order to establish an ensemble together with the refurbished "Blue Factory." This former industrial area is thus gradually developing into an urban residential, commercial, and office district. The elongated, cubic buildings are set into the hillside like a fan, creating flowing interim spaces that expand to form plazas. The colors of the buildings were developed during the various construction phases in collaboration with the artist Harald F. Müller.

House 1
In the long, five-story House 1, constructed parallel to the steep slope that descends down to the lake, 35 apartments are arranged in a variable mix of 3.5 to 7.5 rooms. The two floors adjacent to the Blue Factory hold flexibly dividable office spaces, while a day-care center is provided on the ground floor.

A characteristic of the single-story apartments is the arrangement of the rooms around a central living and dining area, with a connection to the kitchen. Each apartment possesses two loggias that are integrated into the building volume and extend the continuous living space toward the lake and to the south. Floor-to-ceiling windows enhance the sense of spaciousness. These let southern light into the rooms and provide vistas over Lake Zurich to the north and the lakeshore opposite. The outdoor spaces in the penthouses are designed as large patios that

not only open to the façade, but also to the sky. Due to the hillside location, the typology changes to duplex apartments on the two lower floors. Here, the daytime area with living and dining rooms and kitchen extends over the entire depth of the upper floor, while the nighttime area with bedrooms facing the lake is situated on the ground floor.

The grid pattern of the monolithic load-bearing exposed concrete structure defines the exterior. The concrete surfaces of the façade are washed in white, while a metallic note is introduced for the components in the façade openings: in the wood-aluminum window frames, in the blinds, and in the glass parapets' subtly reflective surfaces. Glossy silver paint was used for the elevator cores, while the concrete walls of the staircases are painted a matt yellow-green in some areas, and treated with a transparent glaze in others.

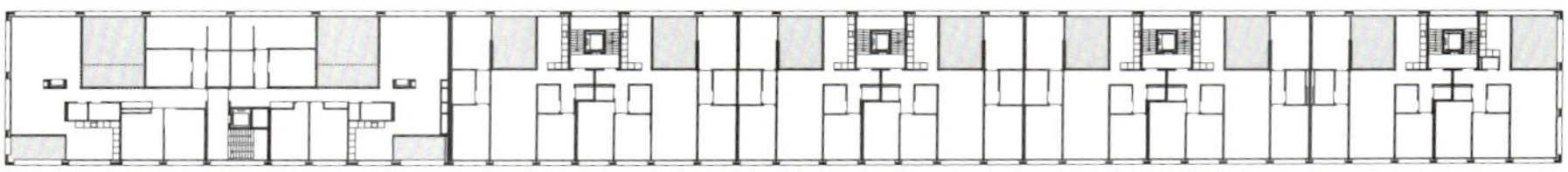

3rd floor

1st floor

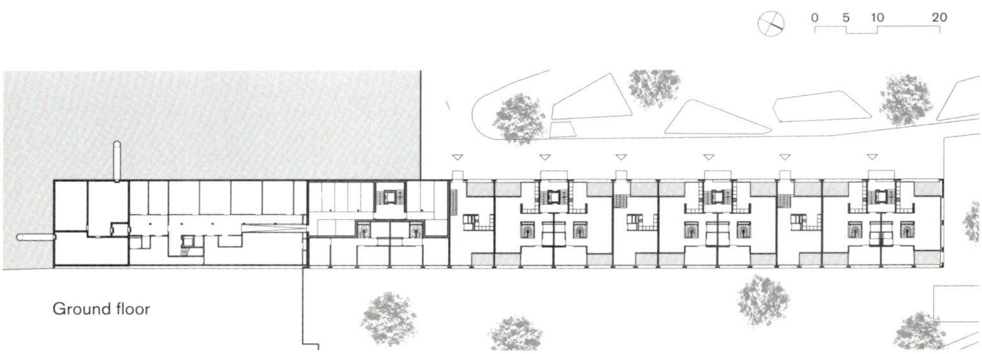

Ground floor

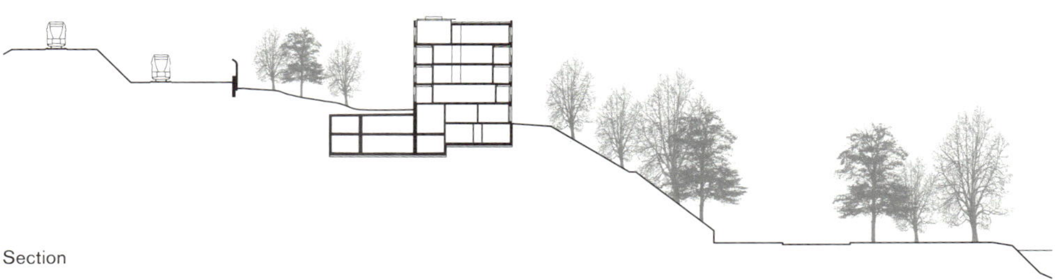

Section

27

5.5-room apartment with patio
3rd floor

5.5-room apartment
3rd floor

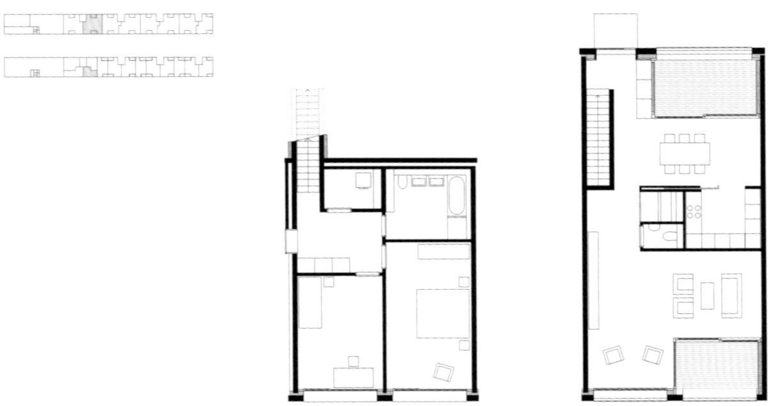

5.5-room duplex apartment
Lower floor and ground floor

House 1

Houses 2 and 3

In the concluding phase of development, two further buildings, with a small park set in front, will complete the ensemble in the northwestern part of the site. In House 2 the emphasis is on smaller, low-cost rental apartments for families, while House 3 focuses on providing housing suitable for older people.

In order to make the most of the sunny southwestern side of the building, which is however exposed to noise, single-story apartments were created for House 2 with a living, cooking, and dining area that runs through the entire depth of the building but which is set at an angle. This floor plan produces a varied assortment of 48 apartments ranging in size from 2.5 to 4.5 rooms. The bathrooms, ancillary areas, and circulation cores are arranged in the central part of each apartment, dividing the living area into two spaces of equal size and hence offering flexible use. In the eastern part of the building the upward slope of the site makes it possible to offer duplex apartments on the ground floor. At the western tip of the building, facing the square, rooms for public use are incorporated into the design.

The compact footprint of House 3 allows for five 2.5- to 5.5-room apartments on each floor. Two apartments are open to the exterior on one side, facing southwest, and two wrap around the corner of the building on the southeast side. The fifth apartment, oriented toward three sides, is located on the northwest side of the building. This floor-plan configuration, incorporating apartments of differing sizes on each floor, coupled with a care facility at ground level, responds primarily to the needs of older residents.

The exterior of both residential blocks uses light beige and pebble-gray glazes. These subdued tones are complemented by brighter colors in the interior stairwells, which are lit from above via skylights.

2.5-room apartment
1st–4th floors

4.5-room apartment
2nd–3rd floors

House 2

Housing Development, Färberei-Areal, Thalwil, Switzerland

Visualizations

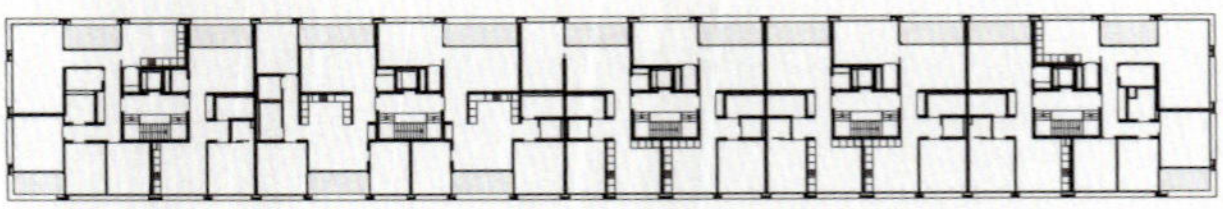

4th floor

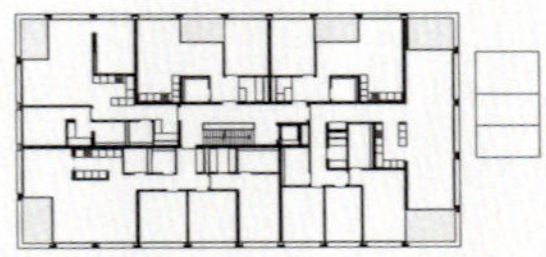

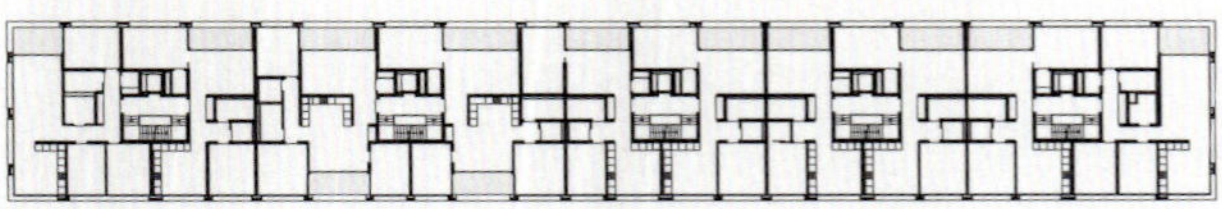

2nd and 3rd floors

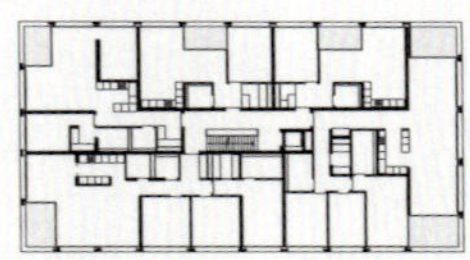

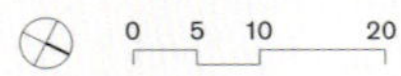

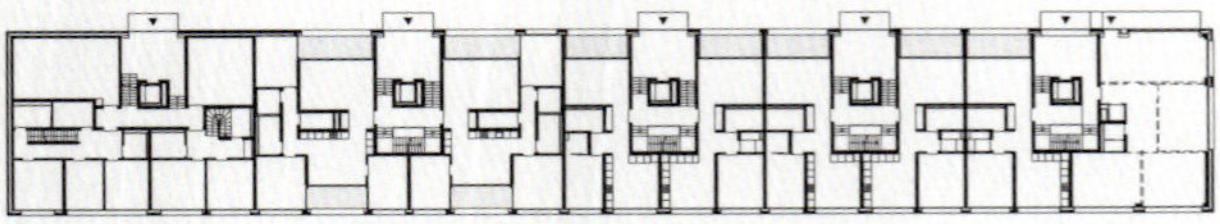

Ground floor

House 2

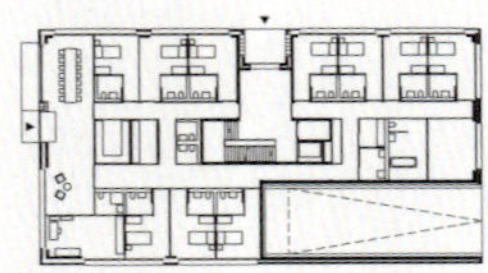

House 3

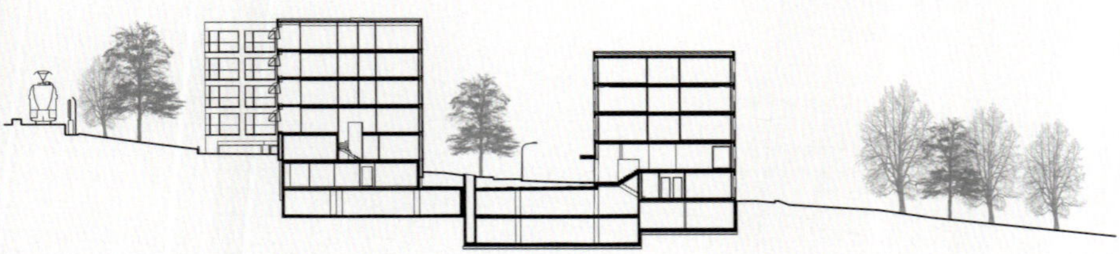

Section

House 5

A site in the southwestern portion of the plot, near the railway tracks and sloping down on two sides, was chosen for a six-story building with eleven condominiums. A range of variously configured single-level units was developed for this building, complemented by specially designed penthouse and duplex apartments. On the upper floors the apartments open to the exterior on three, or even four, sides, affording vistas both over the lake and to the mountain panorama in the south. Due to the steep slope of the site, the apartments on the lower stories are open only on the side facing the lake to the northeast. The design nonetheless incorporates generously proportioned outside areas for all apartments: the two upper apartments enjoy large roof terraces thanks to the slanted form of the building volume, while elsewhere in the building the apartments include either one or two loggias depending on size. In addition, the two ground-level apartments have external seating areas.

Accentuating the play of light in the stairwell, the inner-facing longitudinal wall is painted gold from the top to the bottom of the building, complemented in the entrance area by a pink-painted portion on the facing wall. The load-bearing monolithic exposed concrete façade structure is finished in a brown glaze, while all cutouts in the building volume and all façade openings, loggias, and roof terraces are left unpainted. A subtle golden anodized finish is utilized on the exterior for the wood and aluminum window frames.

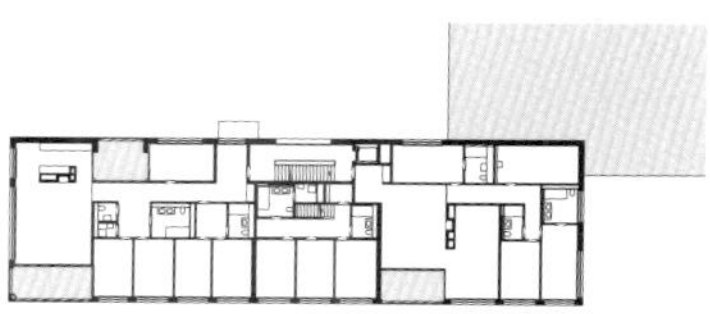

1st floor

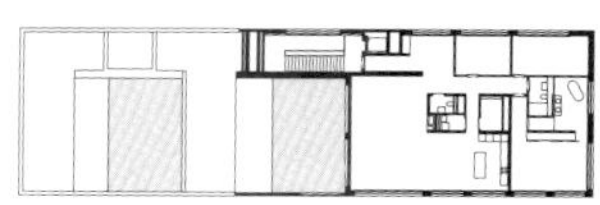

4th floor

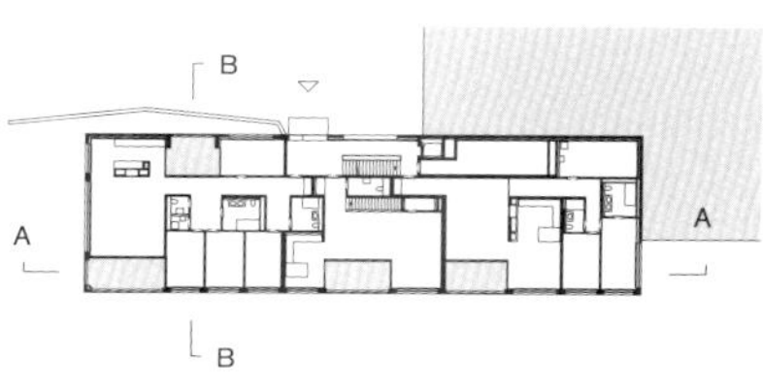

Ground floor

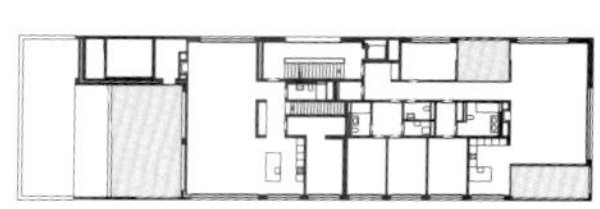

3rd floor

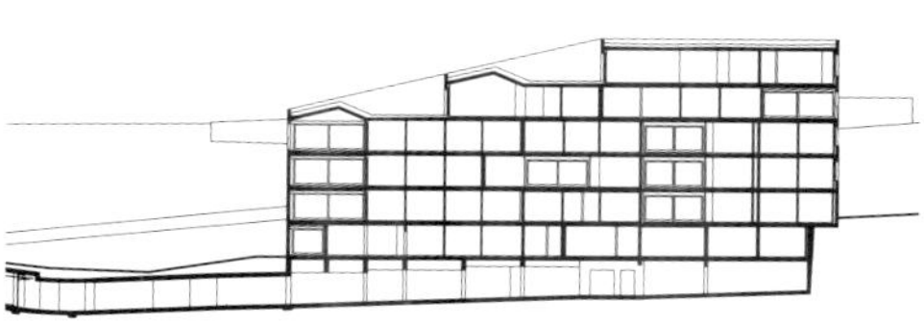

Section A–A

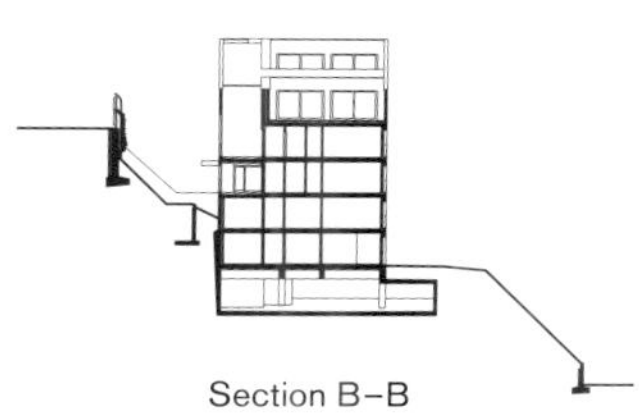

Section B–B

Résidence du Pré-Babel, Geneva, Switzerland, 2003–08 141
Résidence du Parc de Grange-Canal, Geneva, Switzerland, 2003/2007–12 151

The construction of apartment blocks of varying heights and different standards on the former Pré-Babel sportsground and park site pursues the idea of concentrated interventions, aimed at retaining as much open green space around and between the buildings as possible.

The first building phase, Pré-Babel, comprised three apartment blocks 1, 2, and 3 with three stories each, offering a total of twenty-eight condominiums for the high-end market segment. For the second phase, Résidence du Parc de Grange-Canal, three taller buildings with standard apartments were planned, also including subsidized housing in accordance with a special stipulation in Geneva's building regulations. Finding a common architectural language and similar housing typology for all three categories was one of the challenges in developing this park site.

The siting and shape of the buildings create external spaces that are either dotted with trees or left open as lawns. Each apartment type benefits from windows on three or four sides, with views of the expanses of lawn and groups of trees in the park.

The access paths to the buildings 1, 2, and 3 wind through the park and lead to slightly sunken entrance areas. To keep traffic away from the park, the driveways to the garages run underneath it. The entrance hall can be accessed both from the park and directly from the garage. Polished chrome steel parapets open up

this space optically, as does the light gray flooring of terrazzo and cast stone incorporating marble chips. The front doors to the apartments are made of dark oak with an equally wide illumination panel to one side. Exposed concrete walls form a contrast to the refined materials used in the staircases to lend the whole an appropriate everyday quality.

The naturally-lit staircases provide access to two or three apartments and one studio on each floor. The apartments have spacious floor plans and a generous ceiling height of 2.7 meters. From each apartment's entrance area, the space is divided into two main zones: a daytime area with kitchen, dining room, living room, and study, and a nighttime area consisting of bedrooms with connecting bathrooms and dressing rooms. Each unit has a covered balcony and an additional winter garden. One apartment on the top floor of each building has its own private access to the large roof terrace with pavilions.

The building volumes with their composition of horizontal and vertical prefabricated concrete elements are almost classical in appearance. Horizontal gray bands are combined with yellow vertical elements of varying widths, which reference the coloring of the sandstone buildings in Geneva. Sliding windows with aluminum frames alternate with the yellow concrete elements. Reflective glass parapets intensify the play of mirrored trees in the windows and also amplify the impression of the façades forming a "geometric fabric interwoven with silver strands."

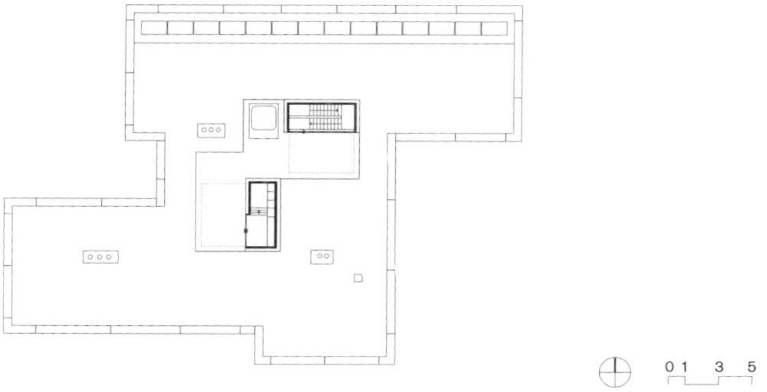

Top floor

2nd floor

1st floor

Ground floor

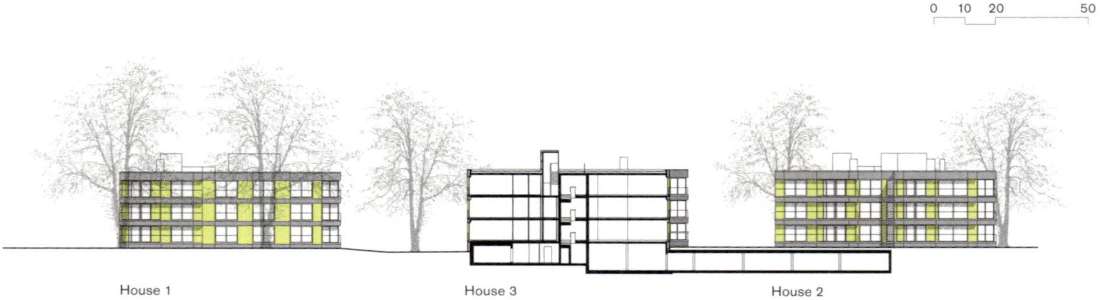

Section

Résidence du Parc de Grange-Canal

The buildings of the Résidence du Parc de Grange-Canal (Houses 40, 42, and 38) are conceived as seven- and nine-story high-rises. They contain eighty condominiums with regulated sales prices as well as fifty state-subsidized rental apartments in House 38, which conform to a simpler standard (with fit-out undertaken by Cerutti Architectes). These are supplemented in House 40 by small furnished units. In these buildings, like those in the first phase of the project, every apartment has a roofed balcony with a winter garden, while each penthouse has a roof terrace.

The yellow-pigmented concrete shell is not designed as a double construction here, but is instead made up of thermally insulated sandwich elements. Rhythm is lent to the façades by black-painted wood-aluminum windows with integrated parapets.

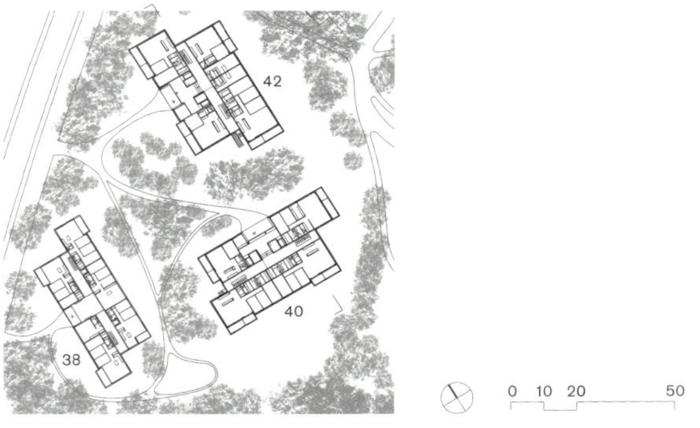

Résidence du Parc de Grange-Canal, Geneva, Switzerland

Section

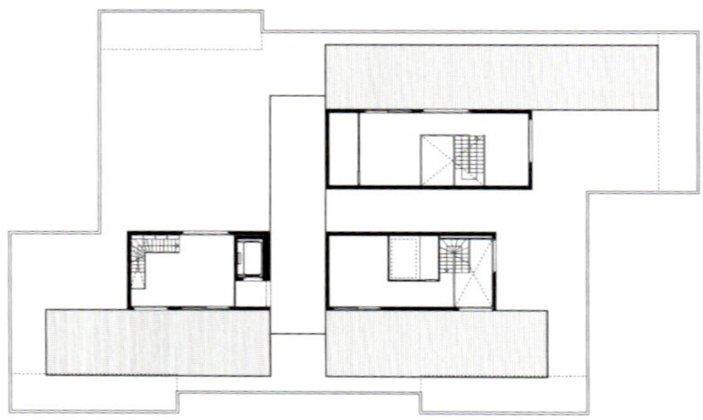

Top floor

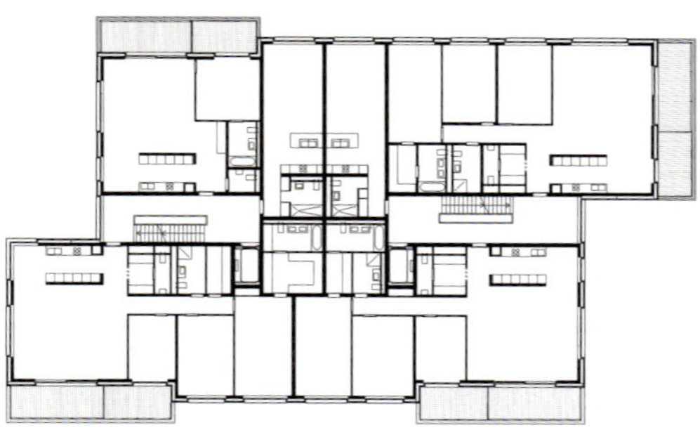

2nd–5th floors

0 1 5 10

Ground floor

House 42

Housing Development Erlenhof, Dietikon, Switzerland 162
2005–09

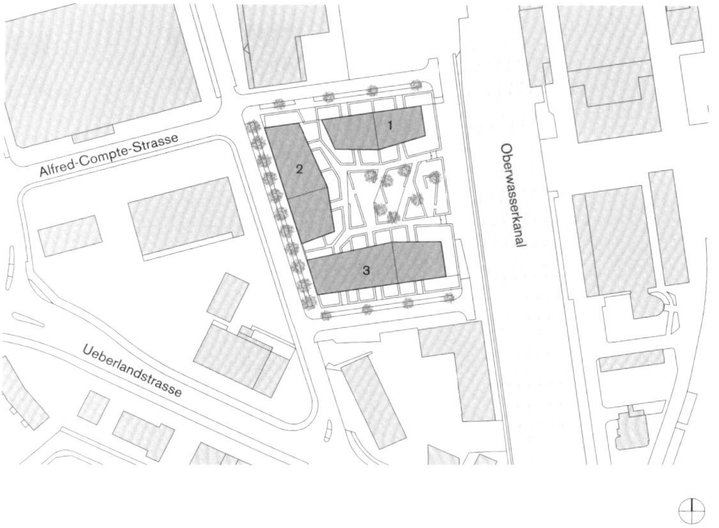

This residential complex, constructed on a former industrial site beside the "Oberwasserkanal," a bypass canal of the Limmat River in Dietikon, gives the emerging district its first truly urban note. Three large built volumes are set above a shared basement level to create a slightly raised courtyard open to the water. Pentagonal ground plans with corresponding gabled façades characterize these volumes. The heart of the ensemble is the courtyard with its large alder trees, which also gives the complex its name (Erlenhof: Courtyard of the Alders). Hornbeam hedges line the perimeter of each of the private gardens outside the ground-floor apartments and articulate the shared outdoor areas. Short flights of steps lead from this part of the ensemble to the promenade along the canal. Rows of trees along the surrounding streets mediate between interior and exterior of the complex; they are the first step in developing a future garden city. This notion also underpins the color scheme for the street-facing façades, which are rendered in a vibrant green that shapes the mood and identity of this pioneering project in what is still an industrial setting. In contrast, the courtyard is transformed into a luminous, light-filled space by pure white façades, with the alders outlined against this backdrop.

Entrance to the buildings is either directly from the street or via passages between the retaining walls of the raised front gardens and continuing up single-flight, well-lit stairways to the courtyard and the apartments. The light here takes on a red hue created by reflections from the paint on the underside of the stairs, contrasting with the green façade on the street and the white space of the courtyard.

The 85 apartments utilize a range of different floor plans to take advantage of the orientation and positioning of the various housing units. The condominiums in Block 1 are configured with loggias set in front of south-facing living rooms and adjacent kitchens, while the other rooms face north. Block 2 comprises rental accommodation of varying proportions, including apartments that open to the exterior on two or three sides. In Block 3 living rooms incorporating open-plan kitchens run through the entire depth of the building, with other rooms grouped around this space, allowing the apartments to open both to the south and onto the courtyard. The gently slanted roofs create high-ceilinged penthouse apartments. Recessed loggias provide each apartment with an outdoor area protected from the weather, while the size and number of the windows are maximized to ensure that all the apartments are flooded with light irrespective of the room depth.

Solid concrete construction was used for the buildings, with load-bearing and bracing cross walls and flat floor slabs formed from in-situ concrete. The façades are finished in plastered external thermal insulation, the basement level in exposed concrete. The slightly slanted roofs feature extensive planted areas.

Color study

1st–4th floors

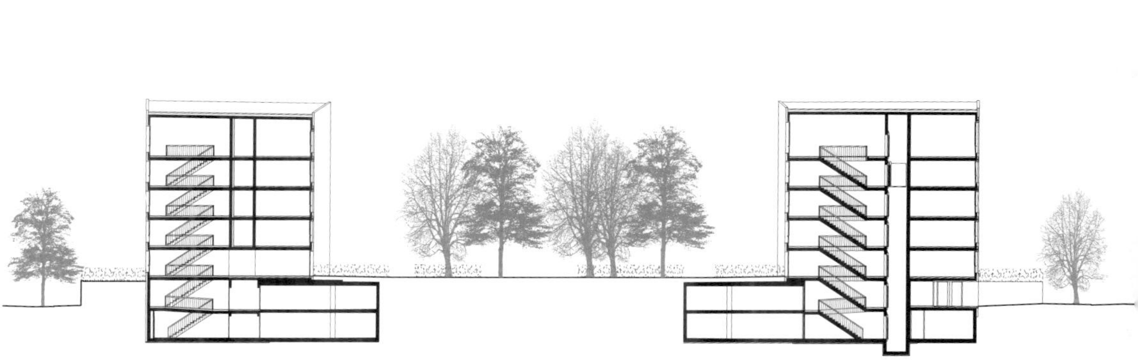

Section

3.5-/4.5-room apartments

Building 3

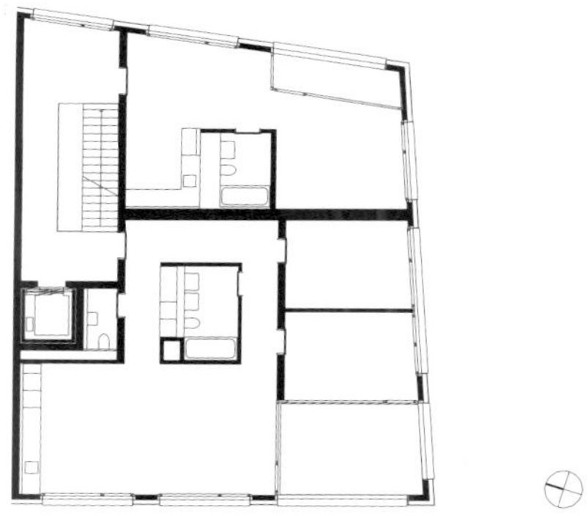

1.5-/3.5-room apartments

Building 2

4.5-/2.5-/4.5-room apartments

Building 2

Typical floor plans

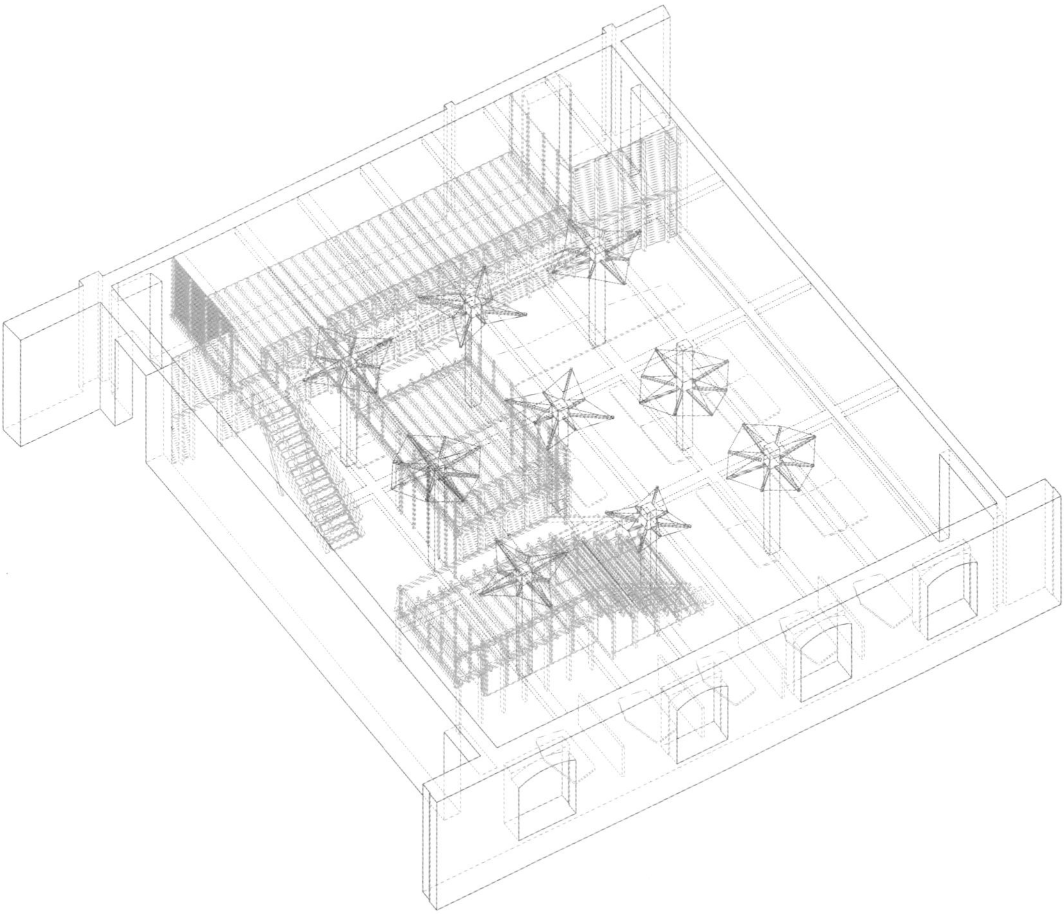

ADAPTABLE

ULMA Trimax